Staten Island: Like It or Not!

Lorenzo Lucchesi

Dedication
To the good, honorable Italians of Staten Island to whom much respect and reverence is owed

Special Thanks

This book would not have been possible without the innumerous contributions of the following individuals, many of whom donated hours of their time to respond to interview questions, summarize their entire lives, and recall their Staten Island experiences. The people of Staten Island have been exceptionally gracious, open-hearted, and constantly welcoming. Such as this work attempts to prove. From restauranteurs to proprietors to immigrants to the hardest workers, an enormous thanks is to be owed to:

~

Mario Ragucci - Maria Marchiano - Frankie Morano - Anthony Supino - John Franzreb III - Joe Montanti - Anne Mikolay - George LeBlanc - Richard Simpson - Maria & Francesco Destro - Ed Drury - Joe Locascio - Victor Popolano - Al Lambert- Michael Ventrone - Walter Buda - Pamela Silvestri - Joseph DiMizio – Michael Notarfrancesco III - Johnny Potenza- Roseanne Abbato - Patricia Salmon - Peter Battaglia - Michele Sherry - Mario Gallucci - Vincent & Liz D'Antuono- Scott LoBaido - Joe Tirone - Ken LiGreci - Wayne Roccaro - Emilie Harting- Sal Carola - Tony & Merry Bisogna - Joseph Pidoriano - Maria Bonamo - Linda Winkler - The Moschella Family - Sal Marino - Mickey Burns - Peter Cundari - Michael Lombardi - Rudolph Macri - Linda Petosa - Anthony Campitiello - Vito Russo Jr. - Vinnie Medugno - Vinnie & Sandra Zummo - Richard Barbato - Stephen Margarella - Paul DeRienzo - Joseph DeVito - Vito Picone - Annette LaRosa- James Carrozza - John Hershkowitz - Richard

Crocitto - Al Csorba & Family - Joseph Sedutto - Beverly
Zinicola - Lee Labita-Stanzione - Stephen & Ciro Licastri -
Addie Andreano-Morton - The Cangiano Family - The
Denino Family - Aida & Victor Scalici - Peter Gati -
Angelo Rizzo - Michael Pistilli - Peggy Ventrudo & Alice
Rizzo – Gus & Deanna DiLeo - Shay La Scalla & Michael
Scaramuzzo - Madelyn & Donny Musto - Donna Comis-
Dolly Garcenot - Alice Bergstromc - Julia Brogna- Michele
& Maria Iammatteo – Carol & Jim Barsalona – Joanne
Bennetti – Thomas Iommi – Lucia Sander & Kenneth
Peters – Bob & Charlie Siclari – Carole Bonnie Reiss –
Ron Castorina Jr. – Lorraine Guerrera & Tony
Maciejowski – Jim Ogden – The Sorrentino Family –
Patricia Borello-Foggin – Joyce Burns – Michele Gambetta
– Gloria Ricciardi – Aldea Simon – George DeRosa –
Msgr. Ferdinando Berardi– Susan Pillarella – Charles
Perrino – Elaine Casazza – Howard Murphy – Carmen
Sorrentino-Higgins – Gina Reginella & Connie Barone –
Enza Mammi – Gloria Santo – Mildred Savitsky – Paul
Mattiola – George Anastasio– Ann Baglio – Anthony
Navarino – Joan Priola – Josie Darrigo – Donna Scarano
Amaturo – Cosimo Parrelli – Marie Dudley – Barbara
Pietracatella – Paul Scamardella – Roger Pucillo – Marilyn
Cucuzza-Ciaburri – John Gatti – Mario Ariemma - Kathy
Mittenhuber – Phil Rosso - Justin Abbey

"I am delighted to send greetings to the residents of Staten
Island as they celebrate the 300th anniversary of the island.
Your community and borough has played a significant role
in the history of our country, and I know that it will continue
to play a vital civic role during the century which is now
opening for you. With best wishes and congratulations" –
President John F. Kennedy, 1961

PROLOGUE & AUTHOR'S NOTE

Staten Island: Like It or Not! (pub. 2019) is an entirely-historical, authentic, and critical examination of New York's "forgotten borough." The subject of much speculation and misunderstanding by other non-Staten Island, New Yorkers, the term "Staten Island" brings to mind an array of distasteful or stereotypical adjectives. However, as proven in this masterful work of literature, the "soul" of Staten Island is a truly complex organism, requiring extended periods of time to study and comprehend. It is a mixture of Brooklyn, Manhattan, Italy, Naples, but more often than not—a convoluted concoction of its diverse, unique personalities. As the reader will discover momentarily, Staten Island is not only recognized internationally for its contributions to engineering, industry, and cuisine, but for its abundance of natural resources, architecture, and scenery. Unlike in other locales in the United States, Staten Islanders are also fundamentaly bound together through either emotional or ancestral bonds, as evident in the strong sense of community embodied by them. *Staten Island: Like It or Not!* is pleased to offer a wide variety of examples sufficiently providing reasonable evidence for all claims outlined in this prologue. Examples are given through individual testimonies taken directly from interviews conducted with Islanders. All information cited in the bibliography with "personal communication" and precise dates attached has been used with permission of subjects. To the best of current historical knowledge, information extracted from archives, and oral tradition, all facts detailed in each section of this book are accurate or truthful. From November 2017 to Februrary 2019, Islanders were posed with a series of questions in three separate categories: genealogical, historical, and editorial. For the former, interviewees recalled in conjunction with records obtained from genealogical archives, birth, death, wedding, and other dates for family members or friends. For "historical," individuals were asked to recall childhood memories or memories pertaining to their businesses and family establishments. Finally, for the latter, each person questioned was prompted to provide commentary on the transformation of Staten Island to its current state. Whether political, religious, or certain forms of secular commentary may interfere with the reading, it is appropriate to respect opinion—recalling the fact that the borough's social and infrastructural change can be attributed to numerous entities (many of which shall be fully chronicled here).

Asides from extracting dozens of amusing anecdotes or fond recollections from hundreds of Staten Islanders, *Staten Island: Like It or Not!* thoroughly investigates the "development" history of the borough through personal perspectives. Through examining hundreds of New York Public Library, N.Y.C. Department of Records & Information Services, and family photographs, a detailed and specific recording of both South Shore and Mid-Island development is given for either the reader's disdain or pleasure. Among Staten Island's most commonly-accepted myths is that its Italian community began to flourish in the later-half of the 20th century. This is nowhere near the truth. The earliest Italians (with few exceptions) began their migration to Staten Island in the late-1800s/early-1900s. Many laid foundations for homes, established sewer systems and other infrastructure, and operated small businesses. Though a large majority of Staten Islanders of Italian descent can trace their roots to southern Italy, a large portion emigrated from the region of Abruzzo/Molise, in particular Campobasso. This unique region of Italy's contributions to Staten Island are extraordinary in character, as they cannot be easily located in other areas of America. The migration of the earliest Italians to Richmond County, with the aforementioned information in mind, then begs the question: "Why Staten Island?" The development of the United States' largest Italian community can be attributed to several factors: proximity to Manhattan, country-like magnificent scenery, immigration technicalities, and miscellaneous happenings (i.e. Julius Weissglass'—the late patriarch of the Weissglass Milk titan family—admiration of the borough in which he was sent to to pick radishes for Luchow's Restaurant in Manhattan). As for immigration technicalities, some immigrants simply stayed, for example, in Rosebank and Tompkinsville due to the Quarantine Station's relative location. Many individuals like Frank Barsalona (the founder of a small seafood delivery company in Tottenville in the early-1900s), however, sought a retreat to the country atmosphere from the crowded streets of Little Italy. The founder of L. Montanti Leather and Findings on Richmond Terr. in fact, was required to leave the polluted inner city to Staten Island by his doctor due to his condition, emphysema. As the Italian community populated rapidly, so did a comical, genuine, and hard-working class of people. It is of utmost importance to recognize these individuals' valuable contributions to American history. Though some Islanders will dissent fervently with the neighborhood names applied to certain businesses or people, all places have been identified using an official map published by the Staten Island Board of Realtors. The general concept of this was to create a sense of conformity and to avoid potential confusion. Footnotes are provided when appropriate to supplement the text with extra information. The structure of the book begins with an "Introduction," followed by a lengthy discourse explaining the earliest industrial activity and construction projects, in addition to the beginnings of "cultural civilization" (chiefly, the German presence in Stapleton in theological, brewing, and other ventures). If the reader desires not to take part in such tiresome subjects, they may advance to "The Neighborhoods and Their Stories" to begin hearing memories of Island childhoods which shall certainly resonate. Though most neighborhoods will be covered through either historial narration or personal testimonials, a special emphasis is placed on the following: Rosebank and

Clifton, Port Richmond, West (New) Brighton, Stapleton, and South Beach. Though several professional editors and the author himself have reviewed the content (along with the revisions made by a number of interviewees during their article previews), it is encouraged that a more perfect telling of history in all scenarios is sought. Therefore, readers may contact the author at the following email address: lorenzolucchesi204@gmail.com

It is with the most profound excitement, I am pleased to present: *Staten Island: Like It or Not!* Enjoy!

Regards,
The Author,

Lorenzo Lucchesi.

OVERVIEW

~

The history of Staten Island is one of intrigue, lore, and longing. The island's tree-lined, suburban streets, traditional dining institutions, and unique and spacious Cape Cod homes hint at a nostalgic past which remains hidden beneath the cookie-cutter, development homes and bustling shopping centers. The blossoming tomato gardens of Italian residents, close intercommunal relations, and luscious hillsides make it inconceivable that such a community could ever be a part of America's great metropolis—New York City. While neighborhoods such as New Springville and Bulls Head teem with police officers, retirees, and middle-class, business proprietors, other areas such as Dongan Hills and Stapleton house retired naval officers, firefighters, and grocers—in direct opposition to Islander's counterparts in Williamsburg and Tribeca who are artists, poets, and neighborhood eccentrics. However, Staten Island additionally remains invariably separated in its civics and political identity. As author Daniel C. Kramer wrote, Staten Island is "a conservative bastion in a liberal city." With no connection by railroad or subway to Brooklyn, and the only link to the rest of the city being the Staten Island Ferry and the Verrazzano-Narrows Bridge (dubbed the [f'in] Guinea Gangplank following mass Italian immigration in the 1960s), Staten Island remains an isolated and stereotyped territory characterized only by the since-removed Fresh Kills Landfill and Willowbrook State School. For decades in fact, Staten Island was and partially remains New York City's dumping ground for the homeless, garbage, and for union bosses' laborers to work when they may have made them angry. Termed the "forgotten borough" by frustrated residents, Staten Island has suffered both financially and morally in its dilapidated infrastructure consisting of overcrowded expressways and outdated bus routes, as well as its geographic isolation. Inhabited first by The Raritan Indians, a branch of the Delaware Nation, then by British military officials during the Revolutionary War, then by persecuted foreigners and fed-up Brooklynites (termed "gavones" by some Islanders), Staten Island has developed contrastingly from the Bronx, Manhattan, Queens, and Brooklyn in every possible aspect—precipitating a founder's effect. Deeply influenced by religious values and a conservative mindset, Staten Islanders remain consistent in their attendance at Sunday services at churches such as Our Lady of Mount Carmel – Saint Benedicta and Saint Anthony of Padua— both churches whose namesakes derive from Italian origins. Staten Islanders, however, have also preserved an accent distinct from any others in the American category (which generally-speaking can amount to four regional 'dialects'). Induced by a variety of influences, including Italian-American gesticulations and lexicon (dramatized by native-Manhattan, Italian singer—Lou Monte), Staten Islanders possess an emotional, song-like way of structuring sentences where they draw on different parts of speech inspired by the plurality of nationalities in their neighborhoods. This includes utilizing spontaneity, incorporating humor, inflecting consonants and vowels, and avoiding monotonous patterns of speech at all times, where many other Americans can either be flat in effect or extremely matter of fact. Such influences on the verbal expression of Staten Islanders are clearly reflected in the borough's demographics which have remained relatively static throughout the decades—with overwhelmingly large Jewish, Irish, and Italian populations retaining their immense sizes. The large number of Italians, in fact, which contribute nearly 40% of the borough's *total* population (and 80% of the South Shore's population), have garnered Staten Island the nickname, "Staten Italy." Many nationalities also found certain niches on Staten Island (e.g. a large majority of the teachers in Eltingville in the 1950s and 60s was Jewish). However, after years of multiple immigrant influxes from the Bronx and Brooklyn, the unique culture of Staten Island has been significantly reduced, if not blended in with the often stereotyped "Brooklynese" which any Islander would have immediately recognized in years past. Furthermore, the incursion of arrivals has also brought about a cultural shift which is clearly reflected in all aspects of everyday Staten Island life, particularly within neighborhood dynamics. For example, two native Islanders out of respect would honor one another's parking space located in front of their homes; on the contrary, a Brooklynite would not (according to various testimonies). This can be largely explained due to the convenient presence of subway/transportation connections to Brooklyn and the lack of parking on city streets. The evolution of such traditions and customs is the subject of much interest and curiosity. One potential source of explanation was the increasingly diversifying racial statistics in neighborhoods such as Port Richmond and other North Shore areas where a large community of African-Americans and Hispanics was developing, prompting mass-departures by European immigrants, as well as decreased home prices and lessening neighborhood appeal. Such patterns of migration led to the formation of "matchbox cities" such as Great Kills and Annadale where an aerial photograph might yield hundreds of rows of houses appearing in a formation similar to several matchboxes.

The construction of housing projects such as the 1,100 acre "Annadale-Huguenot" were attempts made by the City of New York to evenly-distribute out the clumps of residents in the other boroughs. The city's method to initiating these developments, however, was relatively deceitful and unfair to Staten Islanders. Under the guise of "urban renewal" (a term generally used to indicate revitalization of a decrepit, deindustrialized area) due to "unsanitary conditions," the City began a process that was viewed by many as a violation of individual property rights. Early action taken by the City on Staten Island was characterized by miscommunication and willful ignorance. The strident conduct of the city led 1966-1977-serving-Borough President Robert T. Connor (future deputy assistant secretary of the Navy under Presidents Carter and Reagan) to remark, "The comparison, for example, of [enigmatically, arbitrarily deciding where urban renewal is needed] make people wonder whether the city administrations in Manhattan really know what Staten Islanders want." Indeed, those rural areas, despite being susceptible to flooding due to their proximity to Raritan Bay, were perhaps some of the prettiest, most well-maintained in the city. The dream of establishing another Westchester was permanently deferred. Despite the ultimate failure of "Annadale-Huguenot," the proposal and brief action taken by the city administrations forever alienated native Islanders from willingly accepting any development with mild skepticism. Actions such as these were perhaps one of the premier contributions to Staten Island's unofficial adoption of the nickname, "The Forgotten Borough."

The nickname holds as much significance today as it did fifty years ago. Carole Bonnie Reiss—a Richmond County education reformist—testifies to one among many case studies of the painfully accurate description of Staten Island. A native of Bensonhurst, and Ph.D graduate in K-12 Leadership, Reiss served under Mayor Bloomberg's-School District 3, 5, and 6 in Upper Manhattan as Regional Instructional Director. Other education administration roles she has taken have included the position of Dean of Students at F.D.R. High School on 20th Ave. in Mapleton. In 2010, having moved to Staten Island years prior and seen the shortfalls of the public school system as it pertained to her own child, Reiss began her own ambitious project to bring the charter school mentality—that which cultivates a culture of learning in an atompshere of college and career readiness—to her adopted borough. "We like to say any child can be the next President of the United States, but that just isn't the truth." Reiss explained, "Staten Island has suffered so much due to the lack of accountability of elected officials. We cannot continue to ignore the test scores on the North Shore! We cannot foster mismanagement in our city government." At the First Central Baptist Church on Wright St. in Stapleton, Reiss delivered a message to the community, expressing the need for a charter school specializing in Science, Technology, Engineering, and Mathematics (STEM), along with arts (STEAM). Reiss cited the State Board of Regents' refusal to approve a charter school for North Shore underprivileged students, as well as the Borough President's false reporting of the number of dyslexic students on Staten Island with the intent of building another special needs school as opposed to a STEM school as two of many detractors from the borough's educational advancement. "In addition to the need for more charter schools, New York public schools also don't provide instructors ample training with disadvantaged populations. The mentality of enabling academic and social failure is a flawed one. Working as Regional Instructional Director in Upper Manhattan, I created a program called "Junior Nets" in which members of the Brooklyn Nets basketball team came to mentor students in perfecting their basketball skills. In giving students something to look forward to, you create motivation." Identifying favoritism in the school-opening selection process, Reiss nevertheless has devoted her efforts to improving education as a whole on Staten Island. Reiss currently works to secure capital funding with the N.Y. City Council District 49 to provide the North Shore with STEM centers. Persisting since 2008 in combating Staten Island's connotation of "forgotten," Reiss remarked, "It is crucial to recognize how poorly teachers have been treated following the passage of Common Core national standards. We need more training to support the teachers so that they can give high-quality education for every child. The NYC DOE has failed teachers in this area." Education aside, regarding land development and transportation, the borough is more "forgotten," still. Just recently in 2016, Staten Island was excluded from the Five Borough Ferry Plan which aimed at reducing traffic and easing transportation concerns. Ironically, despite being one of only two boroughs surrounded entirely by water, Staten Island must still contend with its isolation dictated by the exorbitant $17+ bridge toll needed to reach Fort Wadsworth from Brooklyn. Former Member of the New York Assembly from the 62nd District (South Shore), Ron Castorina Jr. presents several additional key examples of Staten Island, as isolated culturally. In 2018, Castorina—the receipient of a "Guardian of Columbus" title—spearheaded the movement for the preservation of the Christopher Columbus statue at Columbus Circle in Manhattan. Explaining the statue's importance to Staten Island's Italian community, Castorina (self-described as the "first elected official to speak out" toward this cause) remarked, "The statue is emblematic of a people!" Castorina—a native of Bensonhurst and graduate of St. Francis College who served as Counsel to Minority Leader of the New York City Council, Vincent Ignizio— moved to the Mid-Island (New Springville) section of Staten Island in April of 2001. He is plenty-experienced as a civil ligitation attorney mediating between the city/state and Richmond County. In 2008, due to the lack of sidewalks and other transportation issues, Castorina won a lawsuit against the City of New York which had discontinued schoolbus service for seventh and eighth-grade students on Staten Island. Throughout his term in office, Castorina further helped organize funds for the growing opioid epidemic, assisted the special needs community in the Staten Island public schools, and obtained resources from the state to change the street gradient due to sewer-related issues at Page Ave. & Amboy Rd. Though this project represents only one small issue in the greater illustration of development on

Staten Island, other projects are notoriously burdensome. For instance, in 2004, the International Speedway Corporation, the public arm of NASCAR paid $100 million to purchase the largest vacant private parcel in New York City at 450 acres owned by Staten Island Marine Development (the former site was occupied by the Gulf Port petroleum storage facility). ISC sought to take advantage of an untapped New York market by building an 82,500-seat motor speedway. The plan, however, was met with strong community resistance, political infighting, environmental disputes, and lengthy city approval processes. Islanders cited potential increased traffic and pollution of their already congested roadways as decisive reasons for their resistance to the undertaking. District Attorney Michael McMahon even remarked, "I am glad that the NASCAR people finally understand what I have said all along...that to put a 100,000-seat NASCAR track on the west shore of Staten Island is what my mother would call a schnapps idea." Despite promising more than $350 million in construction wages and a $200 million annual contribution to the economy, the NASCAR track's benefits were ultimately outweighed by its negatives. The failed project is an example of the magnitude of the community resistance Staten Islanders can employ when they are faced with prospects of hostile development. However, as radio personality and former member of Community Board 3 on Staten Island, Frankie Morano, notes, "Staten Islanders aren't opposed to development, they're just opposed to irresponsibility." In fact, the Island has welcomed some enormous projects such as the New York Wheel (once slated to be the world's largest Ferris wheel at 630 feet until its cancellation), Empire Outlets, and Lighthouse Point. Contrary to popular belief, Staten Islanders were vehement supporters of the extension of transportation and commerce to their borough. S. Robert Molinari, Republican New York State Assemblyman from 1943-1944, United Civic League of Midland Beach

President in 1933, and elected member to the Bridge & Tunnel Committees of the Advisory Planning Board of Richmond is a noteworthy example. In 1943, he supported the New York City Board of Transportation's 1938-1943 plans to extend the Independent Subway System (IND)—a rail system acquired by the New York City Subway in 1940—Smith St. Line to Staten Island by virtue of an underwater tunnel. The owner of his own real estate practice and home insurance vendor at 153 New Dorp Lane, Molinari advertised on his office's front: "South Shore Sales & Rentals – Homes Built." But it is clear that Islanders are willing to not only stand up against housing plans, but against major undertakings.

There are, on the contrary, benefits to accepting infrastructure projects. A popular argument in support of Parks Commissioner Robert Moses' extensive creation of freeways and development throughout New York City is that although once regarded as repressively intrusive, those projects are a *current* necessity. The sudden emergence of developer-homes on Staten Island introduced thousands of new neighbors to each other all *at once*, leading to the development of extremely close friendships and sustained bonds that originated from the housing boom in the 1960s. The close-knit community which emerged—the kind where "your mother knew what you had done and was waiting with the frying pan before you arrived home"—remains somewhat in tact today. Though by far one of the most appealing aspects of residing on Staten Island, the neighborliness between Islanders comes with a rather unusual side effect: difficulty selecting a jury. As Mario Gallucci—criminal defense trial lawyer, former assistant to Richmond County District Attorney William Murphy, and co-star in USA Network's TV mini-documentary series *Partners in Crime* (2014-) with attorney Big Lou Gerlormino—put it: "In Staten Island, you run the risk as a criminal defense lawyer of knowing every single person called for jury duty on a given day. Staten Islanders are also inclined to lean more towards conviction and prosecution, which make winning a case significantly harder than in other boroughs." Dedicated toward community improvement, Gallucci—Staten Island's attorney known for his "courtroom theatrics and sartorial style," keeping of 150 ties on a rotation rack at home, annual Christmas distribution of cannoli and Valentine's Day distribution of chocolate to court employees—represents good-hearted individuals who inopportunely find themselves in bad situations. An active combatant of the Island's opioid crisis, Gallucci was one of the main supporters of Carl's House (Carl's Recovery Center) along with founder Marco DiDonno which provides assistance to thousands of people struggling with addiction. Individuals such as Mario Gallucci are moral exemplars of fellow Staten Islanders assisting each other in times of crisis. Others include Peter Cundari and Joe Tirone. Cundari—a native of Carroll Gardens, Brooklyn and former employee for the Long Island Railroad—moved to the Island's South Shore in 1985. Known as the "Fig King" among locals, Cundari maintains a yard with over thirty-five varieties of fig trees, many of which he obtained at the former Bellaclare Nursery on Long Island. Cundari stated in an interview, "People call me from all over Staten Island. I'm like a doctor, fixing fig trees! To many, a fig tree is a symbol of prosperity and new life. When my friend's mother was dying of Alzhemier's, I took a clipping from their tree and planted it in my backyard. The woman's dying words were, 'Oh my God! Our fig tree will live on!'" Fig trees, without entering into a lengthy discussion, are a deeply-rooted tradition in Brooklyn/Staten Island culture. Enza Giordano Mammi, a newcomer to the neighborhood of Annadale in 1986 seeking better quality of education for her children and less congestion, who grew up on Bay 40th St. in Bath Beach, remarked, "I remember being about twelve years old in the time with no air conditioning when Brooklyn families sat on their stoops during the summertime. One particular night, about five of us kids tried to reach over by standing on a red wagon to pluck some figs from the tree in the back of our houses. To our surprise, the owner of the tree yelled, 'Hey! What are you guys doing?' We ran so fast to the front as if nothing happened so our parents would not suspect what we did."

When Hurricane Sandy devastated Staten Island, Cundari went to Casa Belvedere and gave fig clippings away to those who had lost their homes. Cundari elaborated, "These people have nothing, but they want fig trees!" Similarly, Joe Tirone Jr. assisted those who had lost their homes during Hurricane Sandy by leading a community effort to navigate New York State's pilot buyout program. A member of the Staten Island Board of Realtors, Tirone received their Community Service Award in 2013 for his efforts. In addition to this, he was chosen by the *Staten Island Advance* as one of the ten most influential people that same year. Frustrated of the same "flood-rebuild-repeat" cycle, Tirone explained to a Federal Emergency Management Agency representative regarding

[Borough President Robert T. Connor cuts the ribbon in celebration of Tirone's Shoe Store grand opening at 164 Richmond Ave. C. 1974. Courtesy – Joe Tirone]

his

[From the left: "Uncle Sal," Carmelo Tirone, and "Joe the Shoemaker." Taken at 204 Richmond Ave. before the shoemaker shop was put in the back of the store. C. 1940s Courtesy – Joe Tirone]

Oakwood Beach bungalow, "Look, I don't want to fix this house, because I don't want to rent it out, because I don't want to put another tenant in. My tenants...they were hysterical, crying. They lost everything they owned." Tirone's roots run deep in the Staten Island community. His grandfather Carmelo (1885-1975)—a Sicilian immigrant who arrived in 1916—began Original Shoe Repair at 19 Richmond Ave. and later moved to a different location at 204 Richmond Ave. due to business expansion. In 1949, the Tirone brothers (sons of Carmelo) opened a shoe store at the same site, but later moved to 164 Port Richmond Ave in 1975. The oldest retail shop on Port Richmond Ave., Tirone's Shoes gained notoriety for supplying parochial schools with shoes as part of their uniform. Though the store closed down in 2010, Joseph Tirone Sr. still recalled many memories, a prominent of which was when Clarabell the Clown from Howdy Doody came to visit the store. Joe Tirone Jr. remarked, "This isn't the *old* Island anymore...If you want to know how things have changed...In the 1960s, my mother and I were stopped at a stoplight. The minute it turned green, the car behind us honked! My mother looked in her mirror to see if she knew the person and mumbled quietly in an ambivalent manner, 'He kind of looks familiar...I might know him.' After a few seconds, the guy pulled up next to us, flipped us the bird[1], and drove away! I guess that was our welcoming to the new Staten Island."

Despite eye-witness anecdotes from Tirone and other Staten Islanders, the community where everyone knew each other and nobody parked in front of other persons' homes is still relatively present on the *South Shore* unlike in the North Shore in areas such as St. George and Tompkinsville where consistently different settlers moved in at varying periods since Michael Pauw, the wealthy merchant and Mayor of Amsterdam, purchased "Staaten Eylandt" in 1630. Still today, the North Shore of Staten Island remains the most ethnically diverse section of Richmond County with large populations of Mexicans, Indians, Sri Lankans, African-Americans, and Filipinos comprising a large percentage of the area's total residents. Domestic immigration to Staten Island is a part of the three-dimensional process of settling (particularly related to retirement) away from New York's urban center. Residents of Manhattan/Bronx will typically migrate to the spacious areas of Westchester County or Connecticut; those from Queens will settle in either Nassau or Suffolk County in towns on Long Island from Hempstead to Southampton; and those from Brooklyn will predominantly go to Staten Island (and some to the alluring country of "The Garden State"—New Jersey). The pattern repeats itself year after year: Brooklyn to Staten Island to New Jersey to Pennsylvania, as one group tires of the next. The mass-settlement, however, has removed Staten Island's conceptualization as a destination and instead re-affirmed its

---

[1] For those unfamiliar, the phrase "flipping the bird" is an alternative to "giving the middle finger."

official status as a borough. Immigration waves triggered a two-fold population increase from 200,000 to 400,000 residents between 1955-1995, and dismantled the Island's agrarian society, favoring a shift toward a suburban community. This dramatic shakeup was mirrored by the borough's renaming from "Richmond" to "Staten Island" in 1975. The Island's image underwent gradual changes from the outer edges-inward, beginning first with the commercialization of coast side districts such Midland Beach and New Dorp. By the mid-1950s, development had expanded into the inner, rural areas of Richmond County (substituting the word "landowner" with "homeowner"), transforming the Island's countenance forever. Gone were the extensive agriculture and golden fields which echoed the last remnants of a feudalistic-like, European society. Once home to 290 farms—a total of 11,724 acres—Staten Island in the present day boasts only one: The Decker Farm in Heartland Village. Only prior to 1950, surprisingly, was Staten Island one of New York City's major food producers, supplying city restaurants with colorful vegetables and fragrant herbs from tarragon to mint. Describing the farm community, author Emilie C. Harting, granddaughter of Henry Meyer, the German farmer, former president of the Staten Island Growers Association, and central character in her book *The Meyer Farms of New Springville, Staten Island*, states, "I've been told that Italian women... moved along on their knees picking mint in the early 1900s...[singing] songs such as 'O' Sole Mio' and 'Amuri, Amuri'... At lunchtime they sat under the trees on the lawn that sloped down to the creek behind the old Dutch cottage." Greek women in the fields west of Bulls Head sang *kleftika* (Greek ballads) as they strolled about, witnessing the flourishing of their scallion, cabbage, and cauliflower crops. Those who worked on the Greek farms included "Poet Laureate of Harlem" and Harlem Renaissance leader, Langston Hughes (1902-1967). After dropping out of Columbia University in the summer of

1922, Hughes worked for a short period of time at the Criaris Farm at 2289 Richmond Ave. in New Springville "spreading manure, picking weeds, washing lettuce, beets, carrots, onions, tying them and packing them for market" for fifty dollars per month and a bed of hay. His fellow agricultural laborers included "two Greek hired hands, a couple of Italians, and a Jewish boy from Brownsville." Immigrants participating in the agricultural economy of Staten Islanders such as Henry Meyer even hauled their produce on American LaFrance, three-horse hitch carriages directly to market. The rich history of Staten Island agriculture, however, has somewhat retained its legacy. Restaurants such as Basilio Inn, founded by Italian immigrant, Basilio Giovannini in 1921 (making it Staten Island's oldest continuously-operating eatery), still grow produce on-sight as a complement to the restaurant's rustic menu. Other institutions such as Monsignor Farrell High School in Oakwood provide their students dressed in traditional maroon-and-yellow uniforms with exquisite Italian delicacies such as Penne Alla Vodka, Pizza Margherita, and Strawberry Chocolate Cheesecake.

Such epicurean specialties have emerged from a warm, authentic environment fostered in the kitchens and homes of proud Staten Islanders. One specific holiday specialty that exemplifies such prideful Staten Island traditions is the world-renown, Pizzagaina (otherwise known as "Italian Easter Ham Pie") made with cubes of "brahjzoot" (slang for prosciutto—supposedly originating in Borough Park, Brooklyn) or hard salami and a variety of cheeses including mozzarella. Staten Island tradition actually had it that Italians prepare their own, homemade Pizzagaina prior to a family gathering, refraining from purchasing a deli-made version. Individuals who dare violated the sacred tradition were viewed as disrespectful, dishonest, and fake. A similar Staten Island tradition—the baking of Easter Grain Pie (It: Pastiera Napoletana)—also was regulated by akin circumstances. The delicacy resembles a creamy bread pudding, but is much more robust. Those ingredients hidden within family recipes can sometimes be Impastata[2] (a pasty ricotta cheese), candied fruit, or Fiori di Siclia—a pungent extract containing vanilla and citron to culminate the scent of the flowers of Sicily. One of the only remaining delis carrying on the tradition of baking the pie on Staten Island is Novelli's Pork Store in Oakwood. The store, offering a wide variety of New York/Italian products such as bagels, mozzarella bunnies, and arancini, has served New York City for over seventy years, and Staten Island for over thirty. Among its most unique offerings is the famed Easter Grain Pie whose recipe originated from Novelli's Pork Store's owner's grandmother, Lucy Bove. Unfortunately, however, modernity has disfigured the age-old tradition as societal standards for crafting food have been lowered significantly. John Novelli, the owner of the store, even remarked, "You don't see any young people coming in and buying the ingredients. It's a lost art." The desire for fresh, good-quality food and products seems to have also dissipated, not withstanding the agonizing test of time. The encroaching suburbanization movement, rigorously advancing as of 2019, attempts to homogenize sacred establishments such as Novelli's Pork Store by instituting standardized eateries and stores (e.g. a Dunkin Donuts at nearly every gas station convenience store). Throughout the early-1900s on Staten Island, convenience/general stores took on a different glamour—one that did not over extend, yet was a recognizable element of shopping culture. Among the most well-known chains was Roulston's—one of the largest grocery store chains in the five boroughs, started by Irish immigrant Thomas H. Roulston in 1888. Headquartered on

---

[2] *Staten Island Advance* food editor since 2008, Pamela Silvestri noted in the making of Eastern Grain Pie, "Impastata" ricotta or simply Ricotta, cannot be substituted with other ingredients to supplement production costs, particularly the infamous "cottage cheese."

9th St. and 2nd Ave. in Brooklyn, Roulston's grew to over seven-hundred stores in Staten Island, Brooklyn, and Long Island by the early-1940s. It had fifty-eight locations in Richmond County alone. Joseph Husson wrote in *The Commercial Vehicle* in 1915, "All of the stores out of the confines of the Borough of Brooklyn have been made possible by the use of the motor vehicles. These, in turn, have been made possible by the adoption of the tractor and semi-trailer principle, for trucks of the conventional type were tried but proved a failure because of the idle 2-hour loading periods." Roulston's, the old-fashioned grocer whose individual stores resembled more closely "Mom and Pop" stores, characterized itself in a 1921 advertisement in *The Staten Island Advance* as a "logical marketing center for both masses and the classes... conducted so as to give a full measure of service to every one who deals with [them]. A little child or a big business man; the housewife with a limited purse or those who have more...Your nickel is as good as your dollar."

Native-Staten Islanders only reminisce about a time when all sorts of trucks from the Good Humor to Mister Softee to furniture to produce trucks came through the neighborhood selling items directly to individual households. Salesmen such as the Fuller Brush men, and deliverers such as the Weissglass milkmen and Holtermann's bakers came to directly to people's doorsteps. Of course, Staten Island had also been served by numerous regional purveyors, one of which included Sheffield Farms Co. which maintained a depot constructed in 1930 at 170 Lynhurst Ave. in Rosebank. The company—founded approximately in 1880 by Louis B. Halsey who appropriately chose his enterprise's name based on the "Sheffield herd" of cows in Mahwah, N.J. (northwest corner of Bergen County)—was recognized for its reversal of the negative connotation of "milk" adopted following the Swill Milk Scandal in New York in the 1850s-1860s. The Staten Island branch opened on May 22, 1933. Returning to local deliverers, old Italian men such as Emilio Grasso who resided on Hendricks Ave. in New Brighton even delivered homemade hot garlic bread, salami, provolone, soppressata, and mortadella. Other local deliverers included Pillitteri Bros. Italian Groceries, run by Antonio Pillitteri (1876-1967, imm. Aug. 1906) who resided at 24 Austin Ave. in South Beach. Among the only known photographs remaining of the delivery business is of a Pillitteri truck parked in front of Tutti's Bar & Grill, located once at 266 Broadway in West Brighton. For Islanders, as well as for many New Yorkers in other boroughs who grew up prior to 1960, "coal and ice men"—as they were referred to—were also frequent visitors to homes. Often times, the two necessities were provided by the same dealer. Before the usage of natural gas and electricity, coal suppliers were vital for the thrival of Richmond County. Coal distribution yards were too numerous to count. The variety of coal utilized most heavily by Staten Island households, described by American journals as an "essentiality" for "public welfare and health demands," was Anthracite or as it was colloquially known: "blue coal." Anthracite originated from the mountains of eastern Pennsylvania and accounted in 1890 for more than sixteen percent of the nation's energy consumption. The delivery process started at the "miner's pick," and progressed through "the waiting of the railroad car and [the] local dealer's delivery cart." Prominent coal institutions were D.K. Hawkins Coal Co. Inc. at 46 Greenfield Ave., Diamond Coal Co. (also on Greenfield), Southfield Coal & Ice Co. on Olympia Blvd., Springstead Coal Co. on Amboy Rd., and New Dorp Coal Corp. at the southwest corner of New Dorp Lane & South Railroad Ave. New Dorp Coal Corp. in fact had "Lehigh & Wilkes-Barre" written on the side of its facility. Coal yards such as these were positioned conveniently alongside railroad lines where coal would be deposited in carts along the track, and then transported to a silo. Businesses transitioned between delivering coal in the winter, and ice in the summer. Local dealers such as John Franzreb II, Sam "The Ice Man" on Gansevoort Blvd., John DeNora on West Buchanan St. in New Brighton, Christie DeForest in West Brighton, and Joe Rella on St. Marks Pl. in St. George could be seen regularly with their burlap sacks hitched over their shoulder using their large metal pincers to handle the ice. Joseph Rella had among the largest operations, boasting a sizable ice house at 451 St. Marks Pl., currently the site of a weed-infested, empty lot.

As the Italians (incl. the descendants of the fondly-recalled 'ice men') assimilated, elements of both cultures were infused to varying degrees. Italian stores adopted English names on their store awnings. Distinctly Americans products were also added to inventory. Examples include the

[Store owner Antonio Pitarresi celebrates his wedding at Gargiulo Restaurant in Coney Island. C. Apr. 12, 1936, Courtesy – Stephen Licastri]

Eagle Confectionery Store at 239 Sand Lane owned by Antonio Pitarresi—an immigrant from Palermo. A sign directly above the awning reads "Alba Grande Cigars – Estratti L'Italiana" in between two "Forest Lane Ice Cream" signs. Other stores such as butcher L. Dimino & Son at 211

Olympia Blvd. joined American collective grocer organizations such as "United Service Grocers." As ethnic small businesses seemed to flourish, however, a major problem was looming: the rise of the A&P (The Great Atlantic & Pacific Tea Co.). Founded in 1859 as The Great American Tea Co. by George F. Gilman on Vesey St. in Manhattan, A&P was destined to be a national sensation from its very conception. By the 1970s, the A&P had locations across Staten Island from Main St. in Tottenville to Jersey St. in New Brighton to Amboy Rd. in Great Kills. The grocery, pharmaceutical chain dominated competition in the market and posed a threat to local businesses. Author Marc Levinson wrote, "The evidence before Walter Lindley's (a federal judge) court made clear the prices at A&Pwere below those at the competition. As John A. Hartford (longtime president of the company) himself had testified nearly a year earlier, 'We would rather sell 200 pounds of butter at 1 cent profit than 100 pounds at 2 cent profit...U.S. v. A&Pwas the climax of decades of effort to cripple chain stores in order to protect mom-and-pop retailers and the companies that supplied them." A&P, upon its acquisition of the Northeast retailer Pathmark, would be investigated and consequently reprimanded in 2005 by the Federal Trade Commission (FTC) for its monopoly on businesses in Staten Island and in Shirley, Long Island.

Though A&P undoubtedly influenced the childhoods of thousands of Staten Islanders, local deliverers, in particular Holtermann's Bakery, are still fondly remember by many. Among the lesser-known bread deliverers was Dugan's, owned by brothers Dave and Bob, which was headquartered out of Newark. It also maintained a large bakery on 222nd Street in Queens, however. Harry Roman wrote, "[Dugan's] local delivery trucks were small, funny-looking, two-toned vehicle, the front of which always reminded me of a squashed nose. For some reason, the brand name on the vehicles has stayed in my mind – 'Gertenschlagger' – most likely German. These stubby little vehicles zipped around neighborhood streets, replenishing local store stock on a daily basis. Sometimes inquiring local boys and girls managed to liberate a few items when the driver went inside to deliver his products...the power of a sweet tooth is not to be taken lightly." Dugan's was later bought out by Carvel Ice Cream. Perhaps one of the most convenient, door-to-door services offered was that of John Iammatteo in his 1963 Chevrolet service vehicle—knife sharpening. His business was established by his father Pasquale in Brooklyn and was later carried into Staten Island. His truck, purchased on the day of President Kennedy's assassination, would come to be associated with excellent sharpening of knives, scissors, and push mowers. Many Islanders have said, "When you heard that bell ringing, you knew to come running out with your knives in your hands." The sales and service trucks such as those of Iammatteo and Dugan's maneuvered around numerous road closures due to the presence of block parties or children playing in the street, like those who frequented the fields, playing heat-relieving sports such as softball, along Amboy Road in 1924 (preceding the heightened availability of air-conditioning in the late-1960s).

Due to the evolution of American society, however, as well as numerous safety concerns associated with unsupervised play, children stay inside more often, though less so in Staten Island due to the family-friendly, law-and-order atmosphere. In fact, the borough is widely-known for its reputation as a police-heavy division, supplying the New York City police force with more officers than The Bronx. Staten Island's law enforcement-history, furthermore, isn't restricted to the large number of patrol officers, but to all aspects of life including homelessness and mental disability. When Geraldo Rivera received his first big break positioning shipping pallets to jump the fence at Willowbrook State School to document horrendous conditions inside, a new epoch of tolerance emerged, but as did an unexpected phenomenon. The mentally ill were now abound in Richmond County, roaming the streets, much to the demise of residents—indicating a previous boundary separating two polarized classes had been broken. Though Willowbrook State School itself closed in 1987, the issue of handling certain segments of society is by no means obsolete on Staten Island. The debate arose yet again in 2017 when Mayor Bill de Blasio proposed his initiative "Smaller, Safer, Fairer: A roadmap to closing Rikers Island." The plan entails closing New York City's main jail complex, favoring the placement of more jails in individual boroughs. Though widespread dislike among city council members for the idea of a jail being constructed in their districts was imminent, Staten Islanders' fear of the city imposing itself once again on the "Forgotten Borough" not only compounded with a vehement dislike of de Blasio (determined through election statistics), but also with previous experience with other city projects. To further chronicle the law-and-order history of Staten Island, the founding of the North Shore neighborhood, Westerleigh, rooted in the temperance movement, is to be noted. Following the market revolution and shift toward manufacturing, particularly with the development of textile mills, the temperance movement soared—propelled by women who sought an alcohol-free household to ensure minimal domestic abuse. In 1877, a temperance group purchased a large area of land just less than two miles south of the Kill Van Kull, founding National Prohibition Park in 1888. Still today, remnants of the neighborhood's founding remain apparent, with street names such as Neal Dow, Clinton B. Fiske, [Mary A.] Livermore, Maine, Ohio, New York, and Colorado referencing fervent Prohibition activists, politicians, and "dry" states.

Characterized by its unique neighborhood charm, each Staten Island neighborhood resonates with different historical aspects that belong either to a foundation (such as those associated with the temperance movement in

Westerleigh), an ethnicity (distinctive areas predominantly populated by a certain group), or a farm (like that of Henry Meyer in New Springville). It was this separation, individualism, and these periodic immigrant influxes that paved the way for Staten Island's unique formation and development. Only toward the quarter point of the twentieth century did the isolationist philosophy diminish as connections such as the Goethals Bridge and Outerbridge Crossing, both opened in 1928, connecting New York City to New Jersey, appeared. Pro-development sentiments were expressed in signs similar to the one alongside Forest Avenue in 1927 which read: "What the Brooklyn Bridge has done for Brooklyn, what the Queensboro Bridge has done for Long Island, what the Philadelphia Bridge has done for Camden, the Elizabeth Bridge will do for Washington Manor." The bridge's opening was followed by several development and investment booms, particularly in the areas closest to the bridge and on the South Shore—including the erection of Giffords Gardens. The housing project (now covered by Giffords Lane in Great Kills; taking the name of local surveyor/commissioner, Daniel Gifford), developed by "Commonwealth Associates" in anticipation of the bridges' opening, commenced in 1927. The project, similar to the one in Laurelton, Queens, planned the construction over two-hundred Spanish villas, sold with a complimentary automobile, but would ultimately fail as the Great Depression wretched the housing market through the 1930s. Only seven of twenty-two villas actually constructed remain.

As briefly mentioned above, certain areas of Staten Island were founded or inhabited entirely by a single ethnic group, sometimes by complete coincidence (e.g. Italians in the South Shore), and at other times as part of a joint venture. Perhaps the most notable example of a collective settlement was Spanish Camp (Spanish Colony)—a former private community located on the eastern shore near Annadale. The small 1929-founded colony was established by members of the vegetarian, anarchist Spanish Naturopath Society—an organization established in the 1920s to promote "healthy alternative[s] to modern medicine" by residing in the countryside. The community soon attracted dozens of other Spanish emigrants, building up the colony from a series of tents to an array of winterized bungalows. The most famous resident of Spanish Camp was activist, Servant of God, and co-founder of the Catholic Worker Movement, Dorothy Day. Initially a radical journalist living life alla Bohemian in Greenwich Village, Day experienced a conversion on the South Shore of Staten Island where she had purchased a bungalow at Spanish Camp from the film rights she had earned from her semi-autobiographical book published in 1924—The Eleventh Virgin. She found work as a gardening columnist for the *Staten Island Advance* while she established her mission of feeding the homeless and practicing civil disobedience. In the six summers leading up to her death in 1980, Day would spend her time enjoying the sea breeze from Raritan Bay in her modest cottage. She is now buried at Cemetery of the Resurrection. Day's cottage would too meet its own demise in 1997 when developer John DiScala, owner of Volpe-DeSimone Inc., purchased the 17-acre Spanish Camp from the S.N.P. Society for seven-million dollars with the intent of building dream homes "rivaling [those of] Beverly Hills or Saddle River." With 30-day eviction orders underway, the developer advanced his plans to build forty luxury homes, expected to sell for one-million dollars a piece. DiScala's bulldozing of Dorothy Day's former summer retreat came precisely during the official process of designating the cottage as a landmark under protected status. Journalist Wayne Barrett wrote, "[DiScala] had...been sanctioned...for painting the brick façade of an East 74th Street landmarked residential building he'd bought in 1997. He'd already demolished fourteen camp cottages without permits, provoking seventeen Buildings Department violations. He'd denounced the Day cottage as 'rubbish.'" Many criticized the three-and-a-half-year complacency of Jennifer Raab, chair of the city's Landmark Preservation Committee, for the demolition of the historic site. Though plans to move forward with developing would stall for over a decade due to "legal wrangling," the construction of twenty-one homes on the former Spanish Camp property would commence in 2009.

A similar struggle—parallel to the spiritual significance of Day's Spanish Camp cottage—was experienced on Fingerboard Rd. where developers remain in the process of paving over the remains of Mt. Manresa. Founded as the first retreat center in the entire country by Fr. Terence J. Shealy, S.J. in 1911, Mount Manresa derived its namesake from Manresa, Spain—the town in which Ignatius of Loyola developed the practice of spiritual retreats. "The fifteen-acre property is an ecological gem, replete with hills created 20,000 years ago by a receding glacier...Manresa is surrounded by a pristine, old-growth forest containing almost one-hundred native oak, tulip, and black tupelo trees estimated to be at least one-hundred-fifty years old." Despite the formation of groups such as Save Mount Manresa and political advocacy from high-profile inidividuals, the Jesuits entered into a private contract with the developer, Savo Brothers Inc. in 2013. In 2014, Jesuit spokesperson Rev. Vincent Cooke stated, "We are making a strategic decision. Prayer and meditation can take place anywhere, and a special house is not an essential element." The retreat house, whose selling price reached fifteen-million dollars, was scheduled for a transformation into a two-hundred-fifty townhouse development. The sale had gone against previous intentions signaled by the Jesuit community in that they had assured in unofficial statements in 2011 the existence of Mount Manresa would persist for the "next century." Confronted with the reality of maintenance and improvement fees, charitable donations and taxes acquired through Staten Island residents were viewed as non-option for the center's sustainability. Borough President James Oddo endured a contentious fight for preservation of the site, but was ultimately unsuccessful. His final retaliation came in two forms, one with a longer-lasting effect than the other. Following the company's scandalous track record with lying in official documents about the presence of asbestos in several developments, Oddo encouraged investigaton into the project and the company before proceeding with development. Next, as possessing the powers of borough president, Oddo named several streets in the project after evil characteristics—believed by Savo Bros. to be an "abuse of [his] discretion." Oddo gave the names "cupidity," meaning greed for money or possessions; "fouberie," meaning deceit, trickery, guile; and "avidita," meaning greed, avidity to the three streets encompassed by the developer's plans.

The signs of Staten Island's great transformation were gradual and progressive. A brochure published in 1906 by Wood, Harmon, & Co., a real-estate/development firm, shows "Father Knickerbocker," a member of one of New York's oldest Dutch family alluding to 'New York City,' stepping onto Staten Island from Manhattan. The drawing reads: "Father Knickerbocker finds a new home for his children. South New York, formerly (Staten Island)." By 1930, posters advertising immense amounts of acreage available for purchase were an increasingly-visible sight in South Shore neighborhoods, collectively known as "The Sticks"—a term for a rural, heavily-forested area—such as Annadale. On the corner of Arden Avenue & Amboy Road in 1926, several real-estate brokers' signs, including from S.P.E Realty Associates and Hugh W. Murphy from Dongan Hills and Manhattan (demonstrating outside interest in the borough's development) read, "Bungalows and Bungalow Lots" and "Nine Acres—House and Barn." Bungalows, in fact, particularly near the coast, were among the earliest dwellings constructed on Staten Island. Mildred Savitsky (b. 1923) of New Dorp, recalled summer outings from

Greenwich Village in Manhattan to Marconi's Hotel (an Italian villa-type building) at 236 Mill Rd. in preparation for the family's moving to 13 Weed Ave.

Further signs of a suburban shift were evident in coast side communities such as Annadale Beach in 1925 where E.A. White Organization Inc. advertised its constructing of model subdivisions along with "guaranteed complete street improvements" to ease customers' suspicions. A subsidiary of E.A. White Organization Inc., the East Annadale Beach Corp. purchased "nearly one-hundred acres from James W. Hughes, whose property adjoined George Barclay's (where the name of today's Barclay Ave. originates)." The pre-Depression land grab occurred throughout the South Shore, but this development in particular centered around the southwest corner of Holdridge Ave. & Hylan Blvd. Lured by prospective benefits, Constance (b. 1892) and Filippo (b. 1888) Paterno migrated from Nagle Ave. in Upper Manhattan to the East Annadale Beach Corp.'s near-waterfront property in 1930 after a real estate agent pointed to a "steady stream of cars" along Hylan Blvd. as a factor for operating a successful business. That year, Paterno's Hotel & Restaurant opened. By a mere several years into the venture, however, weekend outings to the South Shore during the summertime and decreased automobile traffic could not sustain the operation. The Paterno's in the late-1930s moved to 84 Scribner Ave. in New Brighton with their six children where Filippo would become a warehouseman. In 1968, the building on Hylan Blvd. was "deemed an unsafe structure, and in 1969, it was demolished." The AdvantageCare Physicians – Annadale Medical Office's parking lot currently occupies the formerly vacant planned-development land. The dirt, gravel roads of the Island's South Shore were undergoing a complete transformation — a signal of the borough's evolution and increasing connectivity with New York City. The North Shore, on the other hand, only slid further into the hands of developers.

The developing firm Minogue & Minogue advertised "one and two family houses" and "lots on reasonable terms" on Mountain View Avenue on the grounds of what was previously a vast meadow dominating Graniteville. The commercial, residential vision for Staten Island emerged the moment the bulldozers unearthed the soil of New York City's last frontier. The South Shore of Staten Island could quite accurately be designated as the area most susceptible to development in 20th-century New York. In 1971 for instance, Republican State Senator John Marchi (with support from Mayor John Lindsay) introduced legislation for the South Richmond Development Corporation. "[T]he plan called for the city to use eminent domain to buy property and transfer it to the Rouse Company, which would also construct residential towers on landfill in Raritan Bay." Met with heavy Conservative Party opposition, the plan—a "new-town experiment"—was the largest of its type, calling for housing for 300,000 new residents (twice the borough's population) on a "major opportunity area." The Rouse Co.—headed by James W. Rouse—had been responsible for the designing of the first-enclosed mall on the east coast – Harundale in Glen Burnie, Maryland – in 1958, and the planned community of Columbia, Maryland in 1967. The unsuccessful South Shore proposal woul have been the largest project undertaken by The Rouse Co. Despite the community's ultimate failure, a significant deal of change would occur on the South Shore. One witness to the transformation of the once rural area was Paul Margarella—a self-made businessman from the region of Campania, Italy who input the sewers on Woodrow Road in the early 1960s. A lifelong venture capitalist since birth, Margarella—already having immigrated from Italy—began his career at the Staten Island shipyards, and after meeting his wife—a seamstress—after seeing an advertisement for sewing machines in the newspaper, began a dress manufacturing company called Gem of Staten Island on Beach Street in

Stapleton, employing his wife's cousins. Margarella, during this period, purchased the St. George Theatre in 1974, the Liberty Theatre in 1955 (which he converted to a bowling alley), and the Ritz Theatre (which his son later converted to the Ritz Super Rink and ran it from 1975 to 1983). His son Stephen, the owner of the 1995-founded Margarella Asphalt & Concrete, remarked, "On Staten Island, growing up in my household, it was pretty much 'Whoever has the gold makes the rules!' I got my first job working at LaRosa's Bakery in South Beach carrying racks, and from there, I never lost my work ethic. When I was thirty-eight I retired, but two years later I got bored, so I decided to fulfill a contract maintenance idea and begin my own asphalt and concrete business." Speaking of gold, the anonymous Italian immigrant proverb is of special relevance in Stephen Margarella's case: "I came to America because I heard the streets were paved with gold. When I got here, I found out three things: First, the streets weren't paved with gold; second, they weren't paved at all; and third, I was expected to pave them." Margarella explained, "Not too long ago, my company had the opportunity to pave the entirety of 34th Street from the Hudson to the East River." Margarella's company is a precipitator

[Margarella Concrete & Asphalt in action in Manhattan. Courtesy – Stephen Margarella]

of change on Staten Island, but is also critical in responding to emergencies, hazardous conditions, and needed repairs.

The Island's previous history, although partially reconciled in its incorporation as a borough in 1898, was being placed under direct attack by large groups of people in a large part who sought an escape from the wretchedness of the city to the lusciousness and open-space Staten Island guaranteed. Some migrated from other parts of the city to enjoy better air quality; such was the case with Luigi Montanti, founder of L. Montanti & Sons Shoemaker & Leathercraft Supplies in Port Richmond, whose condition— emphysema—prompted family members, as well as his doctor to suggest he move to the "country" from Manhattan. Developers paved over valuable artifacts of history such as iconic houses and blossoming daisy fields, nearly erasing an entire legacy of intrigue and mystique. Meadows in Great Kills in which children used to build forts made from tree branches, creeks along which native Islanders used to trap muskrats and hunt pheasants such as those leading out to Poppy Joe Island Beach (and sell periodically for $6-8 a pelt in the early-1910s), and endless green fields such as those at Mount Loretto which looked out onto Raritan Bay, were replaced by semi-detached homes, soon to be inhabited by the passengers embarking from Brooklyn on the Verrazzano-Narrows Bridge on the thousands of moving vans headed west.

TRANSFORMATION: BRITISH HISTORY – DEVELOPMENT

~

A survivor of the urbanization movement is the Voorlezer's House in south-central Staten Island—a once Dutch Reformed (a Calvinist sect founded in 1571) Congregation, school-house, and residency. The house was purchased by two of the oldest families on Staten Island— the Van Pelts and Rezeaus (of whom a cemetery is also named in Richmondtown)—and was later deemed the "nation's oldest schoolhouse," having been built in 1696. The home's previous owners, the Van Pelts, also owned several other properties and fields, ever since the turn of the 17th century. A son, John Van Pelt Jr., was a Captain during the Revolutionary War, accompanying George Washington across the Delaware River. His son was also a militia captain during the War of 1812. Although Mr. Van Pelt was originally from Staten Island and served in the United States' military, he did not fight in the Battle of Staten Island which took place between the 2nd Canadian Regiment—a division of the Continental Army—and John Campbell's British forces on August 2nd, 1777, following General Howe's withdrawal of troops to New York City and attempted peace negotiations with the American Patriots. On September 11, 1776, Admiral of the Fleet Richard Howe, participant in the War of the Austrian Succession, Battle of Quiberon Bay in the Seven Years' War, and American Revolutionary War, met with Dr. Benjamin Franklin of Pennsylvania, Edward Rutledge of South Carolina, and John Adams of Massachusetts at the Conference House at the very southern tip of Staten Island: Billopp's Point. Riding on a Patriot-held-Perth Amboy-departed boat waving the "flag of truce," the three men arrived at the Christopher F. Billopp House anticipating a cessation of the violence which had erupted in April of 1775. The three-hour conference produced minimal results: nothing beyond an atmosphere of false exchanges. graceful greeting rituals, and untrue assurances. "[Lord Howe] entered in a discourse of considerable length which contained no explicit proposition of peace except one, viz. that the colonies should return their allegiance and obedience to the government of Great Britain... [the delegates] mentioned the repeated humble petitions of the colonies to the King and parliament, which had been treated with contempt, and answered only by additional injuries... His lordship then saying he was sorry to find that no accommodation was likely to take place, put an end to the conference." The conference ultimately failed due to Lord Howe's ability to only issue pardons and Benjamin Franklin's assertion that "independence was now an unchangeable fact, and Britain had better face it, and negotiate with Americans as a separate country."

The Conference House today, located at 7455 Hylan Blvd., remains one of Staten Island's oldest edifices, having been built in the Dutch Revival/American Colonial style. The home's former owner, Christopher Farmar Billopp, is also the subject of much historical interest. In popular Staten Island folklore, he is said to have been the individual to secure the Island as a part of the State of New York. In 1675, the Duke of York proposed a contest for the acquiring of Staten Island which lied on the west side of the Hudson River. He proposed for a man to circumnavigate the entire approximately 36-mile isle in less than twenty-four hours— a task successfully achieved in roughly twenty-three by his nominee: Christopher Billopp on his boat "The Bentley." In exchange for his victory, the duke granted Billopp over 1,100 acres of land. Compounded with his previous holdings, the land's acreage amounted to over one-thousand six-hundred acres of land—an area second only to Governor Thomas Dongan of New York. On June 10, 1687 Billopp, whose roots derived from Beverely in the East Riding of Yorkshire, was appointed as surveyor for highways of Staten Island. He was also commander of "England's finest ship, the *London*," and operator of the Perth Amboy Ferry. His great-grandson, Christopher, would perhaps become the most well-known of his entire family. Born in 1737 in Bentley Manor (the "Conference House"), Christopher Billopp would become a representative for the State of New York, New Brunswick assemblyman in Canada, Superintendent of the Police of Staten Island, and lieutenant colonel—nicknamed "Tory Colonel"—for the Loyalists. The target of several Patriot attacks, Billopp would successfully be captured twice in 1779 while crossing over to Perth Amboy. "On one of these occasions he was confined in the jail at Burlington. The patriot Commissary of Prisoners, Mr. [Elias] Boudinot, in the warrant of commitment, directed that irons should be put on his hands and feet, that he should be chained to the floor of a close room, and that he should be fed bread and water, it is said, in retaliation for the cruel treatment of two Whig officers who had fallen into the hands of Royal troops." His home would be the site of numerous gatherings with General Wilhelm von Knyphausen after the arrival of his 6,000 troops from Bremen, Germany, and Colonel John Graves Simcoe.

It is a little-known fact that the last shot of the American Revolution was fired off the coast of Staten Island on what would come to be known as "Evacuation Day" on November 25, 1783. Under the direction of the commander-in-chief of British forces in North America, Guy Carleton, the 1st Baron Dorchester, the remaining British "government personnel, remaining troops, and refugees" boarded the HMS *Ceres*, as the American flag was raised at Fort Amsterdam (Fort George) in the Battery, Manhattan. A grave sense of humiliation reigned over the defeated soldiers who only eight years ago, would grasp control of the city they were now abandoning. In 1776, General Howe sat reading the American Declaration of Independence to his soldiers at the Old Rose & Crown Farm House, and British soldiers lodged at the Black Horse Tavern in New Dorp. Seven years later, a British cannon fired off the coast of Staten Island in the direction of Fort Wadsworth, officially ending an entire era of British control. The final British forces departed from Staten Island on December 4th, forever extinguishing the Loyalist presence in Richmond County. A poem from *"Evacuation Day", 1783: Its Many Stirring Events: with Recollections of Capt. John Van Arsdale...* by James Riker, commending the celebration, reads: "Of conquest then despairing, / With Refugees and Tories, / George for his bulldogs sent; / They Yankee vengeance fearing, / *Greased the flag-staff*—and went!/ Then Yorkers, let's remember/ The Refugees and Tories, / The five and twentieth day/ Of the bleak month, November, / When the Cow-thieves sneaked away!"

Before departing for New York City, Lord Howe, who genuinely attempted to negotiate peace at Billopp's residence, and his army camped out at St. Andrews Protestant Episcopal Church (a vehement supporter of the Loyalist Cause on Staten Island), now located immediately next to the Voorlezer's House. St. Andrews was founded by Reverend Aeneas Mackenzie in 1705 in response to the growing number of English on Staten Island and Church of England's desire to maintain a devout congregation in the colonies. St. Andrew's even received a royal charter from Queen Anne in 1712. It is one of the oldest parishes in America and on Staten Island. Its history precedes that of Roman Catholicism in the borough, which would be carried over in the traditions of newly-arrived Irish, Italian, and French immigrants who would establish the first Roman Catholic Church on Staten Island in New Brighton—St. Peter's—in 1839). Immediately behind St. Andrew's Church are two other historical sites—LaTourette Hill and

Lookout Place—both which offer a unique look in time at Staten Island's strategic location during The American Revolution. On Lookout Place (a British fort), located on the LaTourette estate, soldiers chopped down mulberry trees to view the surrounding areas of New Jersey and New York in case of an attack. Staten Island's three-thousand residents in 1777 were avid supporters of the British and did not exhibit one strand of Patriot sympathy. Describing the Anglican hold on Staten Island even before the beginnings of the Constitutional Convention, historian Phillip Papas writes in his book *That Ever Loyal Island: Staten Island and the American Revolution*, "[The Moravians] argued that the Anglican Church was a monolithic obstacle to political and social advancement not only in the community but also throughout America... Anglicans answered these charges by portraying the dissenters as a small group of fanatics who were trying to satisfy their personal ambitions at the expense of the social order." The Island's Revolutionary history alludes to a time period when Staten Island and Manhattan were two entirely separate entities, both politically and geographically. Staten Island's blossoming mulberry trees, which can still be viewed off LaTourette Golf Course, behind which British soldiers used to hide are now but a rare sight in modern, developed Richmond County in which Henry David Thoreau once enjoyed the solitude of the landscape while tutoring Ralph Waldo Emerson's nephews. Though Staten Island's vast wetlands and voluminous meadows have indeed been spared a great portion of New York City's urban development, they were once a near-helpless foe to the notorious New York City's Parks Commissioner, Robert Moses's urbanizing agenda.

Upsetting nearly every neighborhood organization, destroying numerous public parks, and serving the interest of developers and industrialists, Robert Moses, the controversial "master builder" and "power broker," held no special sympathies toward the secluded lifestyle of Staten

Islanders. In 1963, Moses brazenly announced "Staten Island's days of being shrouded and saved by its isolation are about to end." The following year on November 21, the Verrazzano-Narrows Bridge (at the time, the world's longest suspension bridge) opened, signaling an end to an entire period of native history. Michael Lombardi (b. 1952), the son of a waitress at The Golden Q and a naval officer who survived kamikaze bombings, who grew up at 29 Legion Pl. in Concord, recalled "I can remember my bed rumbling the day they began building that bridge! It was the beginning of a whole time to come." The plan, however, was only one segment of an entire colonizing timetable intended to connect the entire tri-state (NY-NJ-CT) area through a series of freeways and bridges. The idea of developing a series of highways and a public park system through Staten Island, however, wasn't in reality a slightest new proposal. In 1870, Frederick Law Olmstead proposed a park system for the Island. Additionally, in 1902, the Staten Island Chamber of Commerce's Committee on Parks proposed creating a network of "parkways" and "driveways" which would model Boston, Massachusetts' Commonwealth Avenue. That very plan would almost identically model Moses' twenty-eight years later. In 1930, Moses proposed the construction of the Richmond Parkway, also known as the Korean War Veterans Parkway—a project completed in 1972, traversing Arden Heights, Annadale, Huguenot, Prince's Bay, and Pleasant Plains. In 1964, the Staten Island Expressway (a part of Interstate 278) reached completion—tracing the route of Little Clove Road, Victory Boulevard, and Goethals Road. By mid-1964, Interstate 278 connected Throgs Neck, Bronx to Astoria, Queens via the Triborough Bridge, Bay Ridge, Brooklyn to Fort Wadsworth via the Verrazzano Bridge, and west Staten Island to Elizabeth, New Jersey via the Goethals Bridge. Clearing space for the 13,700-foot Verrazzano, Robert Moses (angered over the rejection of his proposal for the Brooklyn-Battery Bridge linking Lower Manhattan to

[The construction of the Verrazzano-Narrows Bridge. C. 1960s. Courtesy – Joseph Sedutto]

Red Hook, Brooklyn) astonishingly took a sledgehammer to Bay Ridge, Brooklyn and Fort Lafayette constructed during the War of 1812, and permanently threatened an entire island's way of life. To further aggravate aesthetic matters, Moses proposed Shore Front Drive, a never-materialized highway linking the Verrazzano Bridge to the Outerbridge Crossing (following a route similar to Father Capodanno Boulevard), and the Willowbrook Parkway, beginning at the Bayonne Bridge and running perpendicular through Rockland Avenue. Taking barely any precautions, in 1962, Robert Moses advanced his urbanizing, tyrannical agenda and bulldozed over two-hundred bungalows on New Dorp Beach, preparing for a highway whose fate would never be realized.

The Verrazzano-Narrows Bridge [3] commends the revolutionary sailing voyage of Giovanni da Verrazzano

---

[33] On October 1, 2018, upon the signing of a bill by Governor Cuomo, the bridge's spelling was rightfully adjusted to include two "z"'s in "Verraz[z]ano." The original spelling was dictated by Governor Rockefeller who sought to anglicize the word.

(1485-1528)—the famed Italian, Florentine explorer who made history as the first to sail the entire Atlantic Coast from Florida to northeastern Canada. In January of 1524, Verrazzano, sponspored by King Francois I of France, departed the Portuguese island of Madeira to North America. That April, he became the first individual to sail through the Narrows. Nearly three-hundred forty years later, Mayor Robert Wagner Jr., Brooklyn Borough President Abe Stark, and President of the U.S. Steel Corp. Roger Blough stood alongside each other during the bridge's opening ceremony. The first paying customers were Staten Islanders themselves. Curtis High School Association of Alumni & Friends (CHSAAF) Board of Director George Scarpelli '60 "paid the first fifty cent toll (a Kennedy half dollar) and drove his 1959 light blue Cadillac convertible across the bridge from Staten Island to Brooklyn...A 52-car motorcade followed." In his car were classmates Robert Caplan, Ben Goldsmith, Anthony Lenza, Frank Picone, Richard Rimaglia, and Ronald Sacoff. Stationed at the No. 7 tollbooth two days before, the troop had received reluctant approval for their "camping out" by the Triborough Bridge & Tunnel Authority persuaded by Borough President Anthony Maniscalco. Due to the volume of traffic crossing over to Staten Island, the boys were forced to take the 69th St. Ferry back home. Following the opening of the bridge, a publicization brochure produced by the Staten Island Chamber of Commerce at 130 Bay St. advertised "[m]ore than 64,000 dwelling units, 80% owner occupied...in Richmond Borough, commonly known as Staten Island, one of the five boroughs comprising the City of New York." Staten Island may have been destined to be a suburb since at the least the beginning of the 20th century. In his book *Crabgrass Frontier: The Suburbinization of the United States*, Kenneth Jackson cites New Brighton as one of several potential "first" suburbs in the United States. During the postwar period of 1946-1956, however, the idea of Staten

Island as "suburbia" was to a slight degree inaccurate due to the unpopularity of rowhomes and subdivisons. Despite his conquest of the topography of Richmond County, Robert Moses nevertheless observed, "Staten Island is fortunate in its terrain. It has big hills, deep valleys, and meadows, woodland and waterfront. There is still an opportunity here to avoid errors of the past, save what natured has provided and build for the future with intelligence and restraint." This representation of the developer's personality was more often than not overshadowed by his broken promises. "In its first full year of operation, the bridge's traffic volume of seventeen million vehicles overshot engineers' estimates by thirty-four percent." Furthermore, in 1967, due to the bridge's popularity, a six-lane lower level was added to the structure. Though the source of intense suburbanization, the Verrazzano-Narrows Bridge was noted for its immaculate architecture. The design was charted by Swiss engineer Othmann Ammann, the chief engineer of the Port Authority of New York from 1930-1937, noted for his previous engineering creations—the Bayonne Bridge, the George Washington Bridge, and others. The receipient of the National Medal of Science by President Lyndon B. Johnson in 1964, Ammann once remarked, "It's a crime to build an ugly bridge." The $320-million-dollar project, whose toll was falsely promised to be eliminated by the time the construction costs were paid off, was extraordinary in several respects. For one, the bridge's 4,260-foot center span surpassed that of the Golden Gate Bridge's in California by sixty feet. Second, "[t]here would be enough wire in the Verrazzano's cables to circle the earth five times around at the equator or reach halfway to the moon." Augustine Friedrich also notes there was "enough concrete in its anchorages to pave a single-lane highway reaching all the way from New York to Washington." Third, to honor its beauty, three U.S. postage stamps (1964, 2006, 2014) were created using an image of the Verrazzano. Many on both sides of the Narrows strait have even likened the bridge's blueish lights attached to the cables to a Tiffany "string of pearls." The construction of the Verrazzano-Narrows Bridge came as the final, successful development push which could not be ignored in a thriving New York City. Other attempts were surprisingly frequent, but futile. The first push was in 1888 when the Baltimore & Ohio Railroad attempted to tunnel the strait. The next attempt was made under the administration of Mayor John Hylan which "accrued the considerable sum of $500,000 in appropriations to begin a combination freight and passenger tunnel." One of the final significiant proposals came from structural engineer David B. Steinman who called for the construction of "Liberty Bridge" connecting the two New York City boroughs. The measure however, was blocked by Mayor LaGuardia who not only felt insufficiently prepared for such a project, but felt the interference of the private sector was inappropriate in this case.

Though many of Moses' projects would dismantle an enormous share of residential society, none of his achievements would be scorned more by Staten Islanders than the Fresh Kills Landfill—a two-thousand, two-hundred acre dumping ground for New York City opened in 1948. By this time, environmentally-speaking, the city administration and Staten Island were already at odds. Between 1926-1941, the city operated an incinerator at the current Great Kills Park. The dumping site was used relatively unmindfully in that the garbage remained largely uncovered, allowing a putrid stench to penetrate the atmosphere. Three years after its closure, until 1948, the city would embark on a project to transform the former landfill into a park, using waste material to fill in the wetlands and increase the usable land footprint. Professor Ted Steinberg wrote, "In all, 467 acres of marsh and underwater land was nullified so that Great Kills Parks could open in 1949. Moses had put the 'great' back in Great Kills, or so he argued. If Great Kills Park came at the expense of a salt marsh, it came in a borough with still plenty to spare." Though many Islanders would not know it at the time, the consequences of constructing this public park would not emerge until decades later. In a report written by investigative reporter Paul DeRienzo, it is estimated that out of fifteen million cubic yards of garbage used to fill Great Kills Park, 265 acres contained radiation spots 200-times normal background levels. The toxicity has prevented people from entering certain, hazardous areas of the park, and could require both millions of dollars and extended periods of time to clean up. The radioactivity was initially attributed to medical waste, in particular tiny radium needles used to treat cancerous tumors in the early 20th century, but the enormous area of contamination tells a different story. In September 1940, Belgian businessman and director of the Union Miniere du Haut Katanga in the Belgian Congo, Edgar Sengier (having learned of the calamitous capabilities of uranium from English chemist Sir Henry Tizard) ordered the shipment of 1,050 tons of 65% uranium ore, after private purchase negotiations with Major General Kenneth D. Nichols (the reason for the private arrangements remains unclear, and the presence of ore on Staten Island remains one of the enduring mysteries of the Manhattan Project), from Africa to the United States. The ore arrived to Staten Island and was stored at the J.A. Dean & Co. mill property of Archer-Midlands, just under the Bayonne Bridge in Port Richmond. The ore, from which would be extracted the largest single amount of uranium for the construction of the first initial bombs of the Manhattan Project, would be stored in burlap sacks in a desolate corner of the mill. The Manhattan Project is speculated to have played a role in the 2005 discovery of radioactivity in Great Kills Park. DeRienzo explained, "Much of the waste from atomic bomb testing from the Manhattan Project has gone missing without any explanation. Large amounts of radioactive waste from the bomb project have turned up at locations near the numerous and far flung locations where the bomb was developed, such as West Lake near St. Louis or sites near the chemical plants involved in uranium processing outside of Buffalo, New York. The radioactivity in Great Kills just happened to be discovered because of a post-9/11 helicopter block-and-lot search which was undertaken by the Department of Energy's National Nuclear Security Administration (NNSA) to establish baseline levels of naturally occurring background radiation in large metropolitan cities than can be used in the event of a dirty or nuclear bomb threat by comparing the baseline data to unnatural spikes in certain types of radiation in an attempt to identify the location of a bomb or bombs. The radioactive hotspot in Great Kills Park was one of about eighty discovered in 2005. Though the sources of such findings are still uncertain, such exorbitant amounts of radioactivity could have come from waste related to the Manhattan Project and its immediate aftermath: atomic bombs.

Regarding Fresh Kills Landfill, its opening was to be temporary: a five-year holding place. However, by 1961, it had reached over a thousand acres, and was polluting the surrounding neighborhoods of New Springville, Arden Heights, and Rossville with a smell so repulsive, it forced thousands to stay within the confines of their home with the windows sealed tightly. This was in spite of large trucks spraying massive quantities of pine sol in an attempt to mask the hideous odor. On the contrary, however, some residents of Eltingville, many of whom were children of New York City Department of Sanitation workers, possess fond memories of passing guard shack-like buildings to dump any household item, breathing in a peculiarly sweet smell, resembling neither a pleasant or bad scent. Various reports described the multitude of items lying atop the one-fifty foot mountain of trash (dubbed "Mount Trashmore") covered nearly entirely with seagulls, as "refrigerators, discarded lumber, furniture, kids' games, cans, bottles, etc." By 1991, the acreage had reached its maximum size, making it the largest landfill in the entire world. The madness would rage on until March 22, 2001, when borough president and future borough president, Guy Molinari and James P. Molinaro, would witness the last barge of garbage entering Fresh Kills through the Arthur Kill. Suing the mayor's office for a violation of the Clean Air Act of 1963 and for an unequal distribution of the city's trash burden, Guy Molinari successfully erased the lifetime scar perpetrated by Robert Moses, the 20th-century zeitgeist developer who would change the face of the nation's most populous city. Fresh Kills Landfill would later be reopened temporarily to intake garbage from the 9/11 Terror Attacks (which resulted in the death of over two-hundred Staten Island residents). Consequently, due to the presence of human flesh in the remains, Staten Island would also see an unwanted surge of lingering vultures which still are a frequent sight in the Staten Island skies. Developing and waste management aside, Staten Island's evolution was also propelled by a number of factors, including the discovery of lucrative resources and profound economic niches.

~

Mining, Linoleum, and Procter & Gamble

One such discovery was that of iron ore in the serpentine rock, west of Castleton Corners and in Todt Hill. In the latter half of the 1800's, a large deposit of limonite (also known as Brown Hematite; often used for pigments) was unearthed alongside Jewett Avenue, only six feet beneath the surface. The fifty-six-acre property would be controlled by the Richmond Iron Mining Company (whose captain would reside at a farmstead on Westcott Blvd. & Kemball Avenue on the previous grounds of "Diamond Lake"; his property would later be acquired by the mercantile business, J.W. Cochrane & Co.), and produce over twenty-one thousand tons of ore in its first year of operation. Noting the ore's production-purpose, chemist and mining geologist C. Elton Buck writes in his study *Report... Upon the mines of Staten Island of the Richmond Mining Co.*, "In addition to the legitimate demand for this ore for furnace purposes, a new use has been adopted for it in this city—namely, for the purification of illuminating gas, and already the New York Gas Company have consumed a considerable quantity in their purifiers." At the time of this study requested by the mining company itself, 1868, the United States' demand for furnacing, freight power, and gas lighting was increasing exponentially. The mines on Staten Island proved to be an extremely reliable source for the acquisition of fuel and energy. Additional mines were discovered in Todt Hill, termed "Ijzer Berg—Iron Mountain," by the early Dutch settlers. These mines were first exploited by the H.W. Johns Manufacturing Company for the most-commonly encountered form of asbestos—chrysotile. Founded in 1858 in New York City, the Company utilized the chrysotile asbestos for the manufacturing of fire-resistant shingles (patented immediately before the Civil War). The mining's outcome produced a stunning hilly, curvy topography and an approximately 443-foot hill atop which the Richmond County Country Club sits today. Further discovery of iron ore in Todt Hill lead to the rampant practice of strip mining—a variation of surface mining in which minerals are extracted from relatively flat terrain. Fragments of Staten Island's great mining industry can still be seen in the present day with "Iron Mine Drive," west of the Jefferson Avenue Railway Station, commending the forgotten industrial epoch. Though Todt Hill's opulent greenery and hillsides went unscathed for nearly a decade after the mining industry on Staten Island dissolved, Robert Moses unearthed various shreds of those memories when he attempted to construct the Richmond Parkway. Although he was ultimately unsuccessful in his audacious attempt, he traumatized Staten

Island communities for decades, having unearthed a fair-size portion of land, destroyed several local, historic businesses, and created a man-made mountain (called Moses' Mountain) littered with excavated serpentinite intended for the Parkway's construction. Other remnants of the mining era included several severely dried-up ponds along Victory Boulevard in which ore from the Todt Hill mines was washed; the ponds have since vanished under the façade of modernity—a collection of Italian and American businesses including a pizzeria serving fried calzones—Pi[4], and a deli. Directly west of the mines once operated by the Richmond Mining Company is another intriguing piece of Staten Island Revolutionary history—the colonial home on Watchogue Road of Daniel Blake, grandson of the romantic English poet and painter, William Blake. Once the Captain of the Richmond County Police Department and later, a captain in the New York Police Department, Blake foundered to police unlicensed drinking establishments in violation of the excise law. Another testimonial of him was written by historian Ira K. Morris in her book *Morris's Memorial History of Staten Island, New York, Volume II,* describing Blake as leading a procession of "a squad of mounted police... [a] group of Kickapo Indians, [the] Fort Hamilton Band... [a] chariot containing a representation of the Goddess of Liberty; a section of the Fifth United States Artillery" from the USS Vandalia—an 18-gun sloop-of-war commissioned in 1828, docked at Stapleton.

Another neighborhood which boasts a rich industrial history which has since dissipated includes Travis (named

---

[4] Pi is the site of the former Al's Pizzeria which was known for its $0.15 slices in the 1970s, chicken parmesan heroes, baked ziti, and slogan of "You name it, we'll make it." Tony Bisogna, a former electrician for Seaview Hospital, whose grandfather owned Bisogna's Bakery on Jersey Street in New Brighton, recalled, "Al would run a special every so often: $2 for a whole pie." Bisogna specially built the electrical generator for Al's brother Girard's pizza mobile which Girard would drive to Susan E. Wagner High School and sell pizza to the students after school.

for Captain Jacob Travis), home of the borough's annual Fourth of July parade. In Travis, another micro-economy boosting Staten Island's development (though certainly not its reputation) emerged—"Linoleumville." Termed "New York's worst neighborhood name ever" by *Ephemeral New York*, Linoleumville became the headquarters of the American Linoleum Manufacturing Company in 1872: becoming the first linoleum factory in the United States. Originally named Joseph Wild & Co. after the ambitious, fatigued South Brooklyn resident and founder, Joseph Wild (for whom Wild Avenue is named), the linoleum producer was a joint-stock corporation that purchased three-hundred acres in the west shore neighborhood of Travis, previously-known as Long Neck. Between January of 1875 and 1931 (though mostly following the turn of the nineteenth century), the company continued to produce 90,000 square yards of the "unusual, wear-resistant, elastic, noiseless, and sanitary" linoleum per week, in addition to plank inlaid, cork carpet, wall hangings, feltings, Smyrna, damask Chinese, and Mendota rugs, employing steam boats to haul the material to Manhattan and New Jersey. The factory's linoleum would become known as "Battleship Linoleum" because of the company's installation of 777,470 square feet of the material on fifteen United States Battleships (e.g. USS Mississippi, commissioned in 1917; USS Texas, commissioned in 1914). Revolutionary industrial breakthroughs associated with the factory include its early use of electricity on Staten Island, as well as the invention of the signature process for manufacturing linoleum by superintendent, David Melvin (for whom Melvin Avenue is named). Local linoleum installation, mainly of the darkish/brown variety, to public schools and office buildings on Staten Island was achieved via trucks dubbed, "Linoleum Express." The express delivery vehicles were noted as one of the first successes of the less-costly, one-ton, commercial cars, having replaced the traditional three two-horse teams. The initial models utilized by Joseph Wild & Co. were the Smith Form-a-Truck made by Smith Motor Truck Corp., Chicago, Ill., and the Ford truck manufactured by Hayes-Diefenderfer, New York, N.Y. Other companies in the linoleum industry were located in Port Richmond: The Elm Park Linoleum Works (whose property was later purchased by the Lincrusta Polish Works) and the J.A. Dean & Co. Linseed Oil Mill; the latter whose annual output of linseed oil amounted to 500,000 gallons. The factory's 20th-century, seven-hundred-person workforce consisted of a largely Central/Eastern European, particularly Polish base—many of whom resided in the worker boardinghouses and would help establish the brick-and-stone, $17,000, St. Anthony's Church on January 1, 1910. The first-celebrating pastor, Reverend Joseph Brzoziewski ("Father Joe") was born in Poland in 1878, ordained by Cardinal John Murphy Farley in 1902, and initially appointed to St. Adalbert's Church in Port Richmond. He would go on to serve at Our Lady of Peace in Perth Amboy in the 1950s. For decades until the present time, St. Anthony's has remained the pillar of the local Polish community. The parish owes much to the previous linoleum-manufacturing industry. Since the close of the factory, Travis's Polish community has lived within the confines of the isolated, secluded, and natural Staten Island neighborhood. In fact, the rural neighborhood (a substitute for Kansas) was the backdrop for Elia Kazan's 1961 film *Splendor in the Grass*, starring Warren Beatty and Natalie Wood. Throughout time, much of the Travis Polish culture has disintegrated, resulting in the closure of numerous neighborhood establishments. Among the most prominent was Gadomski Bakery. Former Travis resident Peter F. Battaglia, calling back to mind a lost Staten Island era, reminisced: "some Sunday mornings all I want is to be able to go back to Gadomski's for their Russian Rye Bread, Polish Jelly Donuts, and Crullers...they were amazing...Mr. Gadomski baked in a brick oven at his home on Shelley Ave, and if you were on Victory Blvd. early enough you'd seen him in his baker's whites pushing his baker's racks loaded with treats down to the store. I can hear the bread slicer going. Mrs. Gadomski was gruff and scary, but it was worth it for those baked goods." Linoleumville was one of several major factories along the western shore of Staten Island. Another—located four miles in the northern direction in Howland Hook, "Port Ivory"—was the manufacturing plant for the soap company, Procter & Gamble. The Staten Island location, the company's third plant after its headquarters in Cincinnati, Ohio, and facility in Kansas City, Kansas, opened its doors in 1907—the same year in which William Cooper Procter, the grandson of P&G's co-founder, rose to the company's presidency. The factory would become the Island's largest employer, boasting over 1,400 workers. Seniority ranged between 35-50 years, and employees, who in the 1930s made under $2,000, enjoyed a 48-week, employment-guarantee plan (beginning on August 1, 1923), and a generous profit-sharing plan (beginning in 1887). By 1937, P&G had distributed $12,000,000 in cash bonuses and stock dividends to its employees across the United States as part of the plan. The distribution of dividends was often accompanied with celebratory festivities, such as a trip to the St. George Theatre. The factory was financed by the issuing of $3,000,000 in common stock, thereby increasing the common stock 50% from $6,000,000 to $9,000,000. The plant's original six structures were constructed by the Cramp & Co.—a construction firm headquartered in Philadelphia, notable for its building of the Bronx Opera House and several public schools in Pennsylvania. During its years of operation, the facility produced Crisco shortening, Solo, Lenox Soap, glycerin, Citrus Hill Orange Juice, Mr. Clean, Tide laundry detergent, Duncan Hines cake mix, and "99 44/100%" ivory soap or commercially nicknamed, "the soap that floats." Ivory soap, known to have originated from the accidental mistake of leaving soap for an extended duration of time in a soap-mixing machine, was used for hygienic purposes, supposedly inducing a youthful quality to the skin. The June 1954 special-edition of the company's magazine, Moonbeams, commending P&G's 75th anniversary, depicts a young jubilant baby alongside the words, "That Ivory Look: Young America has it... You can have it in 7 days!" However, as pointed out by Procter & Gamble's book *Unusual Uses of Ivory Soap*, originally published in 1916, one could also mix ivory soap with ammonia and kerosene, producing a "snow-white jelly," and use it to clean all porcelain-lined bathroom fixtures and sinks. Furthermore, one could use a bath of ivory soap on plants to ward off aphids, thereby "[promoting] luxuriant growth, and [giving] rich color to the leaves." By 1917, only ten years after the opening of the Staten Island P&G plant, the ivory soap product line's immense success contributed to the company's $128,549,649 in gross income.

Beginning only with 77-acres, the plant, upon "[adding] soap power to its mix in 1912," would expand to over twenty-eight buildings, spanning over a 129-acre site, "producing a million cases of Ivory Soap each year." Prior to World War II, the facility's products were shipped off via fully-loaded car floats to the Erie, Delaware Lackawanna & Western, Long Island, and New York Central Railroads to reach New England and Canadian markets; the float bridge, operated by the Baltimore & Ohio Railroad, only one of two used by private companies in the New York Harbor Area, was established in order to avoid traffic delays at Arlington Yard run by Staten Island Rapid Transit. Following the War, the P&G plant would be provided with freight interchanges by the Baltimore & Ohio Railroad until the late-1980s when the New York, Susquehanna & Western Railway would service both Procter & Gamble and the adjacent shipping line—US Lines. The end of the War also brought about the disuse of the complex's four piers which handled "export lighterage, coastal-size tankers, and tank barges." Their primary purpose was to "[receive] whale oil, which was loaded into tank-barges out in The Narrows from large, steam-powered whaling ships." The shallow depth of the 15-20-foot Kill van Kull did not enable the 31+ foot-oil cargoes owned by P&G from the Ross Sea in the Antarctic Ocean to pass. This was in spite of the 30-foot, 400 feet wide channels completed in 1923. Very few problems arose with the vessel discharging system, other than one major tragedy—the sinking of the Atlantic Oil Transit Corporation-claimed-Fred E. Hasler steel barge. The 200-feet long by 36-feet wide barge equipped with eight tanks and forepeak and afterpeak compartments, each with two hatches, sunk at 5am on the morning of April 16, 1929 alongside the S.S. Ross at Pier 6. The two vessels operated by the company were the 22,000 ton-S.S. Sir James Clark Ross and the 13,426 ton-S.S. Carl Anton Larsen. The S.S. Larsen maintained a crew of 208 men and operated seven hunting boats, one which "killed 19.5 whales during the two-month season." The S.S. Ross, captained by Oscar Nilsen, an experienced whaling-veteran from Norway, was responsible for the "largest cargo of whale oil ever to enter the port". During a five-month season, the S.S. Ross consigned 45,000,000 lbs. of whale oil for Procter & Gamble; the enormous shipment, filling the S.S. Ross's 120,000 barrels, derived from 1,117 captured whales. Procter & Gamble also maintained a coal silo used for "heating the buildings, as well as in the manufacturing and rendering processes of the soaps and cleansers, as well as fuel for the locomotive." Coal would be used until 1983 when a new market for fuelwood/firewood emerged; until its closure, P&G's Port Ivory facility would be supplied 200,000 tons of woodchips annually as supplemental fuel for the oil-fired boiler from the pinelands in Atlantic County, New Jersey. The large-scale enterprise proved to be the most-significant source of income for Staten Island. A January 26, 1954 edition of the *Staten Island Advance* reads, "The more TIDE pleases women – the more it means to

Staten Island!" The article goes on to say, "Many of the supplies and services needed in the manufacture of P&G products are purchased here on Staten Island. This means higher earnings for local businesses... increased employment...more 'Staten Island' money in circulation! By spending money and paying taxes locally, P&G—like other leading industries located here—is helping to provide better day-to-day living and greater opportunities for all." Throughout the plant's years of operation, employees would share an everlasting bond with each other—many of them, family members. Margaret Lundrigan and Tova Navarra wrote in their book *Staten Island*, "For many Staten Islanders, working at Procter & Gamble was a family affair... in 1957 there were ninety-one teams of brothers, sixty-nine teams of fathers and sons, thirty-five husband and wife teams, twenty-nine sibling teams, and fourteen father and daughter teams." That same year, during which those employee statistics were recorded, the company held a 50th-anniversary luncheon for all employees on October 15 "under a huge circus tent on the plant grounds. Richard Redwood Deupree, P&G Board Chairman, cut a king-size birthday cake, which was topped by the company's man-in-the-moon trade mark." The plant unfortunately shut down on November 16, 1991, and relocated its soap-making operations to Mexico. The Port Ivory Retirees Club, however, recalls the bonds which existed among the since-retired employees back in the workplace. The club's members enjoy outings to the New Jersey shore, Niagara Falls, and Florida. Members include the since-deceased Geraldine M. Herrmann, former coordinator of banking services at the Staten Island Savings Bank and manager at Majors Department Store in Mariners Harbor, and Stanley J. Putkowski, member of the 505th Infantry Regiment in World War II, Chairman of the House & Grounds Committee for the Mental Health Society, and President of the Staten Island Coin Club between 1966-1970. Humorous stories about the factory are recounted by former employees such as Robert McTavish Coquillette who remarked, "The Russians who were big wartime customers were used to their hydrogenated products having a little fishy taste and odor partly because… their processes were not as good as ours. So, after the pristine Crisco product was made… fish oil was added to give the fishy taste the Russians were used to. The other story had to do with the rumor the Germans were coming to bomb Bayway Refinery just across the Kill van Kull from Port Ivory. The word came from headquarters that all office personnel were to go home and all women working in the factory were to be sent home, but the men in the plant were to stay and keep the factory going!"

The soap brand's legacy also lives on to the present day, having lent the name "soap operas" to the melodramatic serials on television. Between 1935-1945, P&G increased its sponsorships funds by $13,000,000, sponsoring over twenty soap operas; this lead a company executive, Alfred Lief, to remark, "P&G virtually built daytime radio for the networks." The company's brands soap operas include many of the most-recognized names in modern television history: Ma Perkins, As the World Turns, Guiding Light, and The Young and the Restless.

~

S.S. White, Thomas Adams

Staten Island's contributions to public health, skin quality, and hygiene were not limited to Procter & Gamble's extensive ivory soap operations, but also to the S.S. White Dental Manufacturing Co. and the Wm. Wrigley Jr. Co. Samuel Stockton White D.D.S., born on June 19, 1822, in Hulmeville, Bucks County, Penn., the son of William R. and Mary Stockton, was the owner of S.S. White Dental Manufacturing Co. also known as the "Factory by the Sea"—the largest dental equipment plant in the world—on Seguine

Avenue in the South Shore neighborhood of Prince's Bay on Staten Island. His achievements and innovations in the contemporary dental manufacturing industry would surpass those of his rivals, including: Charles A. Blake, Jacob J. Teufel, the firm of Johnson and Lund, and Henry D. Justi. Between 1836-1843, White worked in his uncles' operation manufacturing "mineral teeth" (artificial teeth) in Philadelphia. In 1844, he began his own practice in a building-garret on 7th & Race Streets on the south side of Franklin Square near downtown. This marked the official founding of his company—S.S. White Dental Manufacturing Co. In 1845 White partnered with John R. McCurdy and Asahel Jones to form "Jones, White & McCurdy." Three-four years later, White was awarded a gold medal by the American Institute of New York, the first premium by the Maryland Institute of Baltimore, and a gold medal by the Society of Dental Surgeons of Pennsylvania for his porcelain teeth made with feldspar. Five years later, his invention would win the highest award at the Crystal Palace Exposition in London in 1851. White soon became chairman of the American Dental Association. During the Civil War, he met with President Abraham Lincoln to discuss providing dental services to Union soldiers. His immense wealth prompted him to generously donate $300 to every college in the United States for the purpose of the "development of literature and science." During his years serving as chairman, he perfected the "mineral teeth" model. His improvements concerned "the increased capability of resisting changes of temperature; the added strength with lessened bulk and weight...; [and] adaptability to varying conformations of maxilla." His name would be attached to ten patents, the newspaper *The Dental Cosmos*, and several innovations which include the all-metal-frame dental chair and the SS White Tooth Powder. His employee, Dr. Eli T. Starr, would file U.S. Patent No. 158, 325—a flexible shaft for the high-speed range in the company's dental machines. White was also a large shareholder of the American Speaking Telephone Company. In 1881, two years after White's death on December 30, 1879 in Paris, France, S.S. White merged with the dental equipment manufacturing firm of the Johnston Brothers; their merger produced a joint-stock corporation with a paid-in capital of one-million dollars. The plant of the Johnston Brothers was built atop the ruins of a previous factory erected by Treasurer of the Staten Island Railroad, Stephen Seguine, Isaac K. Jessup of Greenwich, Conn., and Major Clarence Barrett (who will be discussed further in a later portion), intended for the obtaining of oil from palm nuts and later, candle-making. Algernon Knox Johnston, the son of Professor of Natural Philosophy and acting president of Wesleyan University in Middletown, Conn., John Johnston (also a designer of a metal apparatus used for obtaining solid carbon dioxide), co-founded the brothers' dental manufacturing company in 1865 along with three of his brothers including William A., member of the Staten Island Association of Arts and Sciences, future resident director and member of the Board of Directors of the S.S. Dental Manufacturing Co.. Algernon was exceptionally skilled in the engineering and manufacturing fields, having improved the design of the water-proof combustible cartridge. On October 1, 1861, Algernon Johnston and Lorenzo Dow Lewelling, the 12th Governor of Kansas, were awarded U.S. Patent No. 33,393; the cartridge was "made of gun-cotton, paper, or other fabric, as above subsequently treated as described, by an oxygenizing salt, and by a water-proof coating, as set forth." During the Civil War, Dow and Johnston's cartridges were used in .44 and .36 caliber revolvers supplied by the Remington Arms Co. In 1882, Johnston filed U.S. Patent No. 282,107—the wood-screw machine—with blacksmith Edward Nugent of Brooklyn.

The Johnston Brothers Dental Co. was recognized internationally for its exquisite manufacturing, especially of "[dental] chairs, engines, instruments, gold foil, [and liquid] nitrous oxide;" in addition to: lathes, brackets, tooth paste, anesthetic gas, and inhalers. When the Johnston firm finally consolidated in 1881, several patented interests were added to S.S. White's manufacturing repertoire, including "The Wilkerson Dental Chair (the first hydraulic chair, introduced in 1877; The Morrison Dental Chair, introduced in 1872; The Morrison Engine, 1871... The Johnston Adjustable Fountain Spittoon, 1876; The Johnston Engine, 1879; The Johnston Gas Apparatus (Inhalers, Upright Surgeons' Cases, Gasometers, etc.), 1871; The Cone-Socket System of Dental Instruments; The Machine-cut Engine Bur." The new and improved bur, one of the most essential tool to dentists, was patented by factory superintendent and designer, Arthur W. Browne—also a depositor with a number of saving institutions, treasurer of the Richmond County Building & Mutual Loan Assoc., and volunteer firefighter. The factory's newly-processed materials were shipped daily to Philadelphia to retail markets via trucks from the American Motor Freight Corp.; the daily truck shipments weighed approximately 4,000 lbs. The company also maintained a large export business, possessing a warehouse in London. Local deliveries were made by the ¾ ton Lansing, Michigan-R.E.O. Motor Car Co. trucks. S.S. White continued its expansion to all different corners of the globe—to continents/countries/cities such as: Chicago, Atlanta, St. Paul, Peoria, Berlin, St. Petersburg, Toronto, London, Paris, South America, Japan, and Australia. Its foremost products were forceps, "improved pedal-level" dental chairs, hand drills, carbide burs, artificial teeth, mouthwash, and even office furniture. The superior chairs, available in green, crimson, or maroon plush, represented a standard of "substantial workmanship and elegance in finish" in their masterfully designed, metal four-legged stumps and adjustable body. The products were manufactured and prepared in a series of about thirty factory buildings, spanning five acres along the waterfront of Prince's Bay. Conditions in the factory received an irregularly high approval rating; the chief factory inspector of the State of New York declared it to have the best sanitary arrangements per capita of any manufacturing establishment in the state. Employees even received complimentary dental care from a clinic located within the plant; they were also able to socialize in a clubhouse leading up to the factory. Women were employed in packing, labeling, molding, and trimming, while men in the manufacturing processes; in total, employees numbered over 1,900 strong. This made the factory Staten Island's largest employer until its closure in 1972; between 1966-1971, the former S.S. White-owned production facility would be taken over by the Sharples-Stokes Division of Pennwalt Corp.—a manufacturer of biology technology and chemical processing applications. In 1971, the factory evolved into the short-lived 100-shop, Prince's Bay Trade Mart, then the Factory Center. Like the paving over of other historic Staten Island institutions, plans for condominium development were made by Muss Development LLC of Flushing, Queens in the late-1980s. The project failed to succeed, and today, what remains of the factory is a sealed-off area of weeds and gravel due to Hurricane Sandy's proof of the area to be unfit for residential zoning. S.S. White's legacy lives on however at its current location in Lakewood, New Jersey where a century of Staten Island tradition is carried out in the processes once refined in Prince's Bay.

S.S. White's contributions to Staten Island will be remembered for decades. Its executive in the early-half of the 20th-century, Albert H. McGeehan would be responsible for assisting in the establishment of the Pleasant Plains Memorial. Designed by master-architect George T. Brewster, a resident of Tottenville and designer of the statue *Independent Man* sitting atop the Rhode Island State House in Providence, as well as several Soldiers' and Sailors'

Monuments across the country, the bronze Pleasant Plains Memorial (made in the sculpture foundry—Gorham Manufacturing Co.) commends the 493 World War I soldiers of the Fifth Ward. The statue depicts a female figure [standing] on a granite pedestal holding a sword and palm frond high in the air while an eagle with its wings spread sits at her feet. S.S. White's since-deceased employees who have left behind a significant legacy include Frank Pignata, recipient of the Asiatic-Pacific Medal, co-inventor of the Nuclear Buoyancy Elevator, and key designer of Princeton University's Plasma Physics Fusion Laboratory; and Louis "Hollywood Lou" Rossi: singer who frequently performed at the Stapleton Paramount Theatre, the Great Kills Strand and with the Lou DeTaranto Band. During many of the years in which S.S. White operated in Prince's Bay, Wm. Wrigley Jr. & Co. possessed a plant in the northeastern side of Staten Island in Clifton. The factory's opening was only one milestone, however, in the innovative history of Staten Island—the birthplace of chewing gum. Antonio Lopez de Santa Anna, 'Butcher of the Alamo' in the Mexican-American War of 1846-1848 and eleven-time President of Mexico, arrived on the North Shore of Staten Island in May of 1866 after having received a pardon from President Benito Juarez for a conspiracy against Emperor Maximilian I, monarch of the Second Mexican Empire. Facing the prospects of either being condemned to death in Veracruz or remain in exile, Santa Anna chose the latter. The General first lived with Gilbert L. Thompson, son-in-law of Daniel D. Tompkins, and then at the Dubois Mansion in West New Brighton. While a guest at the house of military photographer during the Civil War, glass merchant, and the future scientist and inventor Thomas Adams, Santa Anna chewed a substance called "chicle," made from the latex of the sapodilla trees native to Mexico's jungles. Selling for only 5 cents per pound, compared to crude rubber which sold for $1 per pound, chicle, Adams believed, could serve as a plausible substitute in the manufacturing of carriage tires. After purchasing one ton of the substance, Adams experimented in converting the chicle to a vulcanized rubber-like material to no avail. Santa Anna had hoped to discover a lucrative invention which could fund his re-ascension to head of the Mexican government; his early-departure, however, prompted by his impatience with Adams' experiments, unfortunately left him remaining penniless.

Adams did however, file U.S. Patent No. 111, 798—his signature process for preparing the chicle which involved mixing the substance with hot water and rolling it into balls. He soon invented his own brand of chewing gum: "Adam's New York Snapping & Stretching Gum" in 1871. The line of production made its debut at a drugstore in Hoboken, New Jersey. His son, Thomas Adams Jr., a traveling salesman, introduced the gum in Mississippi; by the time he returned home, orders for the gum skyrocketed. Thirteen years later, Adams invented the clove and licorice-flavored "Black Jack"—the first gum to be sold in sticks. Black Jack would be sold first with the Trenton-based, American Chicle Co. (later renamed Adams') and then with Mondelez International. Three years later, Adam's latest concoction "Tutti Frutti," would be sold in the very first vending machines in the United States on New York City elevated railway platforms; this replaced the traditional way of grocers selling penny candy, gum, and peanuts in glass jars. By 1899, Adams's success enabled him to form a monopoly by merging with six other gum processing firms; the American Chicle Co. (a trust) had now purchased the assets of Sterling Gum Co. of Long Island, established a factory in Newark, and was actively using 5,000,00 acres of chicle producing lands in Mexico, Guatemala, and Honduras. In 1920, fifteen years after Adams' death, the American Chicle Co would construct a 550,000-square foot factory in Long Island City. In the end, Adams would join William

Wrigley's company and in doing so, form a bridge between the once polarized competitors. Adams's brief sojourn with the famed Mexican general on Staten Island—a bizarre, curious encounter—would produce a long-lasting legacy which today remains a product driving the consumer markets.

~

Factoryville, New Brighton

Over fifty years prior to the American Linoleum Manufacturing Co.'s opening in Travisville and over seventy to the construction of Procter & Gamble's Staten Island facility, however, several unprecedented industries' arrival led to the formation of another micro-economy: "Factoryville" in New Brighton. One such industry was the manufacturing of firearms, initiated by Joseph Hall's opening of Hall's Gun Factory (also a fabricator of hardware) on Lafayette Avenue in 1833. His factory would be the sight of Staten Island's first celebration of the Roman-Catholic mass in April of 1839. This celebration would mark the founding of St. Peter's Church—now located at 53 St. Marks Place in St. George. His factory would later move to the neighborhood of Willowbrook, only a stone's throw away from the College of Staten Island, to Gun Factory Road— now simply the southern portion of Willowbrook Road after the intersection of Westwood Avenue. The company's guns would be reviewed in a study conducted by the Corps of Engineers, Washington D.C. entitled, *"Report upon the Results of Firing to determine the Pressure of the Blast from 15-inch smooth bore guns made at Staten Island, New York in 1872 and 1873."* Gun Factory Road in the coming decades would see an enormous amount of change, particularly during the Staten Island development boom of the 1920s and 30s. Beside an antiquated Socony Gasoline Station (Standard Oil Company of New York; merged with

Vacuum Oil Co. in 1931 to form Mobil) on [Willowbrook] Road, a developer's sign read: "BUY Before the Boom Begins! 345 Lots in this Subdivision. Don't Invest Until You Investigate. Buy Today, You May Pay More Tomorrow." Existing around the same time as the gun factory, another manufacturing establishment in New Brighton opened its doors in 1819—The New York Dyeing & Printing Establishment. Encompassing over six offices in Manhattan, Brooklyn, and Philadelphia, the company guaranteed a precise service of "dyeing, cleaning, and finishing" for "gentleman's coats, office coats, velvet cloaks, mantillas, alpaca silks, damasks, feathers, etc." The establishment's products would be sold all over the United States, with the silk handkerchief becoming the most popular item. Illustrating the immensity of the dyeing and printing company's business, historian J.J. Clute writes in his book *The Annals of Staten Island, from its Discovery to the Present Time, Volume II*, "[i]n the [receiving] department about forty females are employed in taking the goods and sewing thread numbers on each article...Next to this is the Silk Fancy Dye House, where fifty men are employed in dyeing all kinds of silk goods...Adjoining this is the Worsted Dye House...Next in order is the Cotton Dye House, where an upwards of thirty machines are constantly running...The steam power is furnished by thirteen boilers, and the motive power by two large and six smaller engines; it requires three thousand tons of coal per annum to supply these boilers." Another similar company was founded in 1850 by Colonel Nathaniel Barrett, the nephew of Major Clarence T. Barrett—a native Staten Islander, captain in Admiral David Farragut's Battle of Mobile Bay (1864), combatant in the Siege of Petersburg, Virginia (1865), Police Commissioner, and Superintendent of the Poor. A bronze statue of him was erected in Barrett Triangle (one block east of the Richmond County Supreme Court) in 1915. The company later merged with The New York Dyeing &

Printing Establishment—producing "Barrett, Nephews, & Co." The dyeing company's complex spanned an enormous acreage and included: several manufacturing buildings, several sets of worker cottages, several smoking chimneys, several horse-drawn wagons, the Barrett Estate, and a pond. The small body of water, termed "Factory Pond," was utilized by the heavily-polluting dyeing and printing company, as well as by ice skaters during the wintertime until its disappearance in 1908. Following Barrett, Nephews & Co.'s move to Manhattan, the land was temporarily used by Albert D. Smith & Co. until 1962 to assemble a variety of textiles. Today, the land is covered by Corporal Lawrence C. Thompson Park—named for Staten Island's first African-American to be killed in the Vietnam War in 1967.

Factoryville's largest establishment was the C.W. Hunt & Co., run by Charles Wallace Hunt (1841-1911) of Candor, NY. A skilled engineer, Hunt served as president of the American Society of Mechanical Engineers between 1898-1899, president of McCaslin Machine Co., and was also associated with the Engineers' Club of New York, the New York Chamber of Commerce, the New York Electrical Society, and the American Institute of Mining Engineers. Mr. Hunt, a graduate of Cortland Academy in Homer, N.Y., and special agent for the War Department during the Civil War, "[was] a man of genial address, of great social tact and affability, and of a commanding, yet winning presence." He possessed over one-hundred patents, most of which pertained to the improved efficiency of coal transportation. In 1871, Hunt opened his business on Shore Road (Richmond Terrace), after having been in the coal business since 1865, in West New Brighton. He would later open a branch factory in Germany. C.W. Hunt & Co.'s main office was located at 45 Broadway in Manhattan. Describing the enormous Staten Island factory, Horace L. Arnold writes in his book *The factory manager and accountant: some examples of the latest American factory practice*, "The factory [consisted] of a number of single-floor structures, and one building having a second floor, occupied as a patterns shop above, and carpenter shop below. The power house contains the steam engine, air compressors and dynamos, the power being almost entirely transformed into electric current and most of the machine tools being driven by independent electric motors belted to the driving pulleys in many cases by very short belts, which are preferred to any form of chain drive." C.W. Hunt & Co. specialized in a variety of things including automatic industrial railways, electric locomotives, coal-handling machinery, noiseless gravity conveyors, grab buckets, steam and electric hoisting engines, manila ropes, railway cranes, coal screens, coal elevators, wheelbarrows, and steam shovels. Mr. Hunt's transportation-efficiency machinery would even be used for the Greenville Terminal of the Pennsylvania Railroad in present-day Jersey City. Countless other companies also purchased coal-handling machinery from C.W., including J. Stephens & Sons Coal Yard, Curtis & Blaisdell's Coal Pockets, Ontario Coal Co., and Lehigh Coal & Iron Co..

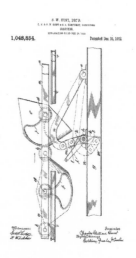

Mr. Hunt sought in every piece of equipment his company designed to ensure safety, speed, and reduction in the breakage of coal.

Hunt set the benchmark for the Staten Island standard

[US Patent No. 1048834. A coal conveyor designed by Charles W. Hunt to improve coal transportation. C. 1912. Courtesy – US Patent Office]

of quality. Although his factory would be bought out in 1920 by Yale & Towne Manufacturing Co. of Stamford, Conn. and later completely shut down during the Great Depression, Hunt had already succeeded in spreading the greatness and opportunity of Staten Island across the entire nation. Perhaps a metaphor for the ever-industrializing, urbanizing Staten Island, Hunt once wrote in a speech he delivered as president of the ASME, "That we live in an age of changes is at once our opportunity and our pleasure. Some of these changes burst upon us, attracting universal notice, while others come so slowly that they are almost unobserved." Factoryville also housed the U.S. Gypsum Co., the J.B. King & Co.'s Windsor Plaster Mills at 561 Richmond Terrace, as well as the Atlantic Salt Co. In 1875, Jose Berre King, "the cement magnate," descendant of a pilgrim on the Mayflower, began his company J.B. King & Co. in co-partnership with his brother, George R. King. Jose's name would be attached to several businesses over the course of his lifetime including: the Wentworth Gypsum Co., the Newport Plaster & Manufacturing Co., the Muralo Co., the Gypsum Packet Co., and the J.B. King Transportation Co.; he was also the first vice-president of the Broadway Savings Institution and member of the New York and Larchmont Yacht Clubs and Building Material Exchange. The 1/3-mile facility, spanning over twenty-five boiler, cooper, storage, and plaster mill buildings manufactured 2,000 tons of wall plaster and cement daily, in addition to paints. The work environment was exceptionally dangerous to the roughly five-hundred employees, paid $1.50 per day: the air absorbed lingering plaster dust and coal, gypsum was constantly being crushed, and the rate at which the machinery operated remained inextricably fast. The gypsum used in the process of fabricating plaster was mined in Windsor, Nova Scotia; Avondale, Nova Scotia; and Hillsborough, New Brunswick. The company possessed warehouses in Buffalo, Norfolk, Boston, and Philadelphia, in addition to a second production center in Roslyn, Nassau County, as well as a main office at 21-24 State Street in lower Manhattan. At the order of J.B. King & Co., the construction of the steel-tug S.S. Gypsum King (completed by the Burlee Drydock Co.—also a designer of the *Richmond* and the *Helen McAllister*) "one of the largest and most powerful ocean-going tugs built in this country" was commissioned in 1899. In keeping with King's "royal" surname, he also operated several other schooners: the S.S. Gypsum Empress, the S.S. Gypsum Prince, and the S.S. Gypsum Queen During off-gypsum-season, when not hauling tank barges filled with gypsum from the Bay of Fundy in Canada, the S.S. Gypsum King transported produce from Santa Lucia, Cuba to Baltimore, Indiana via the Wabash River and to Chrome, New Jersey. The ship's four-day tow from the mines in the North brought back to Staten Island on average more than 4,000 tons of gypsum; the Gypsum King traveled at a rate of nine knots per hour and consumed seventeen tons of coal per day (a relatively efficient ship for its time). Like Procter & Gamble's S.S. Ross however, the S.S. Gypsum King would succumb to numerous collisions including one with the S.S. Woodford off Clifton in 1904, and a fatal accident off Grand Manan Island due to heavy-fog conditions in 1906.

The foremost product sold by the Windsor Plaster Mills was King's Windsor Asbestos Dry Cement of which J.B. King & Co. sold a million and a half barrels of in a period of four years. Soon after its breakout success, the West Brighton company would release a new variation of the initial product, King's Windsor Asbestos Dry Cement Dry Mortar, "[incorporated] with not only a *suitable quality* but *correct quantity* of the best selected, silicious, sharp bank sand, being itself first systematically treated—that is, thoroughly *screened, washed,* and *kilndried*—thus providing a *reliable* and *perfect* wall material." Other products manufactured by J.B. King & Co. include: terra alba (pulverized gypsum), calcined plaster, marble dust, land plaster, ground marble, and marble flour. Plaster did, however, remain the most requested/ordered product, particularly during World War I by the French. The Staten Island placer was also utilized in the construction of the Texas State Capitol building in Austin between 1882 and 1888; a barrel previous filled with plaster reads, "The celebrated Diamond Brand Plastic. Pure white gypsum plaster was quarried from mines in Nova Scotia.". The Windsor Plaster Mills were eventually taken over in 1924 by the U.S. Gypsum Co. of Chicago, Ill; the plant, producing Pyrobar Gypsum tile (a necessity for fireproof commercial buildings), joint compound, sheetrock, drywall, partition tile, and paste paint was one of USG's forty-six plants operating across the U.S. and Canada. "The company's strongest economic growth occurred in its first twenty-five years, when its gypsum board production increased from twelve million board feet to two-hundred million board feet. "In the 1920s, Staten Island manufactured one of the company's leading products—Red Top Plaster.

The acquiring of J.B. King's plaster plant made distribution to East Coast much more economically manageable for USG. Although the company enjoyed early success in the early half of the 20th century, it would eventually close its Staten Island plant in July 1976 and open several other locations in New Jersey. The Gypsum corporation's legacy still, however, maintains a presence all over Staten Island. Between World War II until its closure in 1976, it would produce much of the building supplies for Islanders' home. After a little over a year, East Mineral Inc. of Lowell, Mass. would take over the location for its subsidiary—Atlantic Salt Co. "The 10-acre property is a depot for road de-icing salt for New York State, New Jersey, and Connecticut." The depot stores about 350,000 tons of salt. The Atlantic Salt Co. remains one of the Island's largest employers and treasured industries; the company today seeks to improve transportation efficiency and solutions for

Islanders, in addition to contributing to the fine arts. The Atlantic Salt Co., under the ownership of Leo and Shelagh Mahoney, has collaborated with Nobel Maritime Museum, the Guggenheim Museum, and the Staten Island Chamber of Commerce. The site of the former USG is also occupied by the Gerardi's Farmers Market. Founded in 1985 by Enzo Gerardi, the market (which also operates a garden center across the street) obtains produce from its two farms, totaling forty-three acres, in Atlantic County, NJ. The market, run also by son, Vincent, opens seasonally in coordination with the beautiful/grueling weather of the East Coast.

~

Scrapping

In the South Shore of the Island, yet another industry developed, eventually spreading all across the Island—scrapping. In 1900, Benjamin Lowenstein (1863-1941)—an immigrant from Wallau, Germany—brought his scrap metal business from Manhattan to Tottenville. His initial operations consisted of buying and selling scrap metal, but later, they would involve into a full-scale refining and smelting industry. His business was called Tottenville Copper Co. By 1913, the company was producing one-hundred million pounds of refined copper. In 1931, Lowenstein's company was sold to Western Electric Co. In 1941, it was consolidated under the Nassau Smelting & Refining Co. Marc Pitanza writes in his book *Staten Island Rapid Transit*, "The Nassau Smelting & Refining Company, opened in 1884, was once the largest freight customer on the Perth Amboy Subdivision. It served as the salvage unit for the whole Bell Telephone System, reclaiming various nonferrous metals from obsolete phone equipment for reuse... The complex could handle over seventy freight cars." Nassau S&R Co. also furnished Nassau linotype metal—a metal Lowenstein had gained prominence for refining for the

Mergenthaler 'type impression' machine (forerunner of the modern linotype machine). The Nassau S&R Co. plant on Staten Island played a tremendous role in removing the perception of zinc, copper, tin, and antimony scrap as "junk;" the smelting and refining facility could "stretch" nonferrous metal by constantly reusing it. In 1942, the company did $11,000,000 in business, half of which were nonferrous metals supplied to Western Electric Co. Outworn telephone cables containing two percent tin were sent to Tottenville to be smelted and concentrated to make solder (refined lead) according to Bell System specifications and returned to Western Electric for manufacturing new cables. During the Great Depression, despite hard economic times, Nassau S&R Co. sponsored employee athletic teams, even providing team uniforms and equipment. Over the next few decades, ownership of the Nassau S&R site would vary significantly. The last company to purchase the site—Lucent Technologies Inc. (a spin-off of AT&T)—would operate the former Nassau plant from 1996 to 2001. Five years after closing, Lucent would have the honor of cleaning the 46-acre property from lead, copper, and zinc contamination; "the cleanup entailed covering 450,000 cubic yards of contaminated soil with a thick, unbreakable plastic liner, as well as layers of clean soil." Ten years after the cleanup, the site would be purchased by Bridgewater Capital, along with the Riseman family (Brooklyn-based investors). In 2017, the debate for determining the use of the property began. The initial idea proposed by Bridgewater was to construct 646 luxury senior housing units. The plan was met with fierce opposition, and not only was the project not received with "open arms" by the community, but as Councilman Joseph Borelli and Borough President James Oddo pointed out, "the plan...would require a zone change from manufacturing to residential." Though the future of the old Nassau S&R plant appears to be immersed in developing of some kind, other [previous] scrap areas have either continued their traditions or remained untouched. The Richmond Auto Wrecking Co., which operated an automobile graveyard at 135 Arthur Kill Road (across from the 1908-founded United Hebrew Cemetery) in the 1920s and 30s, for example, has remained virtually unscathed. Another automobile graveyard, operated on the Catherine Breed homestead at 503 Arthur Kill Road, has also withstood the test of time; though both the homestead and the automobile graveyard have vanished, the area is an undeveloped grass lot.

In the North Shore, scrap yards such as those of John Francesco and Anthony Supino still remain fully functioning. John Francesco's scrap yard, founded in 1963, carries on decades of scrap tradition. Descended from Biagio Notarfrancesco, an Italian immigrant from Calvello, Potenza, John's cousin Mike began a career in scrap artistry early on by collecting metal from the streets of the North Shore and Fresh Kills Landfill. *Newark News* special writer Julia Martin wrote, "Junk becomes art in the talented hands of Michael Notarfrancesco and his acetylene torch. From junkyards he picks up venetian blinds, kitchen sinks, old signs, drainpipes, tin cans—any kind of scrap metal—and melts it into original sculpture of all sizes, as small as a candlestick-holder to as large as an eight-foot-high of the sun, clouds, haze, and earth." His eccentric masterpieces were displayed in museums for tens-of-thousands of spectators to visit. Among one of Notarfrancesco's most famous pieces is Largo II—a scrap metal creation inspired by a reef Notarfrancesco saw while in Key Largo, Florida. An innovator for life, Mike would serve as a volunteer producer for Staten Island Community Television (SICTV), and produce over twenty videos which would receive several awards. Mike received his creativity and determination from his father, Mike Sr.—a tinsmith for Bethlehem Steel, senior farmhand who delivered produce from the Ahrend farm in Bulls Head to the Fulton Market in Manhattan, builder of his own Cape Cod house at 27 Eunice Place, and carpenter who due to preferences toward those with Swedish or Norwegian backgrounds was assigned jobs that nobody else wanted. Michael's brother, Vince, also had roots in scrap, having grown up during the Great Depression—a period where salvaging was imperative. In the late 1930s, Vince bought a used truck (a 1923 Reo) and collected newspapers, cleaned out basements, and accepted any job that required a truck. In the early 1940s, Vince began removing scrap metals and scrap equipment at the request of a customers, and bringing it to a recycler for payment. He maintained the business for about fifty years, and passed his genes of scrapping to his two children—John (detailed above) and Benny. Benny would establish a since-closed junk yard in Travis which is currently under development. Just nearby the scrap yard of John

[Michael Notarfrancesco idles in his Vespa at the family homestead at 17 Hatfield Place in Port Richmond. C. mid-1960s. Courtesy – Michael Notarfrancesco, Jr.]

Francesco is the yard of Anthony Supino—founded in 1973 at 2604 Richmond Terr. by Anthony Supino, Sr. Supino Sr.'s mother hailed from Frattamaggiore, Naples, while his father from Monacilloni, Campobasso. His son, Anthony explained, "Running the yard was a phenomenal experience. You had to learn to put yourself on other people's levels." Supino—a native of Giffords Lane and graduate of Tottenville High School—recalls many a gem and tale from old Staten Island.

During the filming of *Splendor in the Grass* in Travis, Supino's mother had the personal privilege of being able to run to the grocer to purchase a bottle of orange juice for actor Warren Beatty. Other memories included attending his first drive-in movie and Fabian's Drive-In near Al Deppe's restaurant. Uncertain about the film's contents, Supino's parents brought him to the 1968 screening of *Rosemary's Baby* in his pajamas.

Across the street from A. Supino at 2581 Richmond Terrace is Lester Kehoe Machinery Inc.—a machine shop owned and operated by Ed Drury (a relative of actor James Drury who appeared in the Western television series *The Virginia* which aired from 1962-1971). A native of the Island, Drury has written for numerous aviation periodicals, is the author of *Staten Island: The Other Cradle of Aviation*, and is also the owner of Drury Enterprises Inc. He is a scholar/historian of Staten Island pilots, airplane factories, and airports, contributing on an occasional basis to the *Staten Island Advance*. His company—Lester Kehoe Machinery— is located within his industrial park consisting of a dredging company, an antique brass works, a linen warehouse, a stair and railing factory, and storage for a museum. His other industrial park—Drury Enterprises—consists of a fork lift company, two steel shops, two woodworkers, an artist studio, four linen warehouses, a computer warehouse, kitchen supply, food truck warehouse, and furniture warehouse; the site is used occasionally for movie and television shootings.

~

Lead & Varnish Works

Drury Enterprises is steeped over a century of Island industry, once housing a Civil War foundry, the Standard Varnish Works, and later the Standard T Chemical Co. Built between 1892 and 1893, the Standard Varnish Co.—thought to be the largest in the entire world—opened in coincidence with the completion of the freight rail link to New Jersey from Staten Island. The contractor for the new railroad system, Colin McLean, built and designed the varnish works' waterfront complex. "Like many industrial buildings constructed during this period, it was designed in the American round-arched style, a variant of the German

[Ed Drury (right), an aviation enthusiast, and his brother, Jack pose at the Staten Island Airport in front of a Cessna 190. C. late-1950s. Courtesy – Ed Drury]

77

Rundbogenstil, and displays such as characteristic features of style as round-arched windows, projecting brick pilasters, patterned brink stringcourses, and bold corbelled brick ornament." When the Standard Varnish Co. was found years before, it became one of the world's largest manufacturers of varnish, enamel, and the first to specialize in automobile varnish. When the highly-successful plant opened in Staten Island, it built miles of underground pipes that filtered oil and turpentine from the docks to large storage tanks in Elm Park...the sun never [set] on products manufactured by the Standard Varnish Works."

Standard Varnish Works would soon expand across continents, enjoying superiority in the production of industrial, railroad, marine finishes, and water-resistant compounds. The company even received a certificate of merit from the U.S. government for its devotion to the production of war materials during World War I. In 1926, the Standard Varnish Works merged with Toch Brothers Inc., and began operating under 'Standard T Chemical Co.' Montgomery Ward & Co.—a mail order—purchased the firm in 1961. Drury Enterprises later acquired the site in 1983. Mirroring the international effects of the Industrial Revolution (from about 1800-1850), Staten Island's industrial production skyrocketed astronomically — particularly within the field of white lead (prepared in the "Dutch" method). In 1842, John Jewett, for whom Jewett Avenue is named, founded John Jewett & Sons White Lead Company on Richmond Terrace; the property would later be acquired by the National Lead & Oil Company in 1890. During the years of Jewett's operation, international white lead production would rise from approximately 5,000 tons to 75,000 tons, with the vast majority being produced in The Netherlands, England, France, and the United States (particularly in Cincinnati and Philadelphia). Until the turn of the 19th century, the Jewett & Sons factory would be the largest in the entire world: covering 374 feet of water front, and an area of 185 by 223 feet across Richmond Terrace. Noting the extent of the company's production facility, consumption, and output, historian Richard M. Bayles writes in his book *History of Richmond County (Staten Island) New York: From its Discovery to the Present Time*, "The works have a capacity for producing three thousand tons of pure white lead annually, and they consume about two thousand tons of coal and employ one hundred men. The quality of their productions is well and favorably known to dealers in all parts of the country." White lead was used heavily as an ingredient in putty and pottery, and as a pigment in oil painting and the painting of wooden surfaces—reducing the likeliness of cracks, water damage, etc. The National Lead Company exploited this demand, inventing the product line, "Dutch Boy," in 1907. White lead's use over the century drastically dwindled, however, due to its poisonous qualities—resulting in the shutdown of the National Lead Company's production plant in Staten Island (though not the company, as it has evolved into "NL Industries") in 1949.

The Jewett Co. and National Lead would leave a legacy extending all the way into the 21st century—contaminating surrounding soil levels with a 24% lead concentration. In 2012, after having collected several soil samples in both the former lead companies' property and Kill van Kull, the Environmental Protection Agency determined the toxicity of the area and removed 4,200-cubic yards of soil to ensure public safety.

~

Oystering

Interetingly enough, lead was not the only Staten Island industry that managed to endanger public health, but also oystering. Since the 1820's, oystering had become a profitable industry in the Kill van Kull and Prince's Bay— prompting the development of the country's first free Black settlement: Sandy Ground (a division of Rossville). Towns along Staten Island's west/north coast extending all the way from Conference House Park to Mariner's Harbor reaped the rewards of the oystering boom, lending Tottenville the nickname, "The Town the Oyster Built." The lucrative fishing industry extended even up the eastern shore of the Island where social organizations such as the Empire City Fishing Club caught fish off the coast of Eltingville. Freemen from the east shore of Maryland and Delaware, though mainly from the small town of Snow Hill in Worcester County, as well as from Bishop and Bishopville, joined the coast-side community, made up of vegetable farmers, based upon the lucrativeness of the millions of oysters lying in the muddy waters. The 350 square miles of water surrounding New York City (particularly in the Hudson River Estuary), containing nearly half of the global oyster population, would even give the Big Apple the name, "The Oyster Capital of the World." The main varieties of oysters found off Staten Island included: the Amboy Bay, Shrewsbury, and Shark River Oysters. After being caught and stored, the oysters would be shipped off to restaurants, markets, and sidewalk-shucking charts from Manhattan to Great Britain. The advantageous trade would sustain the free Black community for nearly a century, sprouting the establishment of institutions such as the Rossville African Methodist Episcopal Zion Church and Cemetery in 1850 and 1852. Although the industry was extremely lucrative, various problems rose to the surface, including pollution and over-exhaustion of resources. In 1840, due to the over-exploitation of native oysters, oyster spat (immature "seed" oysters) were imported from Chesapeake Bay and Great South Bay off Long Island. Additionally, beginning in around 1880, refuse disposed by developing Island towns, particularly of old bricks by the Rossville Brick Company on Arthur Kill Road and Dunn & Dolan Brick Co. in Greenridge (the western portion of Eltingville), contaminated the waters, endangering the age-old oystering industry. The polluted oyster beds, speculated by native-Black fishermen, would produce the beginning of an entire epidemic of typhoid fever: a disease brought on by feces-contaminated food producing symptoms of headaches, diarrhea, and chills. Investigations by Great Britain's government and New York Health Board concluded the distinct source of the typhoid fever/cholera outbreak was Staten Island's oysters. A medical report conducted on May 28, 1904 warned, "[w]hile oysters are being prepared for market they should not be permitted to come into contact with other than pure and wholesome water...The present methods are a distinct menace to the public health, and a person eating oysters, ignorant of their source, is running a serious risk." By 1912, the Department of Health officially shut down the oystering business; by 1915, the importation of oysters from the New Jersey side of Raritan Bay was also banned. Oystering would only continue for a few more years on the east side of the island until the industry's complete demise in 1927. Sandy Ground's Black community would further suffer on April 20 during the Fires of 1963—leaving the ruin of one-hundred, many historic homes.

~

Aviation

Staten Island also pioneered in the aviation industry, boasting five airports, four airplane-manufacturing operations, and twenty landing sites; the foremost airplane-manufacturing site—also the first in America—was C. & A. Wittemann in Todt Hill. Founded by Paul, Walter, and Charles (1884-1967) Wittemann in 1905, the factory would be notable for its construction of two-hundred gliders, thirty-five airplanes, and hundreds of aircraft parts. C. & A. Wittemann would gain notoriety due to its manufacturing of the Baldwin Red Devil II—a Curtiss push-design-like biplane which was powered by a 60-horsepower, Hall-Scott

V-8, and could fly at an impressive 60 mph—designed by Captain Thomas S. Baldwin. Baldwin—a pioneer dirigible airship designer and balloonist—also established Baldwin's Flying Field in Oakwood (1910-1923)—a "fine private field with smooth water frontage" which hosted numerous air circuses. C. & A. Wittemann also constructed a biplane glider plane—exhibited in Madison Square Garden in 1906—used by E. Lillian Todd. Todd—organizer of the first Junior Aero Club in the U.S., and major player in the founding of the Radio Club of America (RCA)—became the first woman to apply for a pilot's license, and the subsequently, the first to fly a plane. Todd even attempted to use Southfield (Hylan) Blvd. as test strip but was ultimately denied by the Commissioner of the Borough of Richmond of New York City. Wittemann also manufactured airplanes at the bequest of Ruth Law Oliver, Cecli Peoli, and Lincoln Beachey. C. & A. Wittemann then became the Wittemann Aircraft Co. in 1915, and later relocated to Hasbrouck Heights, NJ in 1916 as the Wittemann-Lewis Co. (named for the partner Samuel Lewis).

The company would go on to purchase in 1917 a section of land from Walter C. Teter, and established an aircraft-manufacturing enterprise at the Teterboro Airport. "[T]he Wittemanns received the consent of the U.S. Army to convert unused DH-4 aircraft for the Post Office to be used for the first air mail postal service." The aircraft had a capacity for 400-1000 lbs. of mail. Wittemann-Lewis would go on to build two NBL-1 Barling Bombers contracted by the Engineering Division in the 1920s. "[N]o Wittemann aircraft ever suffered a fatal or serious accident." Though the company initiated by the Wittemann brothers was truly the first of its kind, it would declare bankruptcy in 1924; by that time, the Wittemann brothers had brought the inventions of Staten Island to the national stage. The Brothers' Staten Island factory has since disappeared into suburbia, having been replaced with residential housing, long driveways, smoothly-paved sidewalks, greenery, and flawlessly-mowed, bright green lawns. The site of the former factory is marked by Wittemann Place, and borders the menacing Staten Island Expressway. The entire area of Todt Hill began to undergo rapid changes during the 1920s and 30's when real estate companies such as Whitaker & Nutt of New Dorp popularized the phrase "Todt Hill: Highest Point on Coast from Maine to Florida." Variations such as those on the neighborhood's welcome sign read: "Todt Hill: Highest Point on the Atlantic Seaboard south of Maine." Though Witteman Bros. is a forgotten, distant memory, the company gained Staten Island another "first" in innovative achievements. Another locally-based aviation company— The Bellanca (Columbia) Aircraft Co.—would almost make national headlines, having been initially chosen to sell a $15,000 WB-2 to Orteig Prize winning-famed aviator, Charles Lindbergh, for his transatlantic flight from New York to Paris. The company was founded by Giuseppe Mario Bellanca (1886-1960), a 1911-newly arrived immigrant from Sciacca, Sicily and creator of the first enclosed-cabin monoplane in the U.S., who previously operated the Bellanca Flying Academy in Mineola, Long Island from 1912 to 1916. Referencing the academy, Mayor Fiorello H. LaGuardia wrote, "Quite an assortment of individuals were learning to fly at this school. We flew irregularly, whenever we had the time, and whenever the wind was right. I taught Bellanca how to run my secondhand Ford, while we were on route to his flying school." LaGuardia had taken flying lessons from Bellanca in preparation for his entry to the United States Army Air Service during World War I. Bellanca then gained a significant amount of notoriety when he supplied the airplane for Clarence Chamberlin's and Charles Levine's transatlantic flight. Levine—the first passenger ever carried across the Atlantic Ocean—had previously partnered with Bellanca to form the Columbia Aircraft Co. Shortly after, however, Bellanca would split off and found Bellanca Aircraft Co. in Arlington, Staten Island at 3491 Richmond Terrace. After manufacturing aircraft for a period of time afterward on Staten Island, Bellanca would then relocate to New Castle, Delaware (having been lured by Henry B. du Pont Jr.) where he would greatly expand his enterprise; Bellanca Airfield—a service hangar/airfield closed in 1954—bore his name. His former facility in Arlington, despite the development booms plaguing the Island throughout the 1900s, has remained relatively untouched. Though the aircraft manufacturing site is gone, the land has gone undeveloped. Located alongside the former plant is the Mariner's Harbor Yacht Club at 3387 Richmond Terrace; the club, founded in 1910, enjoys a 22,000 square foot property, amenities, and access to various boating activities. Bellanca's plant was also located adjacent to the site of the Downey Shipbuilding Corp. (on which sat the Page House— a lodging site for Hessian soldiers who were "intent on a raiding expedition in Jersey" during Revolutionary Times). Bellanca's plant would then become yet another Island-aviation company—Fernic Aircraft Corp. Located at 3493 Richmond Terrace, the Fernic Aircraft Corp. of Staten Island, N.Y. was founded by George G. Fernic (1900-1930), a young 1927-immigrant from Galati, Romania. A graduate of the Theresianum in Vienna, Fernic would go to Berlin in 1919 and take over the bankrupt-Deutscher Lloyd Flugzueg Werke and assume the title of design director. In 1927, Fernic immigrated to the United States, finding working at Bellanca's Staten Island aircraft manufacturing facility in Mariners Harbor. At the same location, he would then begin Fernic Aircraft Corp. His most famous plane was the Fernic T-9—a three-surface aircraft (a model tandem-wing monoplane)—designed with the assistance of Paul Dronin in 1929. In a series of wind tunnels, Fernic tested the aircraft under the supervision of Professor Alexander Klemin at the Guggenheim School of Aeronautics at New York University.

The airplane would officially be first flown at Roosevelt Field, successfully for twenty-two minutes. In addition to flying and designing aircraft, Fernic also enjoyed racing; in 1927, he, sponsored by Miller and Bugatti, emerged victorious at the Indianapolis 500 held in Speedway, Indiana. Three years later, much to the dismay of the world of aviation, Fernic would die in a fatal wreck during an air race when his Fernic Cruisaire monoplane crashed nose first in Chicago on August 29, 1930 in front of a crowd of 40,000 spectators.

~

Shipbuilding

The Island's largest shipbuilding firm, Port Richmond Iron Works (which for the sake of avoiding repetition will be abbreviated "PRIW"), received national attention when the Shipbuilding Division of Bethlehem Steel purchased the company in 1938. P.R.I.W.—originally a machine shop—was founded by superintendent of the McWilliams repair yard in Jersey City, William Burlee. In 1898, PRIW consolidated with Burlee Drydock Co.; eighteen years later, steel vessel construction would commence upon the addition of a foundry. Burlee was notable for its construction of oil barges which were used by Rockefeller's Standard Oil Co.; the largest barge documented had an astounding carrying capacity of 1,560,000 gallons of oil. Some of Burlee's finer vessels include the ferry boat "Chicago" and the yacht "Norma"—built for William E. Leeds, President of the Chicago and Rock Island Railroad Co. After having been renamed "Staten Island Shipbuilding Co." in 1907, the enterprise would merge in 1929 with five other firms— Theodore A. Crane's & Sons Co., James Shewan & Sons, W. & A. Fletcher & Co., Morse Dry Dock & Repair Co., and New York Harbor Dry Dock Co.—that would be deemed "United Dry Docks" (later known as "United Shipyards"). In

1938 and thereafter, "Bethlehem Steel and the U.S. Navy made substantial additions to the yard in World War II. The yard built vessels up to 416 feet in length and did repairs on even larger ships. Post-war construction focused on barges and tanker and harbor craft repairs. During World War II, there were 47 destroyers, 75 landing craft, 5 cargo vessels, and 3 ocean-going tugs were built at Bethlehem's Staten Island Yard." During the World War II-era, thousands of men and women were trained around the clock, as sheet metal workers, welders, painters, electricians, pipefitters, and machinists. These workers were especially unique across the country because the STATEN ISLAND yard was the only one manufacturing propellers. Between 1950-1951, the Bethlehem Steel Yard constructed the Staten Island Ferry—the largest and fastest ferry until that point able to carry seven-hundred more passengers than the average ferry; Bethlehem Steel constructed ferryboats: Pvt. Joseph F. Merrell, Cornelius G. Kolff, and the Giovanni da Verrazzano. Only nine years after their construction however, the shipyard closed its doors; today, the space is occupied by 1980-founded May Ship Repair Contracting Corp. May Ship Repair, located at 3075 Richmond Terrace, continues the tradition of repairing and constructing vessels, even using previous Bethlehem Steel manufacturing structures for metal fabrication.

BEGINNINGS–
GERMANIC/ENGLISH
INFLUENCES TOWARD MID-19TH
CENTURY STATEN ISLAND

~

Some of the earliest franternizing bodies in the Staten Island German community included the association, the Staten Island Schuetzen Corps (from German "Schützen," meaning "to protect; to shoot"), headquartered at Credo's Hotel on Bay Street in Stapleton, founded in 1872 by brewer, Frederick Bachmann. The Richmond County Schuetzen Camp was located at Julius Raisch's Silver Lake Park Resort.. The organization was one of several German-American social groups on Staten Island intended to foster community amongst German immigrants in a new country. Activities in which the members enjoyed included sharpshooting practice, funeral salutations, and outings into the country. A prominent member of the Schuetzen Corps was an esteemed gentleman by the name of George Bechtel—a Stapleton brewer, Democratic Elector in the Presidential Election of 1888, and wealthiest man on Staten Island (producing nearly 150,000 barrels of beer per year at his father, John's brewery). He was known to have "labored hard and honestly for [his successes]… He was kind, generous, and liberal… [founded] a hospital known as the Bechtel Free Hospital, run by the Sisters of St. Francis." In fact, one year before his death in 1889, Bechtel gifted his daughter Annie a three-story, twenty-four-room Victorian mansion in the Queen Anne style at 387 St. Paul's Avenue. His great successes in the brewing industry were propelled by the rise of organizations such as the Staten Island Schuetzen Corps, made up of predominantly Germans whose taste for the intoxicating beverage also partially-led to the opening of nine additional breweries across Staten Island (though mostly in Stapleton). Bechtel's brewery would then be occupied by Demyan's Hofbrau, owned by prolific painter and vibrant persona, Jack Demyan (1923-1999) aka "Grandpa Moses" in co-partnership with his brother, Frank. The hofbrau, located at 730 Van Duzer Street, featured live top rock groups every Friday and Saturday, accommodated parties ranging from one to seven-hundred, and dished up the Demyan's famous "3 lb. steak dinner for two" at a price of $11.95. It also served ice-cold beer in chilled Löwenbräu mugs. Regular patrons included district judges, lawyers, and even celebrities, including John A. Noble. The son of post-impressionist painter John "Wichita Bill" Noble, John Noble (1913-1983) composed many lithographs including ones depicting Staten Island scenes such as "Ah! Linoleumville." He was revered by fellow artist Demyan who even named a room within the hofbrau after him in his honor, and displayed several of his lithographs in the sailing ship cabin-like interior. Demyan had also mounted several photographs of him with icons such as Richard Nixon, Henry Kissinger, Nelson Rockefeller, and Frank Sinatra. He gained a significant amount of notoriety when he famously catered Francis Ford Coppola's highly-popular 1972 film, The Godfather. The wedding scene was filmed at 110 Longfellow Road in Todt Hill (though the residence as the scene of the celebration is somewhat misleading due to Coppola's erection of Styrofoam barriers to make the Norton mansion resemble a compound), and used 750 Staten Island extras including Staten Island Advance photographer, Tony Carannante. The mansion previously belonged to ex-borough president, Joseph Palma. The cars whose license plates were noted by F.B.I. agents in the driveway leading up to the compound were rented for $75 per day by the crew from vintage car owners who had assembled at Wagner Memorial College the day before to display their vehicles. The crew also filmed the scene following the christening of Michael Corleone as Godfather at Mission of the Immaculate Virgin on Hylan Blvd. in Mount Loretto. Through Demyan's catering of the filming, in which Marlon Brando enjoyed requesting steak on a daily basis, the hofbrau gained the nickname: "Demyan's Hofbrau: Home of the Godfather." The restaurant's Flick Room became a popular drinking place for fraternity and college parties, while the John Noble dining room became a memory-maker for the thousands of Staten Island locals who came to enjoy a variety of sausages, sauerkraut, potato salad, and beer. The upstairs disco room became one of several centers of the Staten Island disco scene (immortalized in the 1977 film *Saturday Night Fever* starring John Travolta which utilizes the Verrazzano-Narrows Bridge as a symbol of opportunity), along with the Park Villa II at 70 Beach Street.

Until his death in 1999, Demyan would continue to leave profound effects on the community of Clifton, gracing residents with both his paintings depicting nostalgic scenes of Staten Island, his personal eccentricities, and acts of services. Memories of the old hofbrau are dear to many Staten Islanders' hearts, particularly to Michael McMahon—a former busboy for Demyan's, future Democratic congressman representing Staten Island between 2009-2011, and District Attorney of Richmond County. "Among [Demyan's] many exploits were serving cake to the passengers and crew of the 69th street (Brooklyn) Ferry on its last run and persuading Governor Nelson Rockefeller to ride a horse through the crowds on the banks of New York Bay in a rainstorm at one his traditional Oktoberfest gatherings." He also founded the American Academy of Art Poetry & Zizhery, and produced over 2,000 tastefully-done watercolor paintings. Unfortunately, business leading up to the 1980s was dwindling due to New Jersey's lowering of the drinking age, thereby removing the necessity for teenagers from that state to travel to Staten Island, and the removal of shipping companies from the Island whose executives regularly dined at the hofbrau. The burning of the hofbrau in 1979 and consequent-shut down of the restaurant, enabled Demyan to concentrate on his work at home; his artistic works include paintings of the Clove Lake Stables, the Columbus Quincentennial celebration in New York Harbor in 1992, and Statue of Liberty celebration in 1986. His restaurateur legacy was maintained by his surviving wife Denise for years later. She operated the Court Tavern at Purroy Pl. & Gorden Street, and later opened a bar in South Beach. What remains of Demyman's extraordinary, well-respected hofbrau on Van Duzer Street is the reoccurring, reappearing phenomenon dreaded by native Islanders—residential housing. Interestingly enough however, a more discreet secret lies beneath the foundation upon which these suburban homes rest today—beer caves. Following Bechtel' Brewery's opening in 1853, George Bechtel ordered the digging of the serpentinite of Grymes Hill to create temperature-ideal fermenting caves for his lager. By 1870, Bechtel's Brewery contained seventeen entire fermenting rooms. Having honed his brewing skills at the American Brewers' Academy (founded by Anton Schwarz in 1880), Bechtel would create a brew so popular, it would do for Staten Island nearly what Schlitz had done for Milwaukee. His ambitious attitude became a microcosm of the entire Island; his devotion and courage would be remembered by many. Bechtel was also a member of Oceanic Hook & Ladder Company No. 1: one of ten volunteer fire departments presently operating in New York City. The need for volunteer companies was halted in 1865 when the city's fire department was professionalized.

The sudden emergence of beer factories would be based on two factors: the capitalization on natural resources such as large underground springs filled with groundwater suitable for brewing, and the large influx of German immigrants—many of whom immigrated due to political tensions provoked during the März-revolution of 1848-49. They would establish a number of breweries on the North Shore of Staten Island, including Bischoff's Brewery, the Constanz Brewery, the Monroe Eckstein Brewing Co at Four Corners., Atlantic Brewing Co. (Rubsam & Horrmann Brewing Co., brewers of "Pilsner Style" beer; later bought out by Piel's), and Bechtel's Brewery. R&H Brewing Co.'s beer refrigerated trains cars (reefers) read, "Drink up Boys – The Brewery needs the Empties!" The R&H symbol would be interpreted by some Islanders as "rotten and horrible." In the present day, Staten Island's beer legacy is carried on by individuals such as Wayne P. Roccaro—"The Beer King of the South Shore." The owner of the Holiday Beverage Center in Eltingville since December 1997, Roccaro maintains a beverage selection of 1,400 beers which range in Roccaro's words from "your grandfather's to your father's to your brother's beer." Roccaro explained, "Staten Island isn't the trend setter when it comes to beer. In fact, Staten Island is taking a long time adjusting to the craft beer craze which has impacted other boroughs at a much faster rate. This however allows me to look ahead of the curve and adequately plan for the future." German brewers remained largely disconnected from politics even after having been attempted to organize into a political force by the anarchist Amerikanische Arbeitersbund or American Workers' League; although, a substantial group of German-Americans part of The Alarm Society of Anarchists would hold celebrations on holidays such as Labor Day at Anton Heil's Park in Fort Wadsworth. The rise in the German population, particularly of the working-class, would lead to the publication of three German-Staten Island newspapers: *Der Deutsche Staten Islander* om 1867, *Staten Islander Deutsch Zeitung* in 1876, and the *Staten Island Post und Sud New York Anzeiger* in 1887. The Staten Island, German brewers based much off their ingredient/water supply off creeping herbs growing wild on the island, as well as boundless supplies of groundwater extracted from the ground Pleistocene moraine deposits beneath the bedrock derived from the approximately 45-inches of annual precipitation. The large supplies of groundwater found on Staten Island are rich in dissolved mineral content and provide great health benefits—many of which can still be discovered in the present day at the mystifying "secret spring of Cloves Lake Park" in West Brighton. Exploitation of these springs by water companies such as the Crystal Spring Water Co., Municipal Water Works, Staten Island Water Co., and South Shore Water Co. commenced in the late-19th century. The four companies operated a total of 1,258 hydrants 9.337 taps in the Borough of Richmond according to the *Annual Report of the State Water Supply Commission of New York, 1906.* The growing German community whose very roots were founded on the abundant supply of groundwater eventually grew so large in Stapleton as to establish several benevolent societies, an Erheiterung, the Klopstock Free & Accepted Mason Lodge No. 760, and the Der Deutsche Evangelische Lutherische Gemeinde zu Stapleton (later evolving into the Trinity Evangelican Lutheran Church). Reverend Frederic Sutter, born in Stambach, Germany, of the T.E. Lutheran Church would be responsible for the moving of Wagner Memorial Lutheran College (previously the Lutheran Proseminary), a training institution for German-speaking future-clergymen of the German Evangelic Lutheran Church, from Rochester to Staten Island in Grymes Hill in 1918. The German community would remain exceptionally religiously-devout and generous. An April 24th ,1889 program for the Klopstock Free & Accepted Mason Lodge No. 760 in Stapleton's jubilee commemorating the freedom of the masonry practice from debt read: "Prayer, by the Past Master, H. Sterzing/ "Old Hundred" (a religious hymn) sung by the singers of the Lodge... Song "Das ist der Tag der Herrn" (Lord's Prayer)/ Oration, by the Past Master, Caspar Schneider... Song, "Der liebe Gott hat's true gemeint" (The

Love God has Meant Faithfully)/ "Frühlingsglaube," (Faith in the Spring) Solo, by Bro. H. Kessler. / Prayer, by W. Master Julius Credo." Another organization which exemplified fraternity among German immigrants was the Staten Island Plattdeutscher Verein ("Low German Club")—an organization, prevalent especially in Wisconsin, intended to preserve the culture and "Plattdeutsch" language spoken in northern Germany/Hamburg and the northeast Netherlands. Many German social, entertainment clubs (as well as the Staten Island Diet Kitchen) held their meetings at the German Club Rooms located on the corner of Van Duzer & Prospect Streets. The Club Rooms hosted a variety of acts and lecturers, and hosted a series of plays/performances. Such acts include: *East Lynne* (based on the 1861 novel by British author, Ellen Wood), the Liebe-Heimlicher Group (a piano-cello-violin trio accompanied with singers), and *Uncle Tom's Cabin* (based on the 1852 novel by Harriet Beecher Stowe) as performed by Caroline Fox Howard. The German Club Rooms were operated for a short period of time by Frederick W. Kost—a native-Staten Islander; well-respected, clever American Tonalist painter whose illustrations would depict the Staten Island wetlands, ships sailing through Great South Bay, and homesteads; and student of renown landscape painter, George Inness.

The German community would further include a theological school and missionary, a restaurant, and an entire factory town—Kreisherville. Originally named Androvetteville for a small Huguenot family inhabiting that area of "Westfield" (one of five divisions of old Staten Island), Kreisherville was founded by Bavarian immigrant, Balthasar Kreischer, in 1854 as a factory town mining clay from the 265-acre Clay Pit Ponds, and producing English-fire bricks, bakers' ovens, fire sand, blast-furnace lining, terra cotta, and retorts. The company would be originally founded as Kreischer & Mumpeton in the Lower East Side in 1845, and expand to over twenty-one New York City lots before transferring the entire property to Staten Island due to the discovery of refractory clay deposits; in place of the old factory in Manhattan would be tenement housing. Balthasar Kreischer was born in 1813 in the municipality of Hombach, located within the Bad Kreuznach district of Rhineland-Palatinate, Germany. His lineage consisted of many brick makers, and Kreischer himself was talented in the field of stone-cutting where he laid the "corner-stone of the fortress of Germersheim"—a fortress whose construction was ordered by Ludwig I, King of Bavaria, against fear of a potential French attack. Kreischer saw opportunity for employment in the fire-brick industry in the United States following the eruption of the Great Fire of New York in 1835. Following his company's opening, in 1878, after the death of his former business partner and addition of multiple sons to the business, the brick factory became B. Kreischer & Sons. During his lifetime, Kreischer would also be granted Patent No. 5174 on March 21, 1871 (later revoked in Fryer vs. Maurer in 1884 due to the invention's realized un-patentability) for a tiling improvement used in fireproof buildings. The invention consisted of "a hollow sectional tile combined with the girders of the building in such a manner that the tiling spans the space between opposite girders, the end sections being supported up or against the girders, and the middle section forming a key to bind the surface together, the whole having a flat undersurface."

Kreischer's factory, with a manpower of two-hundred fifty residing in provided-worker housing, would produce over 7,000 bricks per day (prior to its peak in the 1890s) in all varieties ranging from pressed building to front to ornamental brick. In fact, demand became so enormous such that "a complete plant [was] erected for the manufacture of front brick and... equipped with all the mechanical appliances for making every variety and shape of the highest grade of front or ornamental pressed brick." His incalculable riches enabled Kreischer to gift to his community the

German Lutheran Society of St. Peter's at 25 Winant Place. The Hungarian Congregation would later reorganize the church in 1919 as the Free Magyar Reformed Church whose front pillars would be assembled with Kreischer brick. Kreischer's unrelenting benevolence also prompted the brick baron to give a hefty sum of $75,000 to Henry E. Steinway, founder of Steinway & Sons piano manufacturers in Astoria, Queens; William Steinway was also a trustee of the estate of Balthasar Kreischer. Before his death in 1886, Kreischer would (partially) oversee the construction of two regal, Queen Anne mansions dedicated to his sons, Edward and Charles; the foremost of which was the (Edward) Kreischer House at 4500 Arthur Kill Road Alleged to be haunted by superstitious locals, the mansion was the site of the suicide of Edward B. Kreischer in 1894 and the drowning of Robert McKelvey by Bonnano crime family-hitman and caretaker of the Kreischer House, Robert Young in 2005. The mansion's architecture reigns supreme in the neighborhood, boasting views of Perth Amboy, New Jersey, as well as "fireplaces in every room, incised-leather wallpaper, a turret, twenty-five rooms on four floors, jigsaw bargeboards, decorative chandeliers, and "Van Gogh-like stucco."

In 1855, Balthasar Kreischer would sell a portion of his property to Nicholas Killmeyer: Kreischerville's postmaster, grocer, and hotel proprietor—giving rise to Staten Island's foremost German restaurant, Killmeyer's Old Bavarian Inn at 4254 Arthur Kill Road. The age-old eatery (at one point named "The Century Inn"), originally supplied with beer by the native-Stapleton, Monroe Eckstein Brewing Co., continues centuries of German tradition by serving specialties such as Sauerbraten, Schweinbraten, and Schweinshaxe accompanied with sauerkraut and spätzle. Kreischer's business dealings and civic leadership was further recognized in his title as "Grand Master" of the Grand Lodge of the Free & Accepted Masons of the State of

New York in 1843, 1844, 1849, and 1854, and namesake of the Balthasar Kreischer, Lodge No. 1809. He would also be an investor and devout supporter of the Crary Clay Heater Co., Anderson Pressed Brick Co., and Staten Island Kaolin Co. Kreischer's company would later be incorporated in 1902 by a member of the original-settling family of Kreischerville, Captain Peter Androvette—a transportation manager for B. Kreischer & Sons, founder of an ice, coal, and wood-supply business, one of several founders of the Perth Amboy Dry Dock Co. (a repairer of marine railway ships), founder of the Androvette Towing & Transportation Co. (notable for the hauling of screw steamers such as the *Robert Robinson* built in New Baltimore, New York in 1898), and officer of the Methodist Chapel at Kreischerville. Due to lack of demand and increased competition, however, the Kreischer brick manufacturing enterprise ceased operations in 1927 [year disputed]. In the years surrounding World War I, Kreischerville was renamed Charleston for Charles Kreischer due to anti-German sentiments arisen during the Great War.

Kreischer was nearly unmatched as a German immigrant in his contributions to the betterment of Staten Island; his entrepreneurship would be rivaled by few in the century to come. A pioneer, however, whose aptitude for crafting delectable confectionary creations which remain in the hearts of Staten Islanders to this very day would also gain a similar amount of notoriety, if not more—Claus Hinrich Holtermann. Born on January 31, 1845 in Hepstedt in the current Lower Saxony region of Germany (formerly Prussia), Holtermann received training as a baker in Bremen and established Staten Island's first family-owned establishment, Holtermann's Bakery, in 1878. The business would gradually become "the most trusted name in bakery products," making every product "with love, perfection, and by hand." Holtermann's specialties include long-lost favorites such as Meltaway Cake and Pullman Bread—a bread baked with white flour in a long, narrow pan; at its peak, Holtermann's Bakery's output of the bread was 1,680,000 loaves per annum. The bakery's initial location was in the pre-Revolutionary "House of Buried Treasure" (G. Housman House) in which gold was discovered in 1857 and 1921. During this time, Claus Holtermann assumed the liberty of delivering bread on-foot to his clientele, as well as picking his ingredients directly from the native-peach, apple, and cherry trees to assemble his signatures, homemade pies. Holtermann's then moved to 240 Center Street, immediately behind St. Patrick's Roman Catholic Church, at which point the mode of delivery had upgraded to horse-drawn carriages. Finally, the bakery moved to its current location on 405 Arthur Kill Road in Great Kills equipped with a "4 ½ - bbl dough mixer, flour-handling outfit with conveyor, hopper and automatic seales, molder, three steam ovens, rear fired, and a portable cake oven."

Holtermann's outreach to both Staten Island residents and the underprivileged emphasized the bakery's significance and importance to the community in Richmond County. Portraying the nurturing attitude of Claus Holtermann, author Margaret L. Ferrer writes in her book *Richmond Town and Lighthouse Hill*, "Known as a kind man, during the Blizzard of 1888 he threw a sack of bread over his shoulder and brought it to the children in St. Michael's Home." In the midst of the downpour of twenty-two inches of snow, the fourth deadliest blizzard in New York State history, Claus Holtermann persevered in his trek to the St. Michael's Home for Children—an orphanage in Arden Heights shut down in 1982. The Holtermann brand would achieve high levels of exposure due to its trademark orange, Divco (Detroit Industrial Vehicles Company) delivery trucks which circulated throughout Island neighborhoods. The sound of the truck's engine sent children with a few pennies from their mothers flying to the street corner for an afternoon/afterschool cupcake or donut or slice of plantation marble cake. The brand was characterized by the heavenly smell of baked goods which infested the suburban streets and smiling drivers who wore their charming "Holtermann's" green, orange, and black hats. The portable oven-to-door delivery menu alternated daily; some days promised seeded twist bread, pineapple crumb buns, and 28¢ strawberry iced jelly rolls, while others: chocolate butter cream filled cups, ½ chocolate fudge layers, black walnut flavored buns, and 11¢ Italian bread. Embracing its German heritage, Holtermann's also offers Deutsche honig plätzchen (German Honey Cookies), as well as spicy fruit bars—Fruchtschnitte. The quality of the bakery's products was expressed time and time again. An advertisement in the 1960s for Holtermann's read, "Both call for Perfection and both receive it! Holtermann's Baked Goods & The Verrazzano-Narrows Bridge"—implying the bridge's masterfully-designed architecture.

Holtermann's was only one of several successful German bakeries operating on Staten Island. In fact, the Staten Island baking industry was dominated by Germans/Central Europeans until the rise of Italian-American businesses selling cannoli and biscotti occurred in the 1960s and 70s. Claus Holtermann was rivaled by an adept, innovative genius by the name of Gustave Adolf Mayer—a confectioner and inventor from Weissenstein (now Lauterstein) in the modern-province of Baden-Württemberg. Born on November 5, 1845, Mayer traveled extensively throughout Switzerland and Germany, obtaining an education within the confectionary arts. At the age of nineteen, in 1864, Mayer sought opportunity in the United States and established "Mayer's Confectionery" initially in Manhattan. Less than ten years later, Mayer would move his business and factory to the German-enclave in Staten Island of Stapleton. In his book chronicling the rise of commercialism and specialized industries on Staten Island, *Made on Staten Island: Agriculture, Industry, and Suburban Living in the* City, author Charles L. Sachs describes Mayer's operation: "He designed and patented specialized molds and equipment from which sweet biscuits and wafers were produced and was known as the originator of the "Nabisco sugar wafer" in America. He invented the Vienna Roll, Cigaretta, Carlsbad, Champagne, Fancy Dessert, and Virginia Sugar Wafers… [his] biscuits and confections were served at Delmonico's, Sherry's, and other fine restaurants in Manhattan and throughout the metropolitan region." His pioneering techniques and commitment to his craft led him to file Patent No. 407,935 in 1889—a complicated device intended for the improved process of manufacturing confect-ionery. The invention consisted of a perforated bottom plate, a vertically-reciprocating table provided with spring-actuating keepers for holding the paper for the paste designs on position on the table, and fixed stops beneath the keepers to permit the forward feeding of paper. Gustave Mayer's products came in extravagant, late-Victorian designs, presented on tall platters adorned with intricate ornaments and fixtures; his smaller items such as Vienna Biscuits often were regally advertised and usually came in the vanilla flavor. A prime example is Mayer's "Cigarettes à La Vanille," the finest dessert cigarettes "carefully prepared and from the purest materials." His most-notable creation, the Nabisco sugar wafer, would grow in popularity to such an extent it would become a global sensation, sold by distributors such as Mondelez International. Mayer's specialties were largely novelties of the time period—meticulously-baked treats such as printed biscuits (unleavened flour-based product imprinted with detailed patterns, messages, or designs). Mayer's fortune allowed him to purchase a home for his family in the New Dorp section of Staten Island on 2475 Richmond Road—an Italianate-style villa, appraised for $2,300,000, built in the picturesque ideals illustrated by landscape designer, Andrew Jackson Downing. The house, "a two-and-one-half-story cube capped by a square belvedere with a porch on three sides", was situated in between the polarization forces separating Staten Island— rural and developing. Its magnificent perimeters which provided exceptional views of the country and Raritan Bay enabled Gustave Mayer to innovate as Antonio Meucci had less than three miles away. On February 11, 1913, Mayer filed Patent No. 747,640: a room humidifier "for radiators, comprising a tubular container adapted to fit between the adjacent sections of the radiator." Mayer would also produce birch beer (a non-alcoholic beverage derived from birch beer and birch sap), glass-enclosed concave sign letters, nickel-platted wire candy baskets, and the highly-reflective, "Zinn Brilliant" ornaments. The adornments, handcrafted in special molds, sparkled in the darkness of households during the Christmas seasons, reflecting light against their jewels. His inventions and bakery, however, would become merely a forgotten relic of old Staten Island—succeeded by other European bake works such as Buda Bakers, owned by a Polish, Cracovian family.

Originally from New Jersey, the Buda brothers (initially "Budzinski" preceding World War II), Henry, John, Edward, Adam, Stanley, learned their craft at their uncles'/cousins' establishment, C. Budzinski Bakery on Avenue C in Bayonne. The brothers, who had obtained some knowledge of Polish, attended Our Lady of Mt. Carmel School—located within a predominantly Polish parish in Bayonne, went to public high school, served in the World War II, and returned home to commence baking operations. The bakery possessed four locations: 2110 Richmond Road (formerly on New Dorp Lane) in Grant City, 3956 Richmond Avenue in Eltingville, 28 Barrett Avenue in Port Richmond, and another store in Downtown Bayonne. An offshoot of the family-owned business, "Buda Bakery" was opened in the Tottenville section of Staten Island by brothers Henry and Stanley after having sold their interests in "Buda Bakers." Heightened sales were unfortunately cancelled out by an unexpected labor shortage, brought on by Tottenville's inaccessibility/remote location in Richmond County. Stanley would later run full-time Lieblich & Sons Bakery owned by Max Lieblich at 418 Jersey Street in New Brighton. Buda Bakers would become one of the most highly-respected bakeries in all of New York City, drawing crowds of frequent, far-residing customers who could be seen patiently waiting in an enormous line outside the building or rushing between double-parked cars whose drivers were picking up the bakery's specialty—Ice Cream Rolls. A 1960s advertisement for Buda Bakers stating "Whipped Cream Cakes Made Only With Pure Sweet Cream... Ice Cream Cake, Pastry, Dietetic Products" depicted a miniature baker in full-uniform holding up a cake alongside a message reading, "Quality Service Price." The bakery nearly lifted people from the comforts of their sheets in the late evening, sending a heavenly scent of the insides of a warmed baker's oven heating a hundred rolls of fresh bread into the night air. Customers flocked in from nearly every angle; mothers arrived in their house robes from their bedrooms, children came rushing down Richmond Road immediately after school, and parishioners at St. Christopher's Church on Midland Avenue dressed in their Sunday-best escaped the crowdedness of the wooden pews and disappeared into the scent of a million baked goods arising from the bakery.

Buda Bakers, always open, attracted thousands, serving exquisite products such as rolls, white mountain rolls, crumb cake with big, giant crumbs on top, and the very best cupcakes and black and white cookies. Another specialty was fried-to-perfection golden crullers—a favorite of morning commuters on the ferryboat to the city. The process involved many laborers: the "foreman" who operated several truck-sized dough mixers; four or five "bench hands" who cut and shaped the dough and placed it in a steam box; and the "oven man" who worked from 5pm to 1am placing the dough into the gas-fired ovens that contained revolving shelves like a Ferris wheel. Nevertheless, perfecting timing was always achieved, yielding pure quality. Staten Island's residents' desires for the eternally tempting pastries were expressed in a vintage, 1960s kitsch thermometer of an innocent blond-haired young girl dressed in a summer, white dress and orange hat in a prayerful position looking toward the sky—asking God for a mere morsel of Buda Bakers' infamous sugar-coated jelly donut. The sudden longing for Buda's pastries and unusual, nostalgic cravings echo a decade in Staten Island's history of community and pure bliss. While enjoying a Buda Bakers' pastry, children sat with their parents and siblings watching an episode of the Ed Sullivan Show or scorned, Sunday night episode of the Lawrence Welk Show. Buda Bakers built up a tremendous

[An advertisement featuring Buda Bakers and its products at its three different locations. "Quality Service Price." Courtesy – Walter Buda]

reputation for itself—one that remains a sweet distant memory. Due to advancing illness and age, the Buda Bakers brand dissolved in the early 1980s. The Bayonne location would be replaced by Damian's Bakery, and a nephew of the Buda brothers would later open a bakery on the Jersey Shore.

Despite being unique in its pastries and Polish background Buda Bakers was only one of dozens of family-owned, major Staten Island businesses. Served alongside Buda pastries in Staten Island households was often the notable, Weissglass pasteurized milk supplied by the Weissglass Gold Seal Dairy Corp. As the sun rose above Raritan Bay, the clinking of the quart glass milk bottles could be heard at the doorstep of Staten Islanders' homes who were just preparing to go to work. The delivery vehicles bore resemblance to Holtermann's bread trucks, and even underwent a similar evolutionary process. Beginning first with the horse and carriage and wooden crates, Weissglass employed milkmen who wore an attire resembling that of an Irish leprechaun and Austrian mountain yodeler. The business, originally 'Weissglass Dairy' was run by Julius Weissglass (1872-1946)—an unsuspecting Austrian-Jewish immigrant from Vienna, Austria. Weissglass immigrated to New York City at the age of thirteen in 1887, and found work first at a poison gas factory and then at Luchow's restaurant in the East Village. It was through the latter occupation wherein he served as a dishwasher, busboy, and then waiter, that he fell in love with the Staten Island countryside. On occasion, the young Weissglass was sent to purchase horseradish for the eatery, and spent hours trotting through the immaculate pastures and grasslands. His love for the Island prompted Weissglass, sponsored by an uncle, to purchase a 50-acre farm off Crystal Avenue in Westerleigh on the former grounds owned by the Simonson Family, along with twelve cows, forty ducks, and one-hundred twenty chickens in the mid-1890s. During this time, he resided on Vedder Avenue. After having tired of milking the cows, Weissglass then formed an enterprise in 1899 purchasing milk in cans from farms upstate New York, and selling them to Staten Island residents. At its peak, Weissglass had forty home-delivery routes, several business-delivery routes, five receiving plants in upstate, and a large bottling and pasteurizing facility on 2014 Forest Avenue in Mariners Harbor which produced (with a labor force of two-hundred) over 65,000 quarts of "the milk with more cream," 4,000 dozens of eggs, and 2,500 lbs. of butter annually. After years of operation, Weissglass would become one of the most recognizable brands on Staten Island, distributing products such as chocolate milk, churned buttermilk, and the signature "orange drink." By 1941, the company had also acquired Gold Seal Dairy Products Corp. of Remsen, N.Y., New Dorp Dairy and South Shore Dairy. Certainly the foremost dairy company on the Island, Weissglass was actually only one of numerous dairy businesses whose milkmen also delivered straight to Islanders' homes. Some other recognizable brands were Richmond Farms, Janssen, and Foremost. The Weissglass-Gold Seal ice cream processing plant was located just across from the pasteurizing facility in Mariners Harbor, on Samuel Place. Milkmen began working at around 2am, driving one of twenty delivery trucks, and delivered the famed glass bottles of milk whose lids contained interesting facts about U.S. presidents. An advertisement for the dairy firm read, "You have to get up early in the morning to be fresh for Staten Islanders...We don't really enjoy working while our friends and neighbors are asleep, but it's a family tradition. We've got a reputation for delivering the freshest, highest quality milk and milk products available everyday to our store and home delivery customers. It's the type of reputation you'd expect from Staten Island's only milk processing plant. We intend to maintain it... even if we have to get up early." Though Julius Weissglass passed away in 1946, his three sons, all highly-distinguished individuals: Joseph (1903-1973), Oscar (1907-1988), and Charles (1905-1974), would take over administrative and business affairs by 1920. Joseph was on the Staten Island Advisory Board of the First National City Bank, was a trustee of the Staten Island Savings Bank, and would later become the director of Staten Island Hospital and the Jewish Community Center of Staten Island; Charles would write the ancestral and commercial history of the Weissglass family entitled, "Smiling over Spilt Milk;" and Oscar, the co-founder of the Jewish Historical

Society of Staten Island (JHSSI) in partnership with Dr. Joe Adler, would become the honored namesake of the annual Oscar Weissglass Memorial Seder hosted by Congregation B'nai Israel on 45 Twombly Avenue in Bay Terrace on the first evening of Passover. Until Weissglass' shutting down in April of 1975 due to increases in operating costs and the loss of its sizeable business in New Jersey, the company would be run by the son of Charles—Allan. Allan would later serve as president and CEO of Elizabeth, NJ headquartered-Magruder Color Company Inc., manufacturers in varnishes, paint, ink, and pigmented chips, from 1962 to 2002. Like his uncle, Allan would also receive the Distinguished Citizens Award by Wagner Memorial College, and even go on to become a benefactor for numerous cultural institutions including the Staten Island Museum, a member of the board of trustees of the Metropolitan Museum of Art, and founding member of the Staten Island Foundation. Though the Weissglass family continually remains active in contemporary Richmond County community affairs, Weissglass Dairy itself remains an artifact of the past. Despite the disappearance of the dairy industry's heyday on Staten Island, some are trying to recover this treasured aspect of Island history. In 2018, Native Islanders and businessmen Robert Masucci and Joshua Resnick convinced Ronnybrook Farm Dairy of Ancramdale, N.Y. to begin a milk home delivery service to Staten Island residents. Discussing his reasoning for restoring this lost Island tradition, Masucci remarked, "There is a huge demand nationwide for better quality food... When my parents and grandparents were growing up you didn't have to worry about things like chemicals and different types of things in the food that can do so much harm to our bodies." The non-homogenized milk is delivered via Home DIVVY trucks in the glass bottles whose nostalgic clinging echoes an old Staten Island era. The former Weissglass milk plant in Mariners Harbor is currently covered by Lowe's Home Improvement, across the

Forest Avenue Shopping Plaza. Though the Weissglass name is most often associated with the dairy company, it also bears association with the famous 1/5 mile asphalt Weissglass Speedway on Richmond Terrace & Jewett Avenue near Port Richmond. Although, Weissglass also sponsored numerous sports teams on the Island such as the South Shore Little League. Weissglass Speedway was founded by sports promoter Gabe Rispoli (1921-2006) who owned a baseball field across the street from the stadium. Rispoli saw the opportunity for a speedway as a national interest in stock car racing developed, particularly in New Jersey where the Wall and Old Bridge Stadiums were both constructed, respectively in 1950 and 1953. Using $700 from the Weissglass Dairy Co., Rispoli made needed-improvements to the stadium, and operated the speedway under a NASCAR sanction until 1956. Weissglass remained minimally active with the speedway, sending a business representative only once annually during the "Gold Seal 75" to award trophies. The first races were announced by Chris Economaki (1920-2012)—"The Dean of American Motorsports Journalism." The most-commonly raced cars were the '32 Plymouth and '37 Ford Coupes, in addition to Ford Sedans. The track's most notable racers include Howie Brown and Frank Schneider—winner of the NASCAR Grand National at the Old Dominion Raceway in 1958. Races were held weekly from May to October. The stadium also hosted a variety of sports events including baseball and football games (e.g. Curtis High School's Thanksgiving Football Game), field trials and rallies for the Staten Island Sports Car Club (which awarded trophies at Leone's on Hylan Blvd. or at the Surf Club in South Beach), and boxing and wrestling matches which featured Antonino Rocca and Bruno Sammartino. After nineteen years of operation, Weissglass Speedway shut down in 1973. By this time, the stadium's lease had expired, spectators were few, and Rispoli was making a much more profitable living selling portable grandstands. Furthermore, Rispoli favored local Staten Island drivers, and if he witnessed an "outsider" going too fast during warm-ups, he would find a reason to dismiss the driver from racing. The speedway's legacy is carried on by George LeBlanc who operates the Weissglass Stadium Museum and the LeBlanc Trains & Hobby Center—an authorized Lionel dealer, and vendor of model kits, Carrera slot cars, Aurora AFX, and diecast automobiles. LeBlanc also runs Big-Daddy-George Pinstriping & Lettering at the same location at 28 Hamlin Place, about a quarter mile from the old speedway. LeBlanc is also a repairer of American Flyer model railroads/trains which formerly were repaired on Staten Island at Sterner & LeBlanc. Sterner & LeBlanc, the dominant '50's appliance and television chain on Staten Island, possessed four locations: 245 Jewett Avenue, 751 Forest Avenue, 559 Bay Street, and 3970 Amboy Road. The company sold household items such as W.J. Tappan Stoves and the iconic Cycla-Matic Frigidaire which included four groundbreaking features: a "true" food freezer, heatless defrosting, rust-proof glide-out aluminum shelves, and a butter pre-server. Sterner & LeBlanc would be a precursor to the numerous department stores—Kresges, Major's, Master's, EJ Korvettes, WT Grant's, Woolworth, McCrory's, Fischer-Beer, and Garber's—which ranged from five-and-dime to discount retail. Staten Island's "department store era" (if you will) commenced around the time of the opening of the Verrazzano Bridge, peaked in the mid-1970s, and mostly ended around 1980. Though New York City's second-largest mall—The Staten Island Mall—was completed in 1973, it wouldn't be until roughly a decade later that the small retail chains would be displaced indefinitely. The disappearance of such stores was indeed of a microcosm of the entire country. Today, these memories are recalled to mind by Staten Islanders cleaning out their deceased parents' closets which are filled with discounted double-knit polyester dresses, boxes of vintage records, and piles of never-used linens. Arguably Staten Island's foremost department store was EJ Korvettes (believed to be an acronym for "Eight Jewish Korean War Veterans"), located on the property adjacent to the Staten Island Mall on Richmond Avenue; Korvettes also owned the Korvettes Auto Center, and Hill's Supermarket across the street. The store is remembered by many children who in the 1970s were frequent customers of the soft pretzel and Italian ice stand outside, or rode their mini bikes in the parking lot. Some teenagers even in the mid-1960s on Sundays used the lot as a drag strip, only to be caught by police weeks later. For many Staten Islanders, Korvettes became a central facet of everyday life. The wide selection ranging from pets to sports equipment to records made the department store a highly-sought destination (hence, the chain's jingle: "Korvettes has more of what you're looking for!"). Not to mention, the extremely low prices which prompted Macy's and Gimbels to file a lawsuit against Korvettes under a violation of the 1936 Robinson-Patman Act. Professor Nelson Lichtenstein writes in his book *The Retail Revolution: How Wal-Mart Created a Brave New World of Business*, "[Eugene] Ferkauf could undercut both Macy's and Sears and make money in the process because he held overall labor cost...to but 6 or 7 percent of sales, far lower than the 18 or 20 percent paid by the full-line department stores. Even more important, Korvette's entire inventory was replaced thirty times a year, in an era where the department stores though themselves doing well if merchandise had to be reordered six or seven times per annum." Korvettes even sold their own brand of electronics—XAM, in addition to the newest Panasonic, Fischer and Pioneer stereos; portable and digital clock radios; AM/FM pocket radios; Lloyds 8-track stereo system; tape recorders; 2-speed portable phonographs; Keystone Everflash cameras; and battery-portable TVs. Unfortunately though, by 1970, mismanagement concerning obsolescence and markdowns grew increasingly prevalent; this ultimately led to Korvette's demise in 1980. Even by this time however, EJ Korvettes had assisted in the ushering in of a new era for Staten Island. The department store, built on the former grounds of a chicken farm, completely revolutionized New Springville. The rise of the shopping industry propelled the development of the condominium, townhouse, condensed, busy, tight community that the neighborhood is associated with today. On large, previously forested lots, 200-300 homes were constructed in one sitting. The new encroaches overturned a legacy cultivated by English, French Huguenot, Dutch farmers who first inhabited the area in the seventeenth century. A similar effect was experienced in Stapleton where the F.W. Woolworth Co., along with several other smaller boutiques such as Store of a Million Items, John's Bargain Store, and the Army & Navy Stores made the area a shopping destination; this was in conjunction with the success of the beverage industry: e.g. Piel's Brewery, Imperial Beverage Co., The Old Homestead Dairy, Borden, Meadow Brook Dairy; and profound shipping/dry dock industry (i.e. companies in this field established include Caddell Dry Dock & Repair Co., Port Richmond Iron Works, Staten Island Shipbuilding Co., the Starin Shipyard, Van Cliel's Dry Dock, and Downey's Shipyard). At one point, Texas and Louisiana industrialists even contemplated using Stapleton's derelict piers as a base for oil exploration along the Atlantic Coast. In 1908, a municipal ferry even operated between Whitehall in Manhattan and Stapleton. By the 1920s, however, Mayor John Hylan suspended the service and instead constructed twelve deep-water piers that extended all the way to Tompkinsville, forming a barricade of seventeen ship piers (termed "Hylan's Folly"). Despite several disadvantages and struggles, Stapleton ultimately thrived due to the rise of shopping; Antiques Row on Bay Street was a prime example. On this strip, one could "find anything from a $3,000 banjo to $15 handcrafted jewelry, original art, health foods, and tropical plants." The lavish boutiques and large department, novelty stores also left priceless memories. A well-seasoned Staten Islander remembers at F.W. Woolworth (which also had a location on Port Richmond Ave.) the 40¢ Super Deluxe Ham Sandwich-Baked Ham Sliced Very Thin and Stacked High on Plain Bread, Toast, or Hard Roll, or even the "Extra Rich Ice Cream Soda," Chocolate Malt, or "Super Jumbo Banana Split." The establishment of F.W. Woolworth in Stapleton was clear evidence of a shift in both Staten Island and New York society. The Victorian era of the late-1800's to early 1900s characterized by horse-drawn carriages and extravagant dresses, slowly was beginning to be replaced by automobiles, discount retail, and mass-produced clothing items. In the present day, the cycle of change continues at a rapid pace, particularly in shifting demographics and development. The former Woolworth storefront, having first been occupied by the Department of Health, is currently Oznico Clothing Store at 103 Water St. Since the days of Stapleton's big department stores, the area has since seen an unfortunate, sharp decline. A major point of discussion regarding decline was the erection of the Stapleton Houses—a housing project completed in 1960. The housing projects aligned with a series of other issues including a generational age gap between Staten Islanders, weak policing, increasing taxes, and the controversy surrounding the 1990 construction of the Homeport (Naval Station) military base. In conjunction with shopping and industry, Stapleton (and all of Staten Island, for that matter) relied heavily on its naval/marine capabilities; large shipbuilders and dry docks provided the adequate facilities necessary for wide-range exportation and distribution. These factors were compounded on other appeasing aspects of Staten Island which included a relatively-low cost of living in comparison to the other boroughs, extensive railway/freight connections, an industrious community, and close proximity to Manhattan.

THE NEIGHBORHOODS AND THEIR STORIES

~

The history of New Brighton has been historically compromised, generally in many opinions for the worst. As detailed in previous sections, blocks of family businesses, "Made in the USA" textile plants or factories, and a sterling sense of interracial community, have in many regards met their unfortunate demise. Columbia Meat Market, located 437 Jersey St., is the among the last few standing businesses of the early 20th century in New Brighton. At one time, decades ago, Jersey St. abounded with charming storefronts and intriguing personalities; these included: Lieblich's Bakery [5] (Yetta Lieblich), Rosso's Grocery Store (Jack Rosso), Marotta's Fruit & Produce Market (Emilia Marotta), Bisogna's Bakery (Bisogna family), and Eagle's Department Store (Arthur Eagle). Columbia Meat Market, at the corner of Jersey St. & Scribner Ave., was founded in 1920 by the DeSimone family, and is not only the longest-standing butcher shop in West Brighton, but in all of Staten Island. In the days of its original ownership, the market sold chicken for one penny per pound, and its most expensive cut of meat—rib-eye steak—for five cents per pound (the equivalent of $0.13 and $0.63, respectively, today). Back in the 1920s, "[t]he store was simple, with a wooden floor, a lot of hooks, and the meat in front of the window...This was pre-refrigeration, so there was an ice box, with a rack on top where the blocks of ice were stored."Authentic insights into the neighborhood's past are given by few individuals, many

---

[5] Yetta Lieblich (April 16, 1895 – April 10, 1987), formerly Yetta Bernhardt, a Polish immigrant whose married name translates from German as "lovely," was known in West Brighton for her personality and saying of "If you're healthy, you're wealthy!"

of whom have left their homes for the greener pastures of Pennsylvania or warmer climate of North Carolina and Florida. Among those who have remained is Philomena "Dolly" Garcenot (b. 1931), a resident of Tompkinsville, who spent her primal years at 411 Jersey St. (coincidentally, above the future Dolly's Florists) and then, 76 Jersey St. Her father, possessing the surname "Passarella," had parents originating from the commune of Campobasso—the capital city of the Italian region Molise. On her maternal side, the "Rotunno'"s, had roots in Bari, Puglia. In fact, Garcenot's aunt Mary Barsalona (1909-1977), nee Rotunno, the husband of Peter, was the mother of Frank Barsalona[6]—the New York-based talent booking agent who booked The Beatles' first appearance in America. Garcenot's grandfather, Michael Passarella, raised on York Ave., had the family home built especially for them on Kingsley Pl.; his employment was as a courier of sorts in the late-1930s for the Staten Island News Co. (a subcontractor of Interborough News Co., operated by "one MacAloon," which made no deliveries independent of the Staten Island News Co.) who transported a wheelbarrow from Staten Island to Manhattan, collecting a large bundle of newspapers, and distributed them back on Staten Island. His father, the first to arrive from the Port of Naples, was an urban animal inspector who died after contracting Undulant fever (Brucellosis)—an extremely rare disease—most likely from coming into contact with certain bacteria in animals. Garcenot's maternal grandfather "Giusepp'", however, owned a business of a kind typically associated with early Staten Island—coal and ice

---

[6] F. Barsalona (1938-2012), a native of Lafayette Ave. in New Brighton, spent most of his days living in Manhattan. At G.A.C., working in the mail room, he helped book The Beatles' first American appearance in Feb. 1964. Barsalona went on to found Premier Talent Agency, which represented numerous rock star celebrities. He is noted for "vastly improving the fan experience, working with young promoters around the country to showcase emerging artists at their local venues, and [creating] the infrastructure for the modern day concert touring business."

delivery. Garcenot explained, "My grandfather's company was essentially a one-man-band. He used to keep his horse-and-carriage in an oddly, narrow alleyway on the north side of Pietrangelo's Bakery on York Ave. That alley has since become a paved, cement driveway for the house next to it." Across the street from the aforementioned place was La Morte's Vending—a cigarette, snack vending machine and jukebox company founded in 1955. Just two homes south of Pauw St. at 257 York Ave. was Lombardi's Dry Goods—a very small establishment erased firmly into history. "Across from my first residence in New Brighton was Phil Granito's children's coat factory at 403 Jersey St at the corner of Winter Ave..; my aunt worked there. I'll never forget Conte's Meats or Deodati Pharmacy, or anything that made New Brighton what it was." Garcenot reminisced about the various groups of Italians which concentrated all on certain streets; she recalled calling Sumner Pl. (to the east of Goodhue Repair) "*Vinchiadur* Alley" (after the immigrants from Vinchiaturo, i.e. the Pistilli and DeSantis families). She also remembered learning various colloquial Italian phrases from her maternal grandmother, such as the profanity-laced expression "Va fa Nabe!," short for "Va fa Napoli!," meaning "Go to Naples!" Family outings mainly consisted of weekend trips to South Beach; during such occasions, Garcenot's mother would bring a bottle of wine and place it inside a hole she had made in the sand. "My aunt who didn't know how to swim, would just go to four feet in the water and float up and down on the rope which lead out to the sea!...We didn't have much, but we were grateful for what we had. What I'll always remember most was the way the old Italian ladies in the neighborhood used to cure the malocch'[7] If you went to my grandmother, she would anoint

---

[7] The *malocch'* is the shortened version of "malocchio"—translated from Italian as "bad eye." Another interpretations of the word is "overlook" or jokingly, "The Guinea's Horns." It can be used to refer to malicious glance, an inflicted curse, or a headache.

your head with water, say a litany of prayers in inaudible Italian, and when she poured the oil on your forehead, if it split in two directions, it meant you had a terrible headache. But if you went to the other Italian lady up the street, you would bring her a bobby pin, and she would throw a knife against the front door, and whoever walked by would be transferred the headache. I never understood that one bit..."

The practice of performing the *malocch'* is fondly reminisced by many New Brightoners who "wear their Italian horns in hopes of protection from evil." Among these are Alice Granito Bergstromc—one of many in the Granito ancestral lineage—who stated, "My father used to send me up the hill whenever he did not feel well and grandma would do the *malocch'*." Granito is granddaughter of Francesco (Frank) and Archangela Cutrone (in Italian, meaning the archangel). Her grandmother immigrated in 1908 from Campobasso, and was married to someone she didn't even know. Archangela (b. 1885) was the matriarch of the Granito household at 11 Van Tuyl St.—but in 1945, following her son Carmine's death in the Battle of Okinawa in the Pacific Ocean theatre, Archangela assumed "matriarchy" of a Gold Star Family. Carmine's heroism would be acknowledged in the naming of NY 10304 Legion Post #1296, Granito-Smith Post. In 2013, Lafayette Ave. took the name of Granito-Smith Way. The noted "G.I. Joe" statue of a "lone, rifle-bearing soldier," located originally at York & Brighton Aves. was also moved to Goodhue Park in New Brighton. Regarding her grandmother, Bergstromc remarked, "When I was a young girl, I used to climb roofs and jump off. Not nine stories of course. My grandmother happened to be sitting on her porch and watched me do this. Instead of calling my parents, she started yelling in Italian to me. I did not understand one word, but she kept yelling. I laughed and just kept jumping!" Bergstromc's uncles, Phil and Jimmy each owned coat factories. Jimmy owned the one on Crescent Ave. while his brother had the one on Jersey St.

The most famous Granito family member is Carmine John Granito, also known as "Ron Dante." Dante (b. Aug. 1945), the leader of the fictional cartoon band *The Archies*, gained international recognition for his 1966 recording of Jerry Barry and Andy Kim's "Sugar, Sugar." With Dante's popularization of the song, it was voted "Song Of The Year" in 1969. Though many would also remember him for his 1982 recording "You Deserve a Break Today" for the McDonald's commercials, he also "worked as a producer for Barry Manilow, Cher, Dionne Warwick, Pat Benatar, Irene Cara, Ray Charles, and John Denver."

Similar Italian, Staten Island memories are recalled by Maria Bonamo who grew up on Corson Avenue in New Brighton. The cousin of Dr. John Bonamo, physician to the New York Yankees baseball team, Maria has Italian roots deeply entrenched into Staten Island history. Her grandmother's family owned Filomeno's Bar on Jersey Street; her uncles, Albert, Pat, and Tony (the butcher) ran Butler's Grocery on Bay St. & Hylan Blvd.; and her great-grandparents owned Marotta's—a fruit and produce store— on the corner of Jersey and Corson. Maria exclaimed, "A couple times a week, my maternal great-grandmother Emilia would ride on a horse-and-buggy into Manhattan via the Ferry to the produce market with some money and a gun in her pocket! ... As kids, we were spoiled because we didn't need the delivery trucks to come by and sell us produce; my parents brought home everything we needed from the family store! Growing up, of course, in an Italian neighborhood, all of us, including all my relatives, lived house-to-house with each other. When we wanted cake, we'd go knocking on everyone's door, and if they didn't have cake, they'd give us saltines with butter!" New Brighton at the time was inundated with personalities of all varieties; notable examples include Mike "The Hat" (also known as "The Gevel Man" – Mike Manzione) who would come around in his truck selling gevel—a bleaching agent made behind the buildings on York Avenue, as well as Tony "Gashouse." Maria continued, "Life was so simple back then in New Brighton...At 11pm, when as kids we were ordered to go to bed (of course, we never actually did), we could see downstairs that our kitchen was packed with people. Some nights, at 12am, we ran over to Lieblich's Bakery, knocked on the side door, and Yetta Lieblich would give us some pumpernickel and hot rye bread. I can see her face now! ... In the summers, my family would plant tomato gardens, and in the cooler seasons—Italian Flat-Leaf Parsley and radicchio." "As I was going through my father's old medical bills recently, I was astounded! At one point, they had billed him $2 for anesthesia treatment, and only $5 for the entire hospital stay! And back in the old days, if my dad couldn't afford the exact amount of the treatment, he'd bring Dr. Diamond a bowl of fresh tomatoes from his garden, a few bottles of homemade wine, a loaf of bread, a chicken leg, or whatever else he had to supplement the cost!" Maria Bonamo's cousin, John Gatti (b. 1955) corroborates his relative's account of the close-knit community. "It was a weekly tradition enforced by my grandmother "Mamie" Dizeo Bonamo who kept a detailed attendance log to join together over coffee and cake at the household of the first-arrived-to Staten Island Bonamo's at 17 Pine St. in New Brighton. Many a day did we leave our home in Brooklyn to take the 69th Street Ferry to Staten Island to visit relatives." Gatti, retired Performing Arts Director and instructor of English, History, and "Street Law" at Monsignor Farrell High School in Oakwood, is a native of Bensonhurst, Brooklyn. His father, Gabriel Gatti (b. 1927) was a Parole Officer for the New York State Divison of Parolem and graduate of Lafayette High School. Gatti's paternal grandparents were emigrants from Venice and Palazzo D'Adriana in Sicily respectively. "Their Italian dialects were so different so their entire romance began due to difference in dialects, as an exchange of flirtatious glances and nonverbal communication followed by the proper introductions to the elder relatives (cousins) she lived with when she came to America." Following his father's death in 1965, Gatti, his siblings, and his mother, Gloria departed for Bay Terrace in July of that year, settling on Buffalo St. Like other Staten Islanders and Brooklyn transplants of Italian descent, Gatti is a devout scholar of the spiritual procedure *malocch'*. "My grandmother believed if you had a headache, someone was cursing you. If you felt a headache coming on, you were to immediately place a cold washcloth on your forehead to ward off the evil spirits."

Joanne Bennetti, a board member of the Richmond County Kiwanis—one of Staten Island's premier benevolent societies—grew up in the former Irish, German neighborhood known to reader by this juncture as New Brighton. Bennetti's paternal grandparents—part-German, part-Finnish—met on the boat embarking from Europe to Connecticut. After settling in New Brighton, they bore several children, of which included Bennetti's father John L. Beyar (the last name "Beyar" is an anglicized derivative of the traditional Swedish surname "Beijar"). Beyar (b. 1900), a classically-trained organ player at Trinity Lutheran Church on St. Pauls Ave. and student in Curtis High School's first graduating class, operated the gas station at the southwest

[John Beyar at his gas station on Bay St. with his workers behind him. C. late-1920s. Courtesy – Joanne Bennetti]

corner of Hannah St. & Bay St. across from the former Robbins Reef Motor Co.[8] and was later employed as an engineer at Bethlehem Steel Co. Beyar's maternal grandmother was brought over as a domestic from Ireland in 1880. Bennetti, the ninth of ten children, was raised at 65 Cassidy Pl. Directly across the street at 70 Cassidy Pl. resided Mr. Dominick Manfra (b. 1887), a cobbler who serenaded the Beyar children with Neapolitan songs on his mandolin in the 1950s. At 109 Lafayette Ave. was Walter Marchnak (b. 1892)—a Polish immigrant who resided initially at 84 York Ave., and was a truck driver for a lumber yard; he was also a talented woodworker. At 121 Lafayette Ave. was an Italian owned-barbershop (Bennetti referenced a barber named, "Caruso") which existed sometime in the late-1940s, 1950s. In the 50-numbered homes of Cassidy Pl. was Dan Simone—an iceman who wandered the streets of New Brighton. Bennetti recalled, "In 1944, my older brother decided to hitch on a ride on Simone's ice truck when he fell off and got a double compound fracture in his head. It was a miracle he made it out alive. It was even more a miracle that he ended up becoming a genius. He eventually worked at R.C.A. We nicknamed him 'Egbert' after 'Egbert the Bookworm!'" Other peddlers included Mr. Frank Malandro (b. 1908)—a deliverer of fruits and vegetables—who resided at 149 Brighton Ave.; Malandro also operated a small store at that location. Among Benetti's fondest childhood memories consist of regular visits to the Goodhue Center to

---

[8] Robbins Reef Motor Co., a Buick dealer renown in Tompkinsville for its lighthouse centerpiece, was a pioneering used car dealership. It is written in Hearst Magazines, 1937, "Take trade-ins at the lowest possible allowances, recondition them thoroughly and quickly, price them a little below the market to insure prompt turnover, advertise and display them to good advantage— these are some of the methods which have ironed a lot of the worry out of the used car business of Robbins Reef Motor Co. Staten Island, N.Y…Who wants to buy an abused car? But if the dealer overhauls and dolls them up till they look and act like new, they'll do most of the job of getting themselves sold with minimum delay. More than that, they'll make satisfied customers who will come back to buy used cars again, or maybe new ones."

swim, experiment in the woodworking shop, or dance. She further recalled putting slugs into the Wurlitzer jukebox instead of money into the slot. Bennetti explained, "The employees at Goodhue were so friendly to us! They would buy us records and they also ran the dances. I remember one St. Patrick's Day evening my mother told me, "Don't forget to wear your coat. But being myself, I didn't. When I exited the dance, there was a blizzard. So, I took off my shoes, held them in my hands, and walked all the way home. My body was entirely frostbitten when I entered through the door!" A favorite pastime on Tuesday and Thursday nights was attending the splash parties at Goodhue Pool where the moderator would throw a greased watermelon filled with money into the water. During the snow season, activities involved sleigh riding from the Irving Mansion, owned by two spinsters, down the hill toward Cassidy Pl. Another popular location for sleigh riding was the cobblestone-paved downward slope of E. Buchanan St. Just behind the Bennetti household was a world of entertainment in and of itself. At 154 W. Buchanan St. resided John DeNora (b. 1901)—an ice, coal, and oil deliverer who used to set up amusement rides such as a miniature Ferris wheel and The Whip (a ride in which individuals ride in small containers that force one to a side as corners are passed). De Nora was only one of the many Italians residing on that block of W. Buchanan St. In fact the block was renamed "Caccese Way" in 2014 to honor "three generations of the Caccese family who have compiled a remarkable record of public service." The Caccese American lineage began with Phillip Caccese who immigrated "from Staten Island to Naples in 1910 and worked more than forty years in the NYC Department of Marine and Aviation." Bennetti remembered walking through a small tunnel at the end of "Caccese Way" toward St. Paul's Church on Franklin Ave. Shortly after, she explained, "the man would come out with his shotgun chasing after us!" Other incidents of childhood shenanigans occurred at Sailors' Snug Harbor where the "snuggies" (a nickname for the home's residents) would chase after Bennetti and her childhood playmates after they had jumped the metal fence, attempting to catch a glimpse of the grazing cows and horses. St. Paul's—a Roman Catholic church burned to the ground in the late-1950s—was run by a tiny, little Irishwoman with "flaming red hair," nicknamed "Breidy Bonds." Like St. Paul's, Bennetti's childhood home too went in flames, in the 1980s. Though many original properties saw their final days, many remain, and of course, memories and legacies persist. Joanne's brother Francis "Frank" Beyar, before his death was the owner and operator of Watters Plumbing Supply Corp. at 55 Church St. And as detailed previously, Bennetti herself found a niche in community service. "My love for helping others out began in high school," Bennetti stated, "I was inspired by one of my instructors—among the most famous at Curtis High School—Vince Speranza." Vincent J. Speranza, a resident of Dongan Hills, was a machine gunner in the 501st Parachute Infantry Regiment during the Siege of Bastogne, an American/German conflict during the Battle of Bulge between December 20-27 of 1944. One evening, during the armed engagement, Speranza set off to a local tavern to acquire beer to bring to the troops suffering elsewhere. Despite having no canteen, Speranza filled his helmet with beer, delivering it to the distressed soldiers. He repeated this process. Little to his knowledge, his story would become the basis for legends told across the southeast Belgian countryside; Belgian-brewed "Airborne Beer" commends Speranza's heroism. Bennetti recalled, "Every day, my history teacher, [Speranza] would always say, 'How are you doing today?...Any problems?...You sure?...Well, if you do, I can help you out.' He became my mentor. Little did I know, he had heard gossip about another girl "Joanne" getting pregnant, and he had mistaken her for me. I told him, 'Well, you think I'm pregnant. It's not me! I distinctly remember one time signing myself out of school. He immediately phoned my mother and told her, 'Don't let her call herself out of school! She has so much potential'...I took those words to heart. Vince Speranza and that way of life in the old neighborhood had the greatest impact on my life. New Brighton taught me to be the person I am, and I think I'm a hell of a person!" Bennetti's classmate at PS40, Josie Barnes Darrigo also recalled those neighbors, institutions, and workers who existed as one functioning unit—the community. Darrigo was raised at 320 Glen Ave., a tannish-brown, three-story family residence constructed by her Sicilian grandfather Vincenzo Valentino (b. 1883), a stone mason, in 1930. The household of twelve was surrounded almost entirely by Italians [addresses on Glen Ave – family name]: 294 – Paolucci, 318 – Albini, 311 – Campanella/Monteleone. Other families in the neighborhood included Pistilli, Pizzo (153 Brighton Ave.), Cippoletti, Russo, and Barracato. The Valentino's boasted a distant family relationship with Rudolph Valentino "The Latin Lover"—a noted sex icon and Italian actor who starred in several silent films: *The Four Horsemen of the Apocalypse, The Sheik, Blood and Sand,* etc. Due to Darrigo's location, her mother had an account with F. Malandro in which she paid her bill at the end of each week. Occasionally, Malandro would deliver the produce to the house. Darrigo holds fond memories of sledding down the hill from Castleton Ave. to down the block on Glen Ave, and attending feasts at Church of the Assumption.

In the age when Wall Street brokers rode the Staten Island Railway to the tranquil shores of Lower Bay, Anthony Navarino's great-grandmother, residing with her family in the crowded neighborhood of Little Italy, enjoyed summer outings in South Beach to her bungalow. The bungalow fit about twenty-five people, had an outdoor kitchen, as well as an outhouse in the backyard teeming with feral rabbits. The saddest part of reflecting on days gone by, at least for

Navarino, are thinking about those homes that were forever destroyed in the wake of the Staten Island Expressway—an extension of the Verrazzano Bridge. Navarino (b. 1956), former Superintendent of the Cleaning Service of the Staten Island Railway and B&O trains, lived at Corson Ave. in New Brighton until the age of eleven-months when he moved to 445 Jersey St. His grandfather, Joseph Trentacosta had a horse-and-buggy which delivered fruit and vegetables in Manhattan's Little Italy. His grandfather Anthony, uncle Charles, and father Vincent "Jimmy" had a newspaper route on the North Shore; four-hundred papers from five companies were delivered Monday-Saturday, while Sunday saw distribution of 1500 journals. Navarino's grandfather was a former driver for Staten Island Coach Bus; his father was an electrician on the B. & O. Railroad, later the Staten Island Railway. "When they couldn't pay the rent" Navarino remarked, "My father would move with his family about once a month in the middle of the night!" Navarino once lived as a child at 445 Jersey St., directly upstairs from Vazzana's Deli—owned by the DeSimone family, the original proprietors of the Columbia Meat Market next door. "My mother used to lower a plastic bag filled with some money down from the third floor of the apartment building so I could buy groceries at the Columbia Meat Market. The deli guy used to give me a free, raw hot dog!... I was best friends with Thomas Vazzana (today, a cardiologist on Seaview Ave.) with whom I would play 'Army.' We bought the figurines at John's Bargain Store in Stapleton, and used to divide them into three groups: the Japanese, Germans, and Americans. We used to throw army trucks at the soldiers in order to knock them down. Vazzana's mother was a DeSimone! In fact, when she worked at the Staten Island Savings Bank on Hylan Blvd., I used to cash my check with her every Tuesday." Navarino recalled marches from the Granito-Smith Post on Brighton Ave. to the Church of the Assumption, the time his grandfather—engineer on the railroad—Vincent "Jimmy" Madonia had coffee with then-Massachusetts Senator John F. Kennedy at the St. George Ferry Terminal, and the days when his father took clarinet lessons on Victory Blvd. in the school Frank Sinatra who is rumored to have taken violin. Navarino is currently an accountant at the Stephen Siller Tunnel to Towers Foundation—a charitable organization which constructs house for injured combat veterans. Describing the old Island, Navarino recounted, "In 1964, the Mary Poppins film was featured at the St. George Theatre. I can remember before attending the performance, some woman was shouting, 'Sign the petition! Because someday, you're going to be paying to watch Television!' It sounded so silly then, but fate would prove otherwise!"

Nearly all traces of this prehistoric Staten Island bakery and grocer have been dissolved into history. Various traces of evidence have merely disintegrated into a near-fictitious existence in photographs. The pre-Holtermann's delivery vehicles, which so often characterizes the harmonious Staten Island-1950s atmosphere, could be found at various street corners throughout New Brighton. One image captured in July of 1932 displays the rugged streets at the intersection

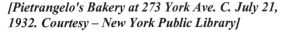

[Pietrangelo's Bakery at 273 York Ave. C. July 21, 1932. Courtesy – New York Public Library]

Jersey St. & Brighton Ave. with Eagle's Department Store and Jack Rosso's Italian grocery in the background. On the southeast corner of that very intersection, currently the site of a fueling station, over eighty-five years ago was captured an everyday street scene with an idle Pietrangelo's bakery truck. Another photograph, this one taken in May of 1929, shows an impounded, somewhat-dismantled "M. Pietrangelo & Sons Wholesale Bakers" truck sitting in the Richmond Auto Wrecking Co. at the foot of Richmond Hill. Pietrangelo's Bakery, located at 273 York Ave. from the early-1900s to the late-1940s, was owned by Michael (Michele) Pietrangelo and his wife Philomena. After the closure of the bakery, Michael pursued his passion of raising gardenias; his spectacular efforts were featured on one

[An M. Pietrangelo & Sons bakery delivery vehicle at the automobile graveyard of the Richmond Auto Wrecking Co. C. May 5, 1929. Courtesy – New York Public Library]

occasion by the *Staten Island Advance*. The young M. Pietrangelo (b. 1883) hailed like many of his neighborhood Italian counterparts in New Brighton from Vinchiaturo in Molise. After a short stint in Argentina earning money to fund the voyage to America, he returned to Italy to marry his wife. Around the year of 1905, the time of his son's birth— the first of eight children (six sons: Carmine, Tony, Andy,

124

Charlie, Pete, and Louis; two daughters: Mary and Margaret) Pietrangelo is said to have founded the bakery. Before that, he was employed at the U.S. Gypsum Co. on Richmond Terrace. The bakery, most notable for its freshly-baked bread, carried barrels of dry goods such as beans, lentils and macaroni, in addition to racks of cold cuts. In the early-1930s, Pietrangelo's wife Philomena opened a soda factory just across the street from La Morte's Vending Inc. Additionally, in the late-1930s, early-1940s Pietrangelo began a side-business catering "football weddings"—traditional Italian, New York ceremonies which involve a "designated quarterback" tossing wax paper-wrapped meat and cheese sandwiches to wedding guests. "All the cooking was done in my grandmother's kitchen, the size of a closet!" Gloria Ricciardi, Pietrangelo's granddaughter, remarked. Ricciardi, a native of Harvard Ave., took her first name from acclaimed actress Gloria Swanson. "When my father operated a private limousine business driving celebrities and actors from Manhattan to Staten Island, Gloria Swanson was the only one that gave my dad a tip!" Ricciardi explained. Ricciardi recalled fond memories of the old bakery and of course, old Staten Island: a particular incident which occurred involved dozens of neighborhood Italian women crowded into the family's mahogany basement to celebrate Victory in Europe Day by drinking themselves into oblivion with champagne. In the early-1930s, Pietrangelo's son Louis went on to own Pietrangelo Funeral Home on Jersey St., in partnership with Patsy Gallucci[9]. Ricciardi recalled a specific incident in which a car came crashing through the windows of the parlor, stopping immediately under the hung crucifix. "Things were so different back then!" Ricciardi explained, "Could you imagine delivering a loaf of bread to a house in New Dorp in 1931! Even the traditions were auspicious. To keep the power of *malocch*—the God-given ability to cure

---

[9] In the 1950s, Louis Pietrangelo established the Richmond Funeral Home on Richmond Rd. in Grant City.

headaches—you would need to say ten prayers every Christmas Eve!" "I can remember during those Christmas Eve dinners the long table of family members. The men were against the wall with narrow space relative to the table, while the women were on the other side because they were always having to get up! You may hear derogatory remarks about Staten Island, but it was the best place to raise children and have a family."

Scarano's Market—a vendor of "Prime Meats"—stood for approximately twenty years in the three-story, green shingle building at 143 Lafayette Ave. in the northwest portion of New Brighton. The store was run by Catiello Scarano, a native of a village near the seaside town of Sorrento, and his wife Louisa Mimmicola of Campobasso. The couple immigrated to the United States to Jamaica, Queens, before residing in an abandoned furniture warehouse on Staten Island. Before opening his market, Catiello regularly went around in his horse-and-buggy, selling fruit and vegetables, through the streets of New Brighton, singing Italian opera. In the mid-late-1940s, Catiello opened Scarano's, and ran it with the assistance of his son Ed—a World War II veteran who saw active combat in the Battle of the Bulge. After Catiello's passing in 1956, Ed and his brother Joe operated the shop, along with the help of certain family members. The brothers' niece Donna Scarano Amaturo explained, "My bedroom was on the top floor's right side. When I was twelve, I began working in the store. At fourteen, my uncle put a knife in my hand and I learned how to butcher. I was mostly religated to the grocery side, however. My grandmother, although not entirely involved, would come down every so often to 'inspect.'" Scarano's was divided into two parts: a butcher in the back, and grocery toward the front door. The market offered homemade sausages, roasting chickens, spare ribs, shoulder steaks, beef liver, soda, ice cream, etc. "My grandmother would yell up the stairs to me in Italian to call me down to teach me how to cook. She used to make an amazing Sofrito with intestines and stomach with sauce and Italian bread" Scarano continued, "We had so many Italians coming in to buy meat. My uncle Ed used to tease the old Italian ladies who came in by hiding an oxtail under the register counter on a butcher board. He'd pretend to reach under his apron and grab the oxtail and say, 'This thing is driving me crazy! I can't get it fixed right.' Then he'd throw the oxtail on the counter and hit it with a cleaver. He had us all on the floor laughing!" Scarano noted a sense of racial harmony which once flourished in New Brighton; customers of all backgrounds were frequent shoppers at Scarano's Market... Among her favorite memories of the area are of her father, James who was a bus driver on the 102 oute (replaced by the S-44). Scarano remarked, "After school, my father would pick me up on the corner and say, 'Mettici cinque sord!' which meant 'Put in a nickel!' The regular fare was fifteen cents, and my father used to give me a two-thirds discount!" Reminiscing about her grandfather, Scarano remarked, "When I was just a little girl, he taught me a children's poem which to this day I can't say without an Italian accent: I see a little a little bird, he go 'Pa, pa, pa.' I say a' little bird, 'How do ya do?' He shake his tail a little, and off away he flew...When people say 'Those were the good old days,' they *were*."

[From left to right: Louisa, Ed, and Catiello Scarano pose for a family photograph. C. late-1910s. Courtesy – Donna Scarano Amaturo]

Scarano's childhood friend, Thomas Iommi of South Plainfield, N.J. shared many similar experiences from childhood in New Brighton. "I can recall in 1965 on a snowy afternoon taking a metal wire trash can from the PS17 schoolyard and putting it in the middle of street. My father— a big Cadillac guy who had recently purchased a Fiat—drove down the street playing games with us as if he was going to go through the pile of snow. Well, he actually did! And plowed right into the trash can! I didn't return home for several days..." Iommi, the son of Anthony "Tom" Iommi (b. 1915), was raised at 22 Propsect Ave. His grandfather and great-uncle ran a produce store "Neighborhood Groceries – Delicatessen," known to locals as "Peanuts" (after his great-uncle's nickname) which operated through the 1930s at 190 Fillmore St. Iommi's second cousin, Anthony F. Iommi was one of the founding members of the British heavy metal band *Black Sabbath*. A member of the English branch of the Iommi family which departed from Italy in two separate directions, Anthony Iommi received the title of one of the "100 Greatest Guitarists of All Time" by magazine *Rolling Stone*. Thomas Iommi's father was a professional photographer in Port Richmond from the early-1950s until 1977 for Lorstran-Thomas Studios [Lors Photography], based out of Newark. Iommi remarked, "Many of the things we did as kids, those adults who helped us do those things would probably be in jail now!...The Signorello family and many of the older neighborhood boys used to take their porcelain kitchen tabletop, remove its legs, and we went sliding down the hill on it on Prospect Ave.!...During the summer-time, when my friends and I played with our band, Mel Ramos—the janitor at PS17— would throw an extension cable out the window to give us amplification. About seventy people would be watching us on those nights!" In era when money was scarce, Iommi concluded, "I can recall when I was just a little boy, Fr. Cascelli coming over to our house to make a deal with father about school tuition when they were first opening the school at Church of the Assumption. Fr. Cascelli said, 'How about you pay your week's salary for tuition every single month.' My father broke out screaming, 'We've been sitting here for three hours, you've been drinking my Whiskey, and you see my family here eating everything on the table, and now you're going to ask me for more money! Get outta here!" Iommi's former neighbor at York Ave. & Propsect Ave., Mr. Joseph DeVito (b. Nov. 22, 1950) described the street being in the 1950s "a two-way gravel road." The son of a longshoreman and a seamstress, DeVito served in the United States Marines Corp. between 1967-1974. Before graduating from New Dorp High School, DeVito in the old neighborhood enjoyed making clothespin airplanes, having an occasional glass of Coca-Cola as a kid at The Brighton Lounge, and going to Hour's Bakery in Concord. One post-service memory in particular which stood out included having to grow a beard for the Bicentennial Parade in 1976. "I can remember as a kid going to Whitey's Ice House at the corner of Hylan Blvd. & Raritan Ave. Our little mischevious group of children would steal empty bottles of soda from the back (about twelve per case), and take them over the fence to get money back. They used to have to give us three cents a bottle! But they caught on shortly afterwards."

Mike Pistilli, an Italian native-Staten Islander with a rich, culturally-significant heritage, withstood the enormous conflict along the Italian-Irish dividing lines which engulfed 20th-century New York City. Pistilli (whose last name translates from Italian as *pistils*—the female reproductive organ of flowers) was raised on Glen Ave. between Castleton Ave. and Stanley Ave. in New Brighton, till the age of five. He was the son of an employee at the Dept. of Sanitation in Manhattan who also owned P. & A. Construction (a small developer which built one to two homes at a time on Staten Island). Early childhood memories included frequenting Jack Rosso's Italian grocery store on

Jersey St., as well as swimming in the pool at the Goodhue Center on Propsect Ave. In 1955, Pistilli moved to New Dorp to 9th St. where his family was the first one of Italian origin; it was in this neighborhood that he would face severe discrimination for his Italian identity. Pistilli descended from peasants who resided in the extraordinary small commune of Vinchiaturo—founded as a prison town in the days of the Roman Empire—in the central Italian region of Molise (formerly, Abruzzo). Pistilli explained, "I remember when I first visited Vinchiaturo in 1972. The mayor declared a 'cease-day,' where everybody was to stop working. Furthermore, my grandfather had installed indoor plumbing just for my visit. Even at this point, they were still using the *baccaus* (Italian-American for the 'back house')...My family was well-respected in the town. My great-grandfather or his brother was believed to have built the *Fontana dei Tre Leoni* (Fountain of the Three Lions) in the *Piazza Municipio* (town square). My grandfather, John always used to say, 'that's where the bums hung out.' Although my grandfather moved to the United States for a short period where he worked either on the Union Pacific or Southern Pacific railroad before returning to Italy, he was a subsistence farmer who performed tasks which were even hard for my athletic, young-adult self. When I asked him, 'How do you do this work at this age?,' he replied, 'I've only ever stopped twice in my life. The first was in World War I where I was captured by the Austrians. The second time, I was forced to fight for the *Tedesc* (Germans) in North Africa.' My grandpa told me he only ever fired his gun directly upward into the air, because he knew his relatives were fighting with the Americans against the Axis powers. Little did he know, they were actually stationed in Europe. When Pistilli moved from New Brighton to the suburbs—New Dorp—he attended Our Lady Queen of Peace School, under the instruction of strict Irish nuns. "They were *extremely* mean to us Italian kids" Pistilli remarked, "We were made to sit in the back two rows of the classroom. One of the nuns used to refer to Italians as 'the butter and egg people.' And aside from the usual insults from neighborhood kids: 'salami breath,' 'garlic breath,' we were often restricted from using the restroom by the nuns. As the nun announced, 'Ok, we don't want a parade going to the bathroom,' some of my classmates urinated in their pants. Our treatment was absolutely repulsive! And when it was Columbus Day or St. Patrick's Day, the school yard was a blood bucket!" Growing up in New Dorp, did however come with some benefits. Guy Molinari lived just behind the Pistilli family; Molinari's brother Bobby—a teacher at New Dorp High School—kept animals upstairs, and occasionally would bring exotic creatures such as a snake to the Pistilli household. Pistilli was also, since the age of seven, a student of the accordion at Steo Accordion Academy on New Dorp Lane, operated by Peter Steo and Marie Elena. Pistilli stated, "Two performances stick out in my mind. My first concert was at the hall at Moravian Cemetery where I played the Clarinet Polka. The second one was at Our Lady Help of Christians, where I played the Beer Barrel Polka; Myron Floren—the accordionist on *The Lawrence Welk Show*— was also entertaining at that event. I'll always remember attending a show at Our Lady of Lourdes where Pete Steo played the Bass Accordion; you needed to be a 'Hercules' to operate one of those!" Pistilli went on to operate Mike & Gary's Candy Store, the former Nat's Candy Store (and even previously, Zucker's) at Rose Ave. & South Railroad Ave. When as a young kid he stole some candy from the store, his mother dragged him all the way back to apologize to the owners and insisted on Pistilli working there till he paid off the full amount he stole. Eventually, Pistilli took possession of the store. "Candy stores were institutions in New Dorp!" Pistilli elaborated, "There were several of them. The most popular establishment was Paul's Sweet Shoppe. Paul's sold egg creams, newspaper, candies, etc. It was the epicenter for Siciliano socialization in New Dorp." Among Pistilli's most precious memories of growing up on Staten Island were exploring the woods in Oakwood and the old lake behind Monsignor Farrell High School, as well as walking the dirt trails which led to New Springville. Pistilli concluded, "Growing up Italian in New Dorp was very hard! All my Irish classmates used to come and eat at my house very frequently, and at one point my mother told me, 'You know, Mikey! All these people come to our house to eat, but nobody ever invites you over!'...When I attended Augustinian Academy, I finally felt welcomed. I was introduced to a beautiful new universe of academia, of education! But despite having to go to Mass at 8am six days a week, being forced to kneel on marbles, and being smacked with rulers, things ended up okay with the Irish. Heck! By seventh grade, I was dating their sisters!"

As observed in New Brighton, Port Richmond too boasted its fair share of Italian restaurants, stores, parishes, and community gathering places. Among those were Gene's Restaurant, Venetian Gardens, Denino's Pizza, Zinicola's bread Bakery, Musto's Deli, Tinessa's Italian Grocery, and Peter Micelli's and Giordano's butcher shops, and Toscana Food Market. Continuing in the Italian vein, Scalici's Florists, run by Victor and Aida Scalici, at 523 Port Richmond Ave. is to be mentioned. Scalici's hothouses, which cultivated among Staten Island's most vibrant Pointcettias, are a common sight for those diners who have exited through Denino's Port Richmond Ave.-side's door and marveled at the sight across the street. Founded sometime in 1955-1956, the florist is being put on the brink of extinction due to retirement, but in part also to the growing popularity of supermarkets, all-in-one shopping destinations for all household/event needs. Victor Scalici, a native of Port Richmond, remarked, "We did everything on this property. We raised our own Thoroughbreds, goats (milked in the back of the house), and even heifers, one which won 2nd place in the State of New Jersey. We hunted, trapshooted, etc. And I had one strategy in business: Don't let them mob you, and Don't let them fool you! Because people will make a dope out of you in two seconds if you let them!" Scalici's brother Jack was also in the horticulture industry, having owned Nature's Garden Center in Bulls Head. Scalici's niece, Julia Franzese Brogna, an employee at the florist in the late-1970s, explained, "We used to arrange bouquets for wedding receiptions at the banquet hall located in the Knights of Columbus building just off of Clove Rd. At one point, Scalici's was doing major business... I remember during the winter season, my uncle Vic Scalici would load all of us children into a sleigh he owned, pulled by a horse, and would take us from where the florist was all the way down to Richmond Terrace! He was a character by all means." Brogna lived initially at 16 Walker St. but then moved to Beekman St., and later Catherine St. Among her fondest memories of the area were her decuple (ten times) daily-trips to Mr. and Mrs. L's candy/general store (owned by two Holocaust survivors) [10] , and purchasing Easter baskets during the holidays. Brogna also recalled Mr. Jimmy Cavaliere "Jimmy the Peddler"—an Italian salesman who roamed the Port Richmond streets ringing the bell on his motorized vehicle, selling cheeses and vegetables in the late-1950s, early-1960s. Brogna's husand, Bob and his partner Fred Tramutola in the 1970s opened the Victory Gourmet, which made an unexpected appearance in the film *Easy Money*, as it was located alongside Alfonso's Bakery. Victory Gourmet was renown for its signature dish— Chicken Victory (chicken breaded with breadcrumbs, slivered almonds, and flavored with Italian salad Dressing). Reflecting on Port Richmond's heyday, Brogna concluded, "The neighborhood was a tight-knit village. Fr. Pasquale Cannizzaro—the pastor at St. Roch's Church from 1950 to

---

[10] "Mr. & Ms. L"—"Mr. Rudi and Ms. Mimi Lindenfeld" were Austrian, Jewish immigrants from Vienna who survived the Holocaust. Rudi, a polyglot of fifteen languages, taught ecology at High Rock Park to children.

1972, used to come over to my aunt and uncle's house to eat and chat. My grandfather, August Improta (1894-1961) used to take me down as a little kid to the Forest Ave. Shoppers Town. We were always together. It's funny the things we remember: the day he died, I'll never forget it. He was my everything."

Gloria Luzzo Santo (b. 1931), Franzese's neighbor at 42 Walker St., recalled a similar tight-knit, traditional environment in the heyday of Port Richmond. Born in a four-room house with no heat except that created from the kitchen stove, Santo described her mother heating up bricks in the oven, wrapping them in towels, and placing them at the foot of her and her siblings' beds to warm the children up. During the night, Santo's mother would place a metal container filled with the freshly-delivered milk on a ledge outside the window to freeze up over night. The first to get up in the morning could drink the cream that had risen to the top. Mixing a healthy splash of vermouth and eggs with the milk, Santo's mother would prepare a hearty beverage for her kids. Her father—a talented grower of peaches—would sell them periodically for twenty-five cents a bag for whoever really admired them. He was also facile with hedge clippers, which he used to carve the family surname "Luzzo" in the home's front shrubs. "Among my least favorite taks was raking my father's chicken coop and collecting eggs from the chickens" Santo exclaimed. "It was hard work. My father would send me down to stoke the belly stove in the basement to shovel out the ashes amidst the coal. The coal came directly from the ice and coal guy on the street" she continued, "there even used to be a banana guy who sold bananas in a bunch for twenty-five cents. All the women would then make banana sandwiches!" Many of Santo's memories were from the many shops which once lined Port Richmond Ave. She recalled her father going with his pitcher, and the other Italian neighborhood men in the summertime with their tin cans to the bar at Gene's Restaurant to bring home beer to supper. She also recalled purchasing White Owl Cigars for her father, Italian Bread delivery from Paramount Bakery, her mother buying live eel for dinners from the fish market, listening to disc jockey William B. William's *Make Believe Ballroom* program over the radio, attending Vaudeville shows for ten cents on Saturday and Sunday at the Ritz Theatre, and sliding on the ice at the brook at the end of Walker St. "When it snowed, they never used to plow the street, so all the neighborhood kids would come out and play. My brother used to pull me up behind his back, and we'd go sledding down Walker St."

"What hits you first is the smell of burnt bread, melting mozzarella cheese, garlic, and sweet, ripe tomato sauce: a smell so rich, it can come only from baking several hundred pizza pies a day, every day." – Ina Yalof. As any description of old South Beach cannot be thorough and complete without mention of the emotion-provoking aroma of Licastri's freshly-baking bread, so the same can be justly said about Port Richmond and the landmark known as Denino's. The establishment began in 1923 as "Denino's Confectionery" at the corner of Port Richmond Ave. and Hooker Pl., serving products such as lemon ice in the days when Ralph's Italian Ices was simply a baseball field (it could be then controversially inferred that Denino's was the original Ralph's). The store was founded, owned, and operated by Giovanni Denino (b. November 21, 1885)—a

[Carlo "Carlie" Denino tends his restaurant's bar C. late-1940s. Courtesy – Palma Denino]

[Denino's Pizzeria & Tavern – currently located at 524 Port Richmond Ave. C. 1960s. Courtesy – Palma Denino]

Sicilian immigrant from the town of Corleone—who arrived in the United States in 1887 at the age of two. In the early-1920s, he purchased the land from a member of the La Forge family[11]—a large land-holding family in Port Richmond. The property stood in front of a small house in the back, and a large, three-story mansion on its south side. Giovanni, a construction laborer who helped in the erection of the Bayonne Bridge beginning in 1928, took turns shifting his family from the back house to the mansion, renting out the mansion when work availability was scarce. In 1925, the Denino family opened a pool hall next door the confectionery, and with the repeal of Prohibition in 1933, the hall began serving beer; in 1937, the establishment became a full tavern. In 1951, however, Giovanni passed away, and Denino's was left to his son, Carlo (b. December 1, 1923). Carlo, affectionately known as "Carlie"—a welder by trade at the shipyard in Mariners Harbor (as well as a veteran of the American Navy)—realized that in order for Denino's to be profitable, a revitalization would be in order. That year,

---

[11] The La Forge family owned several holdings in the area; their landholding legacy is evident in the naming of Laforge Pl. and Laforge Ave. in the near vicinity.

Carlo was given the idea by one of his bartenders to begin serving pizza. Denino's premier pizzas were the regular-round small or large pies, topped with sausage or pepperoni. In addition to this, Denino's served meatball/sausage and ham and cheese heroes. Carlo's wife Palma, who grew up in Mariners Harbor, explained, "Nothing much has changed since Denino's initial days of serving pizza. We're still using the same recipes with the same brick oven! Just instead of rolling all the dough by hand, we have machinery that does that now." The pizzeria has expanded to offer other dinner options, desserts, and espresso. Furthermore, Denino's has grown to include three other locations: Aberdeen, N.J., Brick, N.J., and Manhattan. Palma continued, "Carlie was such an easy-going guy! I actually met him through a friend at the Venetian Gardens—an old Italian restaurant across from Denino's! He used to tell me stories of a friend of his father who used to drive a station wagon to deliver the dead bodies to the morgue! One day, the guy decided in the middle of his route to stop at Denino's bar for a drink. The guy came in; the dead body with him! He placed the body on the stool next to him, while he ordered some drinks. Of course, the body was bent over and had its head buried in its hands. People kept buying, and the bartender kept refilling the body's drinks, because they thought it was a guy who was actually drinking them! The guy who had brought him in just kept taking the drinks placed on the body's side of the counter and finishing them!...Another time, while the guy drank in the bar alone, his vehicle with the body inside was stolen!" "It's so difficult trying to get the real accounts of a story in this family! There's so many Denino's who tell a story a different way. But one thing was always the same in any version—Carlie was the best man anyone had ever met! He never tried to hurt anyone, and he had a big heart! I remember, when Carlie passed away in August 2000, there were thousands, and I mean thousands, of people at his wake! But I'll never forget the day he died. He was playing golf in New Jersey;

and that morning, he said hello and shook everyone's hand who was at the golf course. As he reached for his golf club, Carlie had a massive heart attack! As it turns out, some firefighters were also playing golf that day. They immediately ran over to my husband and attempted to give him CPR. It was useless at that point. But as Carlie collapsed to the ground, a priest, who coincidentally was also playing golf that day, came over to him! As he lay dying on the ground, the priest administered Carlie's last rights over second hole." In honor of Carlo's philanthropist, charitable, and community work, the southeast corner of Hooker Place and Port Richmond Ave. was named "Carlo Denino's Way" in June of 2003.

Zinicola's Bakery was founded originally on 6 Sherman Ave. (later, the street was renamed 'Hooker Pl.') in the Port Richmond section of Staten Island. Mariano Zinicola was an Italian immigrant from the small commune of Tufo di Minturno in the province of Latia in the Lazio region of Italy. Born to parents Giovanni and Catarina in 1855, Zinicola married Rachel Saltarelli, an Italian school teacher, and immigrated to the United States in 1897. Around the turn of the century, Zinicola founded Zinicola's Bakery, and began producing and selling Italian breads. In later years, Zinicola's expanded their selections to include a variety of rolls and, on Sundays, hot pepperoni bread. Though these were by far the Bakery's most notable products, Beverly Zinicola explained, "Zinicola's used to make an Italian Lard Bread known as 'pane con cicciloli', as well as non-sweet biscotti—one plain variety, and one with freshly-ground black pepper. At Eastertime, my grandmother made a sweet Italian Easter Bread with sprinkles and eggs on top. And when Thanksgiving came around, Zinicola's even roasted turkeys for people! You'd walk in and see pans of turkey all over!" Of Mariano's four sons only two remained at the bakery on Hooker Pl., Giosue and Amedeo. In 1921, Giovanni opened his own bakery on King St. in Nutley, New Jersey (one of

Giovanni's sons later opened a bakery in south New Jersey). The fourth son, Oswaldo left to pursue other interests. A popular photograph taken circa 1910 features Giovanni and his brother Amedeo alongside the Hooker Pl.'s bakery's horse-and-wagon, reading "Ask for Zinicola's," in front of the H.E. Walker Graniteville House; the bakery delivered bread along Staten Island's North Shore from their Port Richmond location to as far as West Brighton. The horse-drawn wagons were employed until about 1912 when Zinicola's purchased their first motorized vehicle. When Giosue passed away, his three sons took over the business but a short time later, the eldest son left to open his own bakery on Forest Ave. For residents of the area, Zinicola's would come to be forever associated with the dearest of childhood memories: fresh bread after mass at St. Roch's, a Sunday morning father-daughter stroll to the bakery to pick up some fresh rolls, and buying the hot bread for twenty-five

[Amedeo Zinicola behind the wheel of Zinicola Bakery's first motorized delivery vehicle. The truck still carried the slogan "Ask for Zinicola's bread." Home deliveries of bread were made daily to a large area of Staten Island. C. 1912. Courtesy – Beverly Zinicola]

cents on the way to Little League practice at PS 21. The Bakery was open twenty-four hours a day, seven days a week so the air was always filled the aroma of fresh baked bread. The Bakery was a one-story building, and one would walk in off the street right into the heart of the bread-making and baking areas. They were able to purchase the bread straight-out-of-the-oven. Former Bulls Head resident, Joe Locascio remarked, "I remember both Zinicola bakeries, the one on Hooker Pl. and the other on Forest Ave. & Amity Pl.! Both made the best Bread! That's bread with a capital 'B!' Or maybe I should say 'Pane' with a capital 'P!'" Steven Lombardi, who lived across the street at 20 Hooker Pl. from 1968 to 1975, reminisced, "As a small kid, I remember going in there to get dough and then we would play with it until it was completely dirty or started to get stale. We had to entertain ourselves back then as kids...Between the bakery and Denino's, I remember our driveway being blocked all the time! As a kid, it was a fun time...Always something to do. I remember one time there was a really big storm and the streets flooded. We were at the bottom of the hill on Hooker. We actually swam in the streets a little...until the sewers caught up with the water." In 1975, Port Richmond bakers John Pasquale and John Camoletti purchased Zinicola's. Today, the property is occupied by Melone Bros. (headquartered out of Linden, N.J.), which carries on the traditions of its predecessor. Staten Islanders may still enjoy the pepperoni and other artisan bread, rolls, and those warm loaves which came in brown paper bags for years to come.

Located formerly diagonally across the street from Ralph's Ices, at 474 Port Richmond Ave. at the corner of LaForge Ave., was Musto's Italian Deli—the quintessential Italian specialty shop. The store was founded in the late-1940s by Anthony Musto (6 Aug. 1906 – Jun. 1985)—a native New Yorker with Neapolitan blood whose father-in-law operated a vegetable stand in the Lower East Side. Though it is unclear when Musto arrived on Staten Island, he settled at 685 Bard Ave. in the once-rural portion of West Brighton. With his son, Dominick[12] (1933-2009), Musto ran his Port Richmond establishment for about thirty years to an extreme degree of success. Many passer-by and residents of the neighborhood would recall the 150 lb. provolone cheeses hanging in the storefront window, and the variety of aged, dry salamis which were scattered on hooks throughout the deli. In era without intense FDA regulations, the deliverymen would transport the ricotta in a tall, metal can with ice with a layer of plastic, held by a rubber band, covering the product to the kitchen. Musto's offered an array of Italian cold cuts, canned, imported goods, sausages ranging from fennel seed to chili flake to cheese with parsley, and of course: mut'zadel. In fact, Musto's gained so much notoriety for its mut'zadel that the cheese was employed to bake the lasagna featured in the wedding scene in *The Godfather*. Musto's daughter-in-law, Madelyn explained, "My father-in-law, Tony was basically the businessman behind the whole deli. He never actually made any of the sausage or the pasta; those tasks were assigned to my husband, Dominick... Dominick used to do something known as "Hang Up." If someone owed him money and couldn't afford to pay him back immediately, he'd still let them come in with their family to Musto's and get everything they needed for free. His only rule was: no beer!" In his taxi driving days, before opening the deli, Tony ran the Numbers on Staten Island; he used to keep the betting cards stashed inside his fake radio inside his automobile. When the cops stopped Tony, they would always ask, "We know got the bets, Tony! But where are you hiding 'em?" A clever, humorous individual, Tony often sent his young son, Dominick into bars and restaurants to hand out the tickets; sometimes, because the young Dominick was running in-

---

[12] After serving in the U.S. Navy from 1951 to 1954, Dominick eventually returned to Musto's and purchased it from his father.

and-out of so many establishments all day long, he didn't have the opportunity to eat. "But something happened once Tony reopened the deli" Madelyn continued, "One day, a guy in a huge, black coat with a fedora, just as you see in the movies, came out of a limousine on Port Richmond Ave. and came into Musto's. He was one of the big men in the Colombo crime family. He came in and asked Tony, 'You still wanna play the Numbers?' But Tony had given it up long before then. But the experience shook the crap out of my brother-in-law!...Other than that one time, the Musto's managed to never get themselves into too much trouble. Although, I distinctly remember one time my husband got into a dispute with Peter Micelli who owned Micelli's Meat Market across the street. All I remember was my husband telling Micelli, 'I don't wish you anything, other than what God already has in store for you!'" Dominick's son, Donny elaborated, "My father was an absolute comedian, too honest of a guy! I have some wonderful memories of working at Musto's. As a kid, I remember going to the Richmond Avenue Fish Market next door to Musto's and playing with all the crabs. There was ice all over the store to keep the temperature cool. We were also sent to Zinicola's on Hooker Pl. to buy hot, fresh bread for the store. I couldn't wait to get back to the deli to spread butter all over it!...But I'll never forget when my father purchased Lido Ravioli. He had already told my mother, and when I came home from school, he said, 'Surprise! I bought a ravioli store!' I thought it seemed like a really cool idea at first, but I soon discovered it took a lot of work to keep the shop up." By 1967, Dominick had already moved west to Edison Twp., N.J., where he would raise his children. In the early-1970s, Musto operated a second Musto's Deli on Wood Ave. in Linden, but within a year, found his New Jersey business to be unprofitable. In 1980, Musto sold his deli in Port Richmond to Chucky Palmieri, and purchased Lido[13] Ravioli from the original owner, Rudy V., at 600 Richmond Rd. in Park Hill, next to Auer's Bakery. Lido Ravioli was noted for its ricotta-stuffed and meat raviolis which came in the visually-aesthetically-enticing blue and white boxes. Rudy V. had even given the Musto family special training on how to prepare the ravioli on the kitchen's long, wooden board Despite Rudy's efforts, however, Musto ultimately purchased a $30,000 ravioli machine from Italy which had a greater output capacity. In 1983, Dominick Musto moved Lido Ravioli to the Hylan Shopping Plaza in New Dorp. Having tired of the low levels of customer interaction in Lido's first location, Musto craved socialization in a much more vivacious environment. The move to New Dorp was indeed a brilliant one, having later put the Subway sandwich shop alongside it out of business. At this location, Lido Ravioli supplied ravioli to Cangiano's Pork Store, the Richmond County Country Club, and countless other institutions. The New Dorp location saw a period of expansion where steam tables, along with a greater variety of items (e.g. Panettone, cookies, green egg noodles, gnocchi, tortellini, cavatelli, stuffed shells, and manicotti) were added.

[A typical day working behind the counter of Lido Ravioli. Courtesy – Donny Musto]

---

[13] The word "Lido" translates from Italian to English as "shore." I.e. Lido Beach in Nassau County, Long Island.

An early-1980s advertisement from *The Staten Island Advance* displays the prices for a 50-count Cheese Ravioli box and a pound of Bologna or Liverwurst as $1.19 and

$1.89, respectively. Customers who frequented Lido Ravioli would forever recall not only the delectable ravioli, but the flavorful Bolognese Sauce as well. The once-heavily concealed family recipes goes as follows: first, in a large pot, you cook some braciole and pork with olive oil until it browns. Then, after removing the browned meat from the pot, add more olive oil and several cloves of garlic. When the garlic reaches a golden coloration, you add tomato paste, canned crushed tomatoes, salt and pepper, and fresh-from-the-

[A Staten Island Advance advertisement promoting Lido Ravioli's "Specials of the Week" C. Early-1980s. Courtesy – Richard Barbato]

garden *basinigol*. Donny Musto remarked, "Just whatever you do, do not add sugar!" "We used to make about thirty gallons of this stuff a day—enough for me to take a soak in! But, it was a ton of work making anything at Lido Ravioli. My father used to tell me, 'Get an education, go to school.' But I felt so bad about being away because it was such back-breaking labor for him. I felt compelled to help" Musto stated, "My father could cook miles around anyone. But although he was a lot of things (a talented cook, a Civil War history buff, etc.), one thing he wasn't was a handyman! Sometimes, he'd run out of time trying to assemble me a bicycle for Christmas, so I'd end just having a bunch of wrapped up bicycle parts! He'd yell frustratingly, 'Vaffancul! I can't do this!'" After nearly fifty years in the business, the Musto family finally ended their food-service career. In 1988, due to the landlord's tripling of the rent, as well as personal fatigue, Lido Ravioli shut its doors. On April 9, 2009, Dominick Musto too met his demise. His wife Madelyn concluded, "My husband suffered so much in his final years. He had Dementia. But I'll never forget the moment he passed away. I was sitting on his bedside when I stood up to give him a kiss. With the remaining strength he had, he blew directly into my face and then passed away. It was like he was blowing his soul straight into me. It was beautiful, and I'll never forget it."

"Staten Island used to be such a wonderful place. And you know what ruined it all? *Jersey Shore*." Joe Montanti "Porky Joe Joey"—an independent film maker in Wilmington, N.C. owner-operator of Southern Coast Films, and director of *The Brothers Statue,* saw Staten Island in an era where the tranquil fields of Bulls Head were entirely inconsistent with their substitute: a bustling, overcrowded area. Montanti's childhood friend Joe Locascio commented, "Not much happened in farm country until they started building houses, then the West Shore Expressway, then the LNG tank. When a crane lifting an overloaded concrete bucket tipped over and the boom hit the top ridge of the tank and crumbled into pieces,

[The Montante Leather Findings & Supplies Store at 1939 Richmond Terr. "Shoe Repairing Done While You Wait." C. 1925. Courtesy – Joseph Montanti]

the dome ran down and killed seven construction workers...I also recall my dad's friend falling from the top of the scaffolding they were removing, and was killed, and then LNG tank exploded killing about forty guys! My dad was laid off from that job a week before it happened." John Hershkowitz (b. 1956) of Decatur, Tenn. similarly testified to other "fond memories." Born in the Marlboro Projects in Gravesend, Brooklyn, Hershkowitz moved to his home near the intersection of Richmond Ave. & Amsterdam Pl. in 1969. "I can remember as a teenager sharing beers over the tombstone of Ichabod Crane (the military official sent to investigate the sightings of the Headless Horseman in Sleepy Hollow, New York) in the local cemetery just acorss the street from our house!" At the age of sixteen, Hershkowitz was employed for one day at EJ Korvettes. After finding a snake hiding beneath a package of scarves shipped from India, Hershkowitz ended his job after one day. "Growing up, we'd take our girlfriends with cars, parking in the woods in Willowbrook Park, and then go to Palermo's Flaming Grill...On school days, on our way to Port Richmond High School, we'd spend hours at Perry's Luncheonette on Richmond Ave. having coffee with butter rolls. Some days, we'd sit there for hours, not even going to school!" Like Locascio, Herskowitz also had the privilege of knowing Joe Montanti. The Montanti family (originally spelled "Montante" – meaning "upright") hailed from Canicattì, but later migrated to Racalmuto, both towns in the province of Agrigento, to seek work in the Gibellini sulfur mines. Gabriel Montanti wrote, "The mine is well documented for having harsh working conditions. The mine was particularly harsh for Salvatrice Lauricella (my great-great grandmother), as her husband Giuseppe Lauricella was murdered there. Salvatrice was so grief stricken that she was temporarily blinded, her house raided of all possessions by the locals, which precipitated fleeing Racalmuto with her daughter Marianna." Luigi Montanti arrived in the United

States to Ellis Island on October 6, 1906 and settled at 216 Chrystie St. in Manhattan's Little Italy; only a short time after, he moved to 225 Willis Ave. in Mott Haven, Bronx. Sometime in the early-1920s, having been informed from his doctor that his condition, emphysema required him to move to the "country," Montanti set off for the North Shore of Staten Island. In the early-1920s, Luigi Montanti opened L. Montanti & Sons Leather & Findings at 1939 Richmond Terrace. Joe Montanti explained, "My grandparents traveled steerage class to America. They were what could be described as 'non-W.O.P.S.' (without papers)...My second-cousin Vincent actually was riding on the SS *Andrea Doria* in 1956 when it sank. He was coming back from medical school in Palermo, but he survived the accident." L. Montanti remained in business until approx. 1960; during its time in operation, several affairs are worth noting. L. Montanti & Sons had obtained a contract with the NYPD to repair motorcycle cops' leather jackets. Furthermore, in the 1950s, Montanti recalled his father being called in during a live filming session of *Howdy Doody* in Manhattan to make an emergency "hip" replacement on the puppet; Montanti's father replaced Howdy Doody's wooden joints with leather parts. During the 1940s, one of Luigi's brothers ran a bar on Richmond Terrace just down the street. On one occasion, Luigi's son Carmelo was preparing some chicken soup in the kitchen for the bar's patrons when he ran out of chicken to cook. Carmelo's uncle exclaimed, 'Just dip in the chicken in water!' When L. Montanti & Sons later transformed into a western wear, feed, and apparel shop, it supplied the horse feed to Clove Lake/Franzreb Stables. Joe recalled as a ten-year-old witnessing a blonde man coming into the store to attempt to purchase a certain Stetson cowboy hat the establishment did not supply. That man was Robert Redford. Like Johnny Latanzio of the Tackle Box on Jewett Ave., Carmelo J. Montanti too was involved in groups relating to his recreational interests (e.g. he was affiliated with the

Richmond Co. Sheriff's Mounted Posse). While at the Posse, Montanti escorted Gov. Nelson Rockefeller's during his inauguration as the 49th Governor of New York in 1959, and rode in the Macy's Thanksgiving Day Parade in 1963 and 1964. In a Staten Island that teemed with equestrian locales, which included West Shore Stables, Clove Lake Stables, Moore's Stables, Carl Tuzzelino's Abilene Barn on Willowbrook Rd., and others, the idea of operating a western wear, saddle store was a rather ingenious one. Also like Latanzio, Montanti had a larger-than-life personality. Joe remarked, "My father, while at the Greensboro Overseas Replacement Depot (ORD) in North Carolina, was about to be sent to Burma when World War II just ended. All his life, he told my grandmother, 'When I grow up, I'm going to marry a short, fat Italian woman.' In the South, however, my dad met the woman of his dreams. He sent a telegraph home stating, 'Am discharged, bringing home wife.' And when they arrived at Penn Station, his relatives were aghast when a five-foot nine Southern blonde emerged from the train and said, 'Hey y'all!' Though by 1973, the Montanti store had shut down, and the store's property reduced to an industrial lot, many Staten Islanders will forever recall the shop at which so many memories were made.

~

The story of Sedutto's Ice Cream begins with a man of a third grade education who arrived on the shores on America around the year 1905. Born in 1872 in Salerno, Italy, Joseph Sedutto began his culinary career apprenticing in the old country, learning the art of fine confectionary. Sedutto was originally a Swiss-trained moldmaker (a crafter of molds for use in metalworking, jewelry manufacturing, etc.), and had, before settling in America, traveled from Italy to Argentina to New Orleans, and back. After immigrating to the United States, Sedutto found employment at the IJ Mott Foundry.

148

Sedutto later became pastry chef at the Waldorf-Astoria Hotel, where he impressed the likes of many customers, including President William H. Taft. Although this claim that Sedutto was a pastry chef at the famed hotel is questionable, it is certain that he supplied the kitchen with pastries, as a letter received by the Sedutto family in 1908 from Helen Taft—the president's wife—thanked Joseph Sedutto for the exquisite dessert. Around this time (early 1900s), Sedutto also had opened a pastry shop at 102 Mulberry St. in Little Italy with a man by the name of Pasquale D'Alessio. It is believed that Joseph's brother-in-law later convinced him to go into the ice cream business, as opposed to simply making pastries and cakes. After selling his establishment on Bleecker St. in Greenwich Village in 1922, Sedutto moved to 60 DeHart Ave. in Mariners Harbor on Staten Island. In the back building, Sedutto began the brand known by Americans for decades. The move to Staten Island, however, was a deviation from the original plan to go to where Sedutto had purchased property and intended to construct a factory on Cropsey Ave. and Bay 50th St. in Gravesend, Brooklyn. Ultimately, Sedutto chose to come to Staten Island where he had previously spent summers

[The site of the Sedutto's Ice Cream Factory, as decorated with Santa Claus and his reindeer for the holidays. C. About 1950. Courtesy – Joseph Sedutto]

[A Sedutto's Ice Cream One Half-Gallon Liquid Label. Courtesy – Sal Marino]

vacationing. In 1949, "when the National Lead Co. was selling a new but incomplete 10,000-square-foot industrial building on Richmond Terrace, [Sedutto] bought it and moved in." From 1949 to 1995, Sedutto's thrived at 2000-2012 Richmond Terrace; by 1946, however, the ice cream company's founder had passed away. Sedutto's specialty products included spumoni, biscuit tortoni, nutrolls, ice cream logs, ice cream cakes, all different varieties of ice cream, snow cups, ice cream tarts, mud pies, and more. The quality of such desserts were expressed in Sedutto's Italian trademark "Crema di Eleganza" (Cream of Elegance). These items were sold on the Staten Island Ferry, Manhattan eateries such as Tavern on the Green and 21 Club, as well as elite ice cream parlors and even airplanes and ocean liners. Sedutto was sold aboard Alitalia, US Lines, and the Italian SS Michelangelo. Among Sedutto's most notable customers was Wallis Simpson—the famed Duchess of Windsor and controversial wife of British king Edward VIII—who enjoyed "butter pecan" flavor, and had it shipped directly to Paris. Sedutto's grew to heights never imagined before; it became not only an integral part of Staten Island culture, but that of New York City. A March 7, 1983 advertisement for B. Altman & Co. (a luxury depart-ment store chain) reads, "Even if your idea of exercise is a stroll to Sedutto's for a cone of coffee-mocha-almond, you need new Chaps activewear." In the second to last year of its operation, the Sedutto's North Shore plant would truly embrace its Staten Island identity, having created a "Staten Island's Own" product line. The half-gallon containers of ice cream were blue and gold, displayed an image of Staten Island, listed Staten Island town names horizontally, and were sold exclusively in Richmond County. At its highest, Sedutto's had four stores on Staten Island: 2000 Richmond Terrace (at the factory), 145 Canal St. in Stapleton, 314 New Dorp Lane in New Dorp, and 1351 Forest Ave. in Elm Park. Unfortunately, though the Sedutto's name is still in existence, Staten Island's last link to the brand was severed on Monday, June 16, 2008 when the last Sedutto's parlor in New Dorp was shut down. [14] Joseph Sedutto—grandson of the founder—recalled, "My grandparents created an enormous legacy for themselves! My grandmother, Giovannina was a licensed midwife and delivered Fr. Vincent Capodanno...During World War II, when sugar was being rationed, my grandfather gave sugar to Ralph Silvestro of Ralph's Ices so he could make his product. When my grandfather passed away in the late-1940s, he was so well-respected that people went to great extents to obtain and arrange flowers. At that specific time, for one reason or another, you couldn't get flowers from florists..." Sedutto continued, "Running the business was truly a family affair. All my uncles, my father took part in it. My dad was even driving the trucks into Manhattan when he was fourteen! When Sedutto's eventually became a corporation, they actually issued stock! I still have some of their stock certificates! But they were never listed on a stock exchange." Sedutto concluded, "When Sedutto's went to its location on Richmond Terrace, I remember going inside the factory and seeing nothing but stainless steel everywhere. It was hard work maintaining the plant because all the stainless steel had to be cleaned and sterilized at the end of every day! I never

---

[14] By this juncture, Sedutto's Ice Cream Corp. had undergone several changes of ownership by major-food brands such as Consolidated Foods, Pillsbury, and Schrafft's during the 1980s.

actually worked at the factory. Some nights though, I wish I could just sit down with my grandfather, someone who I never knew who he really was, just one more time."

Of Staten Island's 475,000+ population, roughly half are estimated to have at least heard of Staten Island's "most entertaining car sales-man"—Al Lambert. With roots running over a hundred years in the borough's automobile industry and about sixty-five years in the world of entertainment, Lambert has appropriately coined the expression, "Getting a car from Al Lambert is an entertaining experience." Lambert's great-grandfather Diego Ferrara immigrated from Sicily in the early-19th century and came to Mariners Harbor in 1911. His sons, Lou, Dom, and Angelo opened Ferrara's Garage—a car repair business—at 69 Harbor Rd. in 1927. During the Great Depression, Lambert's grandfather sold the property to the New York Fire Department to build the 158 Engine 128 Hook & Ladder firehouse. Lambert's family once owned the former Staten Island Toyota. He has been a partner in six auto franchises; today, he runs Lambert Leasing, under corporation of Al Lambert Associates Inc., based in Richmond Valley. The commencement of his entertainment career can be attributed to when Mr. Al Quinn put eight-year-old Lambert on stage at PS 44 in 1954. His first paid gig occurred at the age of twelve at Tavern on the Green where he was paid $20 to sing two songs. In 1966, he formed Al Lambert and the Corporation with Charlie Costa, John Trentacosta, and Tom Rybicki. Lambert's wife, Lenore also performs with the group[15]. Over the span of his career, Lambert has performed at many noted venues: Rodney Dangerfield's, the Copacabana, the Plaza, and Carnegie Hall. To date, he has sold 10,000 cars, and performed on over 5,000 occasions. His earliest accomplishments included forming the first

---

[15] Lambert is also the father of Laura—a singer, writer, and portrait artist, as well as Al Lambert Jr.—Harvard Law and MBA Graduate and former Counsel to President George W. Bush in 2007-08.

"Chorus with Special Children" as a teacher at Willowbrook State School in 1969. "The children sang in two and three part harmony...if there was social media at the time, their amazing sound and achievement would have went viral!" Lambert stated. A graduate of Wagner College (BA in 1968 and Master's in 1977), Lambert is estimated to have raised over two-million dollars for charities and not-for-profits in

his sixty-year career in business and community service. A member of the South Shore Rotary for forty-two years, Lambert stated "'Service above Self' is crucial for [that organization]." Lambert remarked, "In my business, you have to stay relevant. Though I'm in two separate trades, I am wholly in one business—pleasing people." The Mariners Harbor and Port Richmond

[Al Lambert (right) with comedian/entertainer Rodney Dangerfield (left). C. early-1980s. Courtesy – Al Lambert]

sections of Staten Island boast many personalities like Al Lambert who have great tenacities for entertainment. Notable examples include Carmine Giovinazzo (b. 1973)— famous for playing the role of Detective Daniel "Danny" Messner on the CBS crime drama CSI:NY, as well as Vincent "Vinnie" Medugno. Medugno, a Broadcasting & Media instructor at Port Richmond High School, private entertainment DJ, CCD Instructor, Eucharistic minister, and professional singer, is a lifelong Staten Islander and native of Elm Park. Personally mentored by artist Judy Torres and disc jockey Joe Causi, Medugno served as "personal assistant and social media manager for the late VH-1 star Angela "Big Ang" Raiola," and has opened for singer Frankie Avalon and worked with Connie Francis. "At the age of ten, I grew up listening to Frank Sinatra, Bobbdy Darin, etc." Medugno explained, "At the end of the school day, I would rewrite all the day's notes from music class on the board..." Though unconfirmed, Medugno's grandfather suggests the family may possible be related to Domenico Modugno—the Italian singer and songwriter famous for his 1958 recording of "Volare" or "Nel blu dipinto di blue." Medugno's roots run deep in Staten Island. His parents met under the instructorship of Grandmaster Peter Siringano, Sr. (1928-1994)—a certified martial arts teacher who owned "Staten Island Jiu Jitsu & Karate Dojo" at 1293 Castleton Ave. In the present day, Medugno works with various Island charities, and participates in the "Miss Special Needs" pageant. He also stars in the annual "Christmas Show" at the St. George Theater.

"Staten Island is only seven miles long and fourteen miles wide. You'll be talking with someone on Staten Island, and you'll know someone they know, and they'll know someone you know. And if you keep the conversation going, you'll find out that person is related to you." Elaine Casazza grew up on the Staten Island in which valuable life lessons were learned, and long bread lines at Cangiano's Pork Store were the main precipitator of people's palms sweating. Raised in Willowbrook, Casazza recalled playing games as children such as "Church" (where Necco candy wafers were used as hosts), as well as a game where Casazza's sister would sing The Shangri-Las' 1964 pop hit "Leader of the Pack" while the neighborhood little boy would fall off a Big Wheel bicycle. Casazza reminisced, "Hylan Blvd., or as we called it 'The Boulevard,' was the epicenter of our childhoods. I remember spending hours in the A&W parking lot, eating fried clams and drinking root beer... If you were cheating on your boyfriend or girlfriend, Hylan Blvd. was not the place to be! I remember on Senior Day, we'd decorate all our cars with our school colors, and go around to all the Catholic high schools and honk our car horns while they were still in session. Then we'd go to a parking lot—South Beach Five—and drink ourselves into oblivion." Casazza's father, Vincent Passaro, came from Brooklyn and had ancestral roots in Messina, Sicily. Originally working on Wall Street, Passaro had six broker dealers and three seats on the New York Stock Exchange and former-American Stock Exchange. When Elaine's cousin—a Greek man who knew only the craft of pizza-making—needed a job, however, Passaro opened Passaro's Pizzeria right outside Major's on Forest Ave. in Mariners Harbor in 1974. Passaro's was noted by the PennySaver newspaper as having "the first Black pizza man on Staten Island." Though the pizzeria was only open a year-and-a-half, Casazza remarked, "My father had me and my three siblings working in there when I was only ten! While my brother made the pizzas, I was waiting tables, ringing people up, and rolling meatballs...When we closed the pizzeria, my father went on to have a microfilming business, and later opened a restaurant called 'The Deck' in Hampton Bays." As an adult, Casazza became a successful Tupperware salesman but moved on to her next career in sales after a bizarre incident. Casazza explained, "There was a woman who called me ten times a day complaining that I sold her a spice container that made her onion powder get hard! After just being worn down for weeks, I finally mailed her some new onion powder. That was the end of that! When I became a bartender later, a friend told me Bacardi needed a new face of sales. Having a pretty face at the time, I dressed up in a little costume and was instantly hired. In my career, not only did I make money hand-over-fist, but I also got to know many people on Staten Island!" Those Casazza has since migrated to sunnier shores away from the forgotten borough, she still fondly remembers those institutions and anecdotes of old Staten Island. Casazza stated, "I remember going to Leone's on Parkinson Ave. & Hylan Blvd. The restaurant had little, quaint tables and was beyond retro! You thought Sinatra was going to come walking out of there! More people probably got engaged at Leone's than at Jade Island...Then I remember going to Skippy's truck on Hylan. They made the best dirty-water dogs[16]!...But I'll never forget one story my mother, Anne told me. She used to go to Weight Watchers, and back then, you had to be weighed in front of everyone. She told me one time a little 4'11" by 4'11" Jewish woman came up to be weighed, and that she gained weight. When the teacher inquired about her weight-gain, the woman replied, 'Fuck Sara Lee!' And we still use that phrase in my household today! One time, my daughter powered through an entire Sara Lee cheesecake. When I told her, 'What happened: you ate it *all*!' She turned around and said, 'Fuck Sara Lee!'"

A staple of Mariners Harbor, Piazza's Restaurant served the community for decades. Originally a bakery founded by Santo Piazza (b. April 26, 1877)—an emigrant from the fishing village of Cefalù, Sicily—in the 1930s, Piazza's was located across the street from the bustling shipyards at the corner of DeHart Ave & Richmond Terr. Piazza's for most of its existence was a "workingman's" restaurant, hosting not only longshoremen from across the street, but also corporate executives from Brewers Shipyard and Procter & Gamble from their Staten Island facilities. A versatile establishment, Piazza's included a bar (the liquor license is dated Dec. 30, 1948), bakery display case, and a complete deli selection case for freshly-made sandwiches as well as pickled lamb's tongue and pickled herring. Santo's son, Salvatore "Sam" later incorporated daily specials into the menu, such as corned beef and cabbage, pot roast, beef short ribs, shrimp

---

16 In New York linguistic terminology, a dirty-water dog refers to a hot dog that is boiled in water which is rarely changed.

scampi, fried fish cakes with spaghetti, fried flounder, liver and onions, steak dinners, etc. Salvatore's daughter, Mary "Pat" Peters also worked at the restaurant, providing homemade rice pudding. Salvatore's sister, Mary Foti ran Piazza's Bakery at 392 Port Richmond Ave. with her husband, Sal. Piazza's is long-regarded by some neighborhood residents as the oldest bakery to make Italian pastries on Staten Island [disputed]. Piazza's was noted for its exeptional bakery rolls, fig cookies, "Bulls Eye" cookies, and of course, its famous "Icebox Cheesecake." After her husband's passing, Foti resided above the bakery until its closure in the early-1990s. Lucia Sander (b. 1949), the daughter of Salvatore Piazza and student in the first graduating class of Countess Moore High School, worked at Piazza's Restaurant between the ages of thirteen-sixteen in the early-mid-1960s. Concerning the restaurant, Sander remarked, "I can remember the kitchen having a three-unit compartment sink with a gas burner underneath one unit to sterilize the dishes. The kitchen had large wooden refrigerators with freeze compartments that held copper ice cube trays. The trays had to be dipped in warm water to release the ice cubes, In the storage area behind the restaurant, it was entirely a dirt floor!" Sander grew up at 38 Hamlin Pl.—her father's second Staten Island home after

[Salvatore Piazza (left) "Sam" serves customers at his restaurant's bar. C. 1960s. Courtesy – Lucia Sander. Photograph enhanced by Kenneth Peters]

DeHart Ave. in Mariners Harbor. "Growing up on Staten Island" Sander stated, "My mother[17] (renown throughout the neighborhood for her beautiful gardens) and I would walk to the shops on Port Richmond Ave., like Loebel's to shop for clothes or Stechman's to see the soda fountain and have a sandwich or Urbach's to buy dry goods. George LeBlanc used to pinstripe all our cars on Hamlin Pl.!" Reflecting on her father's and mother's legacy, Sander concluded, "In his later years, my father—Salvatore Piazza—liked to go to Carvel Ice Cream on Forest Ave. to have a 'Banana Boat.' I used to drive him there every weekend so he could get his dessert. It brought me back to the times when as a child I would go the restaurant with my father on Saturday when he would do paperwork and make preparations for next week. On our way home, we would always stop at Sealtest Dairy on Forest Ave. and he would buy me a container of chocolate milk. These are things I'll always remember about Staten Island!"

~

The famed pizzeria, recognized far-and-wide by native Staten Islanders for its "wood-paneled dining room and glass detail"—Pal Joey's—was founded by Joseph Andreano and Loretta Yaccarino in Sept. of 1958 at 616 Forest Ave. in West Brighton. Joseph Andreano (b. January 19, 1922), the son of a Barese (from Bari, Puglia) iceman, the oldest of his siblings, began his life's work at Aiello's Bakery at 724 Henderson Ave. Aiello's was owned by Andreano's future-wife's Neapolitan family (who were third-fourth cousins with actor Danny Aiello), and specialized in Italian bread. It was here that Andreano met his wife Laura, affectionately known as Lori. After serving in the 102nd Infantry Division in World War II, Andreano married his bride in 1946.

---

[17] Sander's mother, Anne "Mullaney" Piazza", an emigrant from County Mayo in Ireland, would live to the age of 103.

Andreano's primary employment before going into the pizzeria business was a produce manager at the Food Farm on Hylan Blvd., down from New Dorp Lane. In 1958, Andreano—an admirer of Frank Sinatra and fan of George Sidney's 1957 film *Pal Joey* whose name was "Joseph"—opened Pal Joey's Pizza. While Andreano made the pizza, his wife Lori "Mrs. Pal Joey," worked in the kitchen. When their landlord observed their enormous success, he raised the rent tri-fold ($50). Wheeling the pizza oven down the street to 538 Forest Ave.—the address of a dilapidated wooden building—eleven years after their pizzeria's opening, Andreano and his wife opened Pal Joey's second location. The pizzeria served two styles of pizza: the regular-round variety, and the Sicilian-square pies, which were cooked with an array of toppings. In 1958, a slice of pizza was fifteen cents; a whole pie was a dollar-fifty. On Friday nights, the pizzeria baked fresh ziti. Pal Joey's even served spumoni and biscuit tortoni from Sedutto's, and cheesecake. The site of "countless first dates and after-game pizza parties," Pal Joey's also witnessed many first kisses and several marriage proposals. Andreano's daughter, Addie Morton recalled, "My father had me working in the pizzeria when I was seven! Along with my sister, I was making the pizza boxes (my sister could box one-hundred in eight minutes) and washing windows with the Squeegee because my father refused to hire outside help!...I'll always remember the day Pal Joey's opened on 538 Forest Ave.: Wednesday, July 9, 1969. I had just graduated high school, and was supposed to report to my new job at Marine Midland Bank. I worked as a waitress Pal Joey's opening day, and made ninety dollars! And in 1969, that was *big* money! The next day, I called the bank and lied, saying I was going to go to college instead. I wasn't going to make that kind of cash anywhere else!" "There were so many characters working for us" Morton continued, "There was Bobby Smith, the take-out order taker on Friday nights who we called the 'Mayor of Forest Ave.,' because he knew who everyone was and everything about them. He even knew what dog they had! Then there was Ray who drove the Volkswagen pizza delivery vehicles with the ovens in the back that kept the pizza warm. One time around 1969-1970, Ray called my father and said, 'I'm at a customer's house.' My dad said, 'Ok, why are you calling me?' Ray said, 'Well, because the pizza ovens in the car are on fire.' My dad said, 'What are you doing?!' Ray said, 'I'm in the house with the customers eating ravioli.'...I stayed at Pal Joey's until 2001, even after my father passed away and Pal Joey's was sold and moved down the street. When my father took me as a little kid to go see the new building at 616 Forest Ave. back in the late-1960s, the building was made of deteriorated, old wood. As we were leaving, my foot went through one of the wooden panels! And that's why I always tell people, 'I was literally stuck at Pal Joey's my entire life!'...I have so many wonderful memories of the pizzeria. The guys at lunchtime tried to come only when my mom was making the egg and pepper or eggplant parmesan heroes, because she stuffed them till they could be stuffed no more!...And my father: he was such a wonderful person! On Friday nights in the late hours, when him and his employees had finished cleaning up, he'd take them all to the King's Arms diner on his dime for breakfast. He also sponsored Staten Island Boys' Football and Sacred Heart Baseball teams. The kids at PS 45 used to be able to leave school at lunchtime. The parents would only let the kids leave if it was a trip to Pal Joey's down the street for pizza!...Years after my father had retired, his old boss from Food Farm on Hylan Blvd., Mr. Tantleff pulled up to Pal Joey's in a Rolls Royce, and sent his friend into the pizzeria to see if my father was there. I told the man I was his daughter and he showed me to Mr. Tantleff in the vehicle. He was such a nice man! We both cried as we talked about days gone by. When my father left Food Farm to open Pal Joey's, Mr. Tantleff had told him, 'Whatever you do, if something happens, you will always have a place here. There will always be a door open for you. But I will give you one piece of advice: Never borrow money from your family!' And my father never did...In his later years, my father was ill and I had to take him to the hospital to get dialysis three-times a week. As I dropped him off one time, I'll never forget! My father was getting out of the car, when he looked back and me and said, 'God will repay you!' In tears, I looked my father in the eyes, and said, 'He already did.'"

Forest Ave., in particular its West Brighton portion, once highlighting a cultural richness in the meaning of "Staten Italy," is gradually succumbing to those pressures of a rapidly-changing environment. The site of a Taekwondo studio with upstairs office space in the modern times, Stanzione's Deli has sadly disintegrated into a mere memory with newspaper clippings to tell the story of days gone by. Founded by Gus Stanzione (b. July 4, 1900)—a Neopolitan immigrant, married to the former-Rose Macchia, who had been residing prior to his arrival on Staten Island in Argentina—the deli first operated on State St., right off Castleton Ave. In 1936, Gus Stanzione constructed the building at 705 Forest Ave., between Bement Ave. and N. Burgher Ave., and opened "Stanzione's" bread bakery—the last bakery on Staten Island to make the authentic Sicilian bread. When Stanzione's son Edward "Eddy" (1932-2003) took over the business after his father's retirement, he eventually expanded into the grocery and deli market. In 1939, Stanzione's netted Gus and his family, roughly $2,000 (the modern equivalent of $36,000), and was completely a family affair; Rose's brother Alfonsio served as the bakery's delivery boy. Gus Stanzione's daughter-in-law Lee Labita-Stanzione—the head of Wetlesen Realty—whose uncle, a barber and beautician, owned Sunshine and Vincent's Barber Shop, explained, "Stanzione's had a few firsts on Staten Island. They made the Island's first Italian sliced bread—Stanzione's Tasty Crust Bread, as well as the Island's first Italian tomato sauce. People used to ask Rose why she would ever make sauce in West Brighton, a heavily Irish, Jewish neighborhood at that time. She said, 'Well, I'm not going to sell to Italians who make their own sauce!'" Stanzione's specialties included focaccia (the plain and tomato varieties), potato salad, meatballs, sausage, eggplant parmesan, pizza/meatball heroes, macaroni, and of course: bread and tomato sauce (referred to by some as "gravy"); the freshly-baked bread was even featured in the storefront's window. Patrick Casciano recalled, "I asked Stanz for lasagna for twelve. He grabbed the tray, handed it to me, and told me to not bothering washing it, just bring it back. I handed him seventy-five dollars as the dollar signs rolled in his eyes. Stanz was the man!" Stanzione's for many natives of Staten Island calls to mind the most joyous of memories: grandparent-grandson strolls after mass at Sacred Heart Church on Castleton Ave. to pick up a quart of tomato sauce and the Sunday paper, interacting with Ed Stanzione in his apron and his wife while they worked, and ordering simply a pizza without cheese, but plenty of Stanzione's signature tomato sauce. Ed Stanzione's commendable work running the family business was recognized in the naming of the northwest corner of Bennett Ave. and Forest Ave.: "Edward R. Stanzione Place" in August of 2004. Regarding the street naming, it is written: "When he wasn't enjoying food – preparing and eating it too – he was watching his beloved Brooklyn Dodgers." Involved in community affairs, Stanzione also "was a member of the Richmond County Post of the Veterans of Foreign Wars in Port Richmond." Though Stanzione's Deli has ceased to exist, many will still recall the vivacity the establishment brought to the neighborhood; and for some, Stanzione's will forever remain the standard-of-quality to which all potato salads and tomato sauce will be compared.

Next door to Stanzione's Deli, LiGreci's Staaten, one of Staten Island's distinguished catering and banquet halls, has been the site of thousands of lavish celebrations and social activities. The edifice itself was constructed in 1954 by Mike Bilotti with the intent of constructing a catering hall, which if unsuccessful would become a funeral home. The LiGreci family, meanwhile, began their proprietorship across the street. In the early-1960s, the LiGreci's purchased Rainero's Restaurant, owned by Richard "Richie" Rainero, located at 676 Forest Ave.[18] Jack LiGreci, a bartender at Rainero's, was a native of Harlem, and had been brought over to Staten Island at a very young age. His career in the dining universe commenced when he flipped hamburgers at Al Deppe's restaurant in Greenridge, and then at Sunset [Bowling] Lanes in New Springville. After being employed at Rainero's, in 1963 LiGreci took over the restaurant, establishing LiGreci's Bar & Restaurant. The neighborhood institution was renown for its Chicken Francese (flour-breaded, egg-dipped chicken in a white wine, lemon-butter sauce), Salmon Oregonata, and Prime rib. The LiGreci family had roots in Palermo, Sicily, though their last name is typically associated with developers and builders in Agrigento. The LiGreci name as relating to towns or municipalities, today is evident merely in the district, "Contrada San Giovanni Li Greci," about twenty miles from central Palermo. The Li-prefix (similar to more commonly heard, singular version, Lo-) indicates belonging to a certain family or group of people; the word "Greci," meaning Greeks, perhaps refers to the time of Greek presence in Sicily before the birth of Christ. The LiGreci's legacy in America began when Giovanni LiGreci emigrated from Sicily; his son John (1897-1979), along with his Neapolitan wife Giuseppina Peruso, was the one who migrated to Staten Island from Harlem. The couple purchased a house on Oakland Ave. in Randall Manor; when LiGreci's Staaten finally opened in May 1971. Giuseppina LiGreci resided at 472 Bement Ave., on the LiGreci property,

---

[18] The property has since seen several establishments: Kent's East, Donna Lee's, etc. Currently, it is occupied by Bruno's Bakery & Restaurant which opened in 2003

at what was known by family members as "Mamma's House." Since its opening, LiGreci has become Staten Island's largest banquet hall, but has also expanded to include a lunch selection. Jack LiGreci's son, Ken recalled, "I was working at the old LiGreci's across the street from the Staaten when I was just a little kid. I have memories of going down to Hans German bakery on Forest Ave. to purchase Kaiser rolls, cold cuts, and the Sunday paper...Because we lived nearby, we would go down to the Silver Lake Golf Course at nighttime and play demolition derby with the golf carts. One day, the police came storming toward us, so we all took off in every which direction. The one who decided to stay was Tony Bradford—the cleverest one in our friend group—who hid behind a tree. The police caught him and threw him in jail for two nights. The next day, they came down to LiGreci's and fined us all two-hundred-forty dollars! We had to work that money off."

Born in 1924 to Italian immigrant parents Michael and Elisa, Anthony Guido Ajello, whose Italian heritage derived from Caserta, Campania and the Island of Ischia (directly southwest of Naples), was raised in Plainfield, N.J. and Bensonhurst, Brooklyn. His grandfather, asides from being a skilled sea captain, was among the first persons to import Italian tomatoes in the United States. Among his many connections in the importing business was the head of Polly-O cheese, whose company at that time was headquartered on Sedgwick St. in Brooklyn. Many members of the Ajello family became employed at Polly-O; Anthony Ajello himself, after serving in the U.S. Army during World War II, would join his father and brother, Mike at the company. In the late-1940s, Ajello purchased a surplus army ambulance for twenty-five dollars, and began a cheese route through Brooklyn and Long Island. At this time, he was selling mainly Polly-O pizza cheese, ricotta, and mozzarella. Eventually, the young Ajello sold the route to Polly-O and became a salesman for them. It was here and at several other catering/restaurant businesses, he observed the usage of "low-grade" ricotta cheese in the making of Italian delicacies such as manicotti and ravioli. [19] The penurious methods involved in manufacturing the products would become the inspiration for Ajello's desire to fill an expanding niche within the Italian fine-food market. Inclined to "merge his sales experience with his enduring vision of creating a store where customers could purchase fresh ravioli filled with the highest quality ingredients," Ajello opened the first location of the now highly-popular Pastosa Ravioli on solely a shoestring of money (the word *pastosa* translates from Italian as 'doughy'), in 1966 on Avenue N and East 53rd St. in Flatbush. Along with his brother Michael and partner Tony Postiglione, Ajello achieved an unprecedented new height of business, leading the opening of another location in Brooklyn on New Utrecht Ave. and 75th St. in 1972, following the opening of the Staten Island location. Ajello's daughter Elizabeth recalled, "I remember working at the original store in Brooklyn one Christmas Eve. I distinctly remember a little rinky-dink radio playing Christmas songs while my mother and I were helping make the manicotti. I remember my mother telling my father around midnight., 'Everybody has to go home, Anthony! We have to go put the gifts under the tree.' And my father with his hand turned the radio off, looked at my mother and said, 'Rose! I never want you working in this store again! You're too sentimental, and if I don't make money now, then I never will!'" Shortly after the Verrazzano-Narrows Bridge went up, Elizabeth's Uncle Joe contemplated moving to Staten Island; at that time, the bridge's fifty-cent toll was enough for Anthony to discourage his brother from departing Brooklyn. In the end, Joe Ajello sold his *latticini* (dairy products) store in Bensonhurst, Ajello Dairy—the former site of Santamauro's—and moved

---

[19] The word "low-grade" here is used with a certain flexibility. Polly-O's product in Ajello's eyes was already satisfactory; he merely sought to upgrade it.

to Eltingville. Between 1968-1972, Joe ran Ajello Dairies Salumeria at 4105 Hylan Blvd. Despite initial resistance, Anthony later ultimately moved to Staten Island. When he opened the first Staten Island Pastosa location at 764 Forest Ave. in West New Brighton (formerly the Forest Ave, Farmers Exchange) in the late-1960s, Ajello converted the former wooden fruit-and-vegetable stand into a small ravioli outlet that could fit no more than eight people; Pastosa's main competition at this time was Silver Star Ravioli in Brooklyn. During this time, Ajello sold only cavatelli, olive oil, olives, cheeses, manicotti, Italian meats, canned tomatoes, stuffed shells, and of course—ravioli. There were no "prepared foods." Eddy Lombi, a brilliant engineer, sold Ajello the four-up round ravioli machines; the finished products were placed eighteen in a box. As of 2019, the "Pastosa Ravioli" name has expanded to twelve locations from New York to New Jersey. The Staten Island locations are: 3817 Richmond Ave. in Eltingville, 1076 Richmond Rd. in Concord, and the original store on Forest Ave (which the family has since expanded by taking over the two adjacent storefronts). Production has since expanded from several dozen ravioli at a time to thousands. Ajello's son-in-law Vincent D'Antuono who currently runs the Forest Ave. Pastosa Ravioli store with his wife, Ajello's daughter Elizabeth, remarked, "My father-in-law had a tremendous memory. If you played Brisk with him in 1944 in the barracks, he'd

[Anthony Ajello at the original Pastosa location. Courtesy – Vincent & Liz D'Antuono]

166

remember! He also never felt like he was beneath anyone. He'd tell someone, 'You're not ready for our ravioli, try somebody else's!' And he knew he was the best, because his ravioli *was* the best! During the flu season, he'd tell customers at the store, 'The best remedy is two ravioli every four hours!'...The entire Ajello family knew quality, even the dog. When my wife was young, she had a dog named Viette her father received by a friend. The dog knew the difference between and fresh Pastosa mozzarella and the packaged variety! When it sensed the packaged mozzarella, the dog would turn its back and walk away. It waited for that distinctive white mozzarella bag from Pastosa's!...My mother-in-law, Rose had a huge house on Staten Island. It became apparent that Anthony needed somewhere to bring in all the cans of imported Italian tomatoes. We're talking five to six hundred cans at a time. Rose's basement became the unofficial Pastosa warehouse! She couldn't even get in there anymore! At 3am, the trailers would come to the house and unload the palettes of tomato cans near the garage! This went on for less than ten years till she went crazy!" Pastosa's future looks brighter than it ever did. D'Antuono continued, "When Anthony constructed the stores, he did so with very little money but a lot of love for the product. He served everything fresh, and we still do! I've never sold a day-old mut'zadel, and I never will!"

Regarding old institutions in West Brighton, The Franzreb Stables have too disappeared. Portions of the former land owned by the Franzreb family were incorporated into Clove Lake Park, while other portions became the Fountains Apartments located at 1000-1100 Clove Road. The apartments occupy what was once a ten-story ice house used by the Staten Island Hygeia Ice & Cold Storage Co. run by John Franzreb II. Hygeia Ice Co. harvested ice from Clove and Silver Lakes, and employed horses to cut the ice with six-foot rotary blades; from there, ice was floated to the facility, and sent upward to each floor in the ice house by virtue of ten horses which moved in a circulator fashion to power the lift. The ice was insulated with sawdust, shavings, and straw for means of preservation. Hygeia Ice Co. eventually shut down, as refrigeration became rapidly available on the commercial market, and the State of New York officially formed Clove Lake in 1917 to serve as a holding place for water from the Ashokan Reservoir in Ulster County. Though the ice business had just shut down, an entire equine future had just begun to open up; John Franzreb II, the son of John Edward Franzreb I from Buren, Westphalia, Germany, opened Boulevard Riding Academy on Victory Blvd. The twenty-five horses which were previously employed in hauling the ice from the harvesting center to individual households were trained for riding instruction purposes. The academy would later evolve in 1933 into Clove Lake (Franzreb) Stables—the "incubator of horsemanship." Franzreb catered to a wide variety of institutions including elementary schools, high schools, and colleges who instead of simply teaching Physical Education brought their students to learn to ride. For many of the youngsters who were brought to Clove Lake during their school years, learning the art of horseback riding would become valuable as they entered police careers which required the skill. For other young Staten Islanders, who simply rode horses for fun, the activity became an effective showing-off technique to impress their girlfriends. For Italian Staten Islanders, however, Franzreb Stables is most memorable for its delivery trucks which provided manure to fertilize their personal tomato gardens. Franzreb gained notoriety when it supplied horses for mainstream movies filmed in the New York City area; in fact, due to the high demand from film directors, Franzreb kept seventy-five horse-drawn vehicles on hand. The stables' horses would be featured in Gene Kelly's 1969 film *Hello, Dolly*, the Rose Bowl in New York, as well as in the 1976 Macy's Thanksgiving Day Parade; it was during the latter parade that John Franzreb III served as grand marshal along with actress Betty White and actor Lorne Greene while horse-mounted, dressed as Paul Revere, and made to shout, "The parade is coming!" J. Franzreb III has also enjoyed riding sessions with Walter Matthau, George C. Scott (during the filming of Arthur Hiller's 1971 satirical film *The Hospital*), and opera singer, Luciano Pavarotti. Franzreb accredits himself with having secured the filming location of *The Godfather* on Staten Island, persuading his friend whose grandparents had recently passed away to refrain from selling the property; per Coppola's request for true Italian tomatoes, Franzreb even specially ordered tomatoes on the vine from Chicago. Franzreb's Stables was a worshipped pillar of the Staten Island community. Though it ultimately shut its doors in 1982 (a real estate developer having made Franzreb an "offer he couldn't refuse"), it is remembered by many Islanders who still recall riding the horses such as 'Turtle Dove' whose special names were applied to avoid inducing a sense of fear, and encourage ridership. In the present day, J. Franzreb III retains his old sprit for horses which has kept him alive since his childhood. He proudly assumes the title of ringmaster—the chief safety officer during a horse show—in twenty one-week long shows (e.g. The New York State Fair, The Eastern States Exposition) every year. During these shows, Franzreb sports a traditional coachman's attire consisting of "brown paddock boots, canvas leggings, white breeches, stock tie and red coat." This outfit is also Franzreb's wardrobe-of-choice during his playing of the coaching horn, commending Staten Island Chuck (the rival of Punxsutawney Phil), the weather-predicting rodent's early spring/late winter proclamation. Franzreb has presided under mayors Michael Bloomberg's having been bitten by the groundhog in 2009, and Bill de Blasio's dropping of the animal in 2014 (which is speculated to have resulted in Staten Island Chuck's demise two days later). Franzreb's former stables have since disappeared;

although, Clove Lake Park has remained relatively untouched. The park today hosts a variety of recreational activities including the annual Lou Marli Thanksgiving Run/Turkey Trot, hosted by the Brighton Kiwanis Club, which helps collect food for the St. Paul's food bank. Sitting atop an island in Clove Lake also is The Stone House—a rustic, American fine dining venue with lakefront and patio seating. Similarly, the equestrian remnants of several other Staten Island horse stables have also vanished under multistory apartments, public recreation areas, and office buildings namely Teddy Moore's Stables (where mounted police's horses were kept), Franzreb (Clove Lake) Stables and West Shore Stables. Located at 52 Hughes Avenue at the corner of Merrill Avenue in Bloomfield, West Shore Stables, founded in 1968, offered horse-drawn hayrides, English tack, flat and jumping lessons, eight school horses, outdoor, indoor ring, horse shows, and riding lessons in both the English and Western styles. One of the most notable horses bred at West Shore Stables was 'Solider Boy' who made his debut with actor Billy Crystal on the Late Show with David Letterman. West Shore Stables regularly held racing competitions, and hosted horse shows sponsored by the Staten Island Horsemen's Association; the association today aims to preserve the few remaining bridal trails and dwindling equine population due to stable loss. Owned by Frank C. Mastropiero (1934-2002), known by his acquaintances as "Pinky," and Vinny Vigliotti, West Shore Stables became part of the Staten Island Industrial Park in 1974, became remotely-accessible due to the opening of the West Shore Expressway in 1976, and was ultimately shut down in June of 1994. Sitting atop the property today are a collection of hotels, offices, and restaurants, including The Hilton Garden Inn, Hampton Inn, Nicotra's Ballroom, and Lorenzo's Restaurant & Bar. The property is owned by Lois and Richard "the best landlord on Staten Island" Nicotra, the founders of major international fast-food franchise The

Nicotra Group LLC. The duo are trustees of their non-profit Bloomfield Conservancy which aims to preserve the 415-acre protected woodlands and surrounding area in the Corporate Park which once contained West Shore Stables.

As in other areas of Staten Island, particularly Rosebank where parishioners of St. Joseph's Church would enjoy a home-cooked Sunday meal after the church service, the West Brighton community too followed a similar ritual. Berardi's Pizza at 1194 Castleton Ave. saw the majority of its clientele come from the parish of Our Lady of Mt. Carmel – Saint Benedicta; they enjoyed rigatoni, spaghetti, ravioli, and the pizzeria's signature, Clams Oregonata. The eatery's chief proprietor was Ralph Berardi, one of many family members in the Berardi family clan. The Berardi family hailed from Ruvo di Puglia in the Province of Bari. Beginning in 1957, the first segment of the Berardi family immigrated, followed by the remainder the next year. The family settled on Taylor St., just around the corner from the future-

[An advertisement for Berardi's Pizzeria & Restaurant "Fast Hot" Home Deliveries. Courtesy – Ferdinando Berardi]

Berardi's Pizzeria. In 1965-66, after Ralph Berardi had spent a substantial period being employed at the original Al's Pizzeria, Alphonse "Al" Iannacone (1912-2004) sold the business to him. Al's Pizzeria then moved to 965 Jewett Ave. in Meiers Corners. Until the early-1980s, Berardi's was kept within the family, before being sold to Carmine Lacertosa, a mason, who later on relocated the pizzeria. Despite coming from a wide variety of professions—the patriarch Vincenzo Berardi being a carpenter, brother Vito being a tool and die maker, the family nonetheless worked alongside each other in the restaurant. The matriarch Leonarda also contributed in the kitchen. Though Sicilian Pizza was by far the biggest seller, an advertisement from the mid-1960s for Berardi's features "Heros, Calzones" in an "Air-conditioned dining room." The restaurant's location, 1194 Castleton Ave. is given with the Plaza Casino at 1171-1175 Castleton Ave. being the reference point. Occasionally, the Berardi's would commemorate their Barese history by serving one of Puglia's staple dishes—orrechiette with sausage and broccoli rabe, alongside a basket of hot focaccia. Ferndiando Berardi as a seminarian also worked in the pizzeria and upon ordination in November of 1977 was assigned to be an assistant priest at Blessed Sacrament on Forest Ave. recalled, "The customers on Friday would come in asking for a sausage pizza. But I always told them, 'No, you can't, it's Friday.' Then my brother would yell at me from the kitchen, 'Don't remind them what day it is!'" Berardi, a graduate of Cathedral Prep Seminary (High School) in Manhattan (1965-1969), Cathedral College of the Immaculate Conception Seminary, Douglaston, Queens (1969-1973), and St. Joseph's Seminary in Yonkers fondly remembered preparing tomatoes in the kitchen, cutting the cheese and vegetables, manning the register, and serving tables. Berardi, now a Monsignor serving as the Superior of the Casa Santa Maria, the Graduate House of Studies of the Pontifical North American College in Rome, remarked, "I couldn't have asked for a better preparation as a priest and pastor than working at Berardi's. As being a servant of God requires involvement in peole's lives, I learned to be a good listener, to be a judge of people's hearts. Customers would open-up to me about anything on their mind—their marriages, their finances, anything." "If there's something I miss most about the old days on Staten Island, it's the community. I can remember walking back home with the day's proceeds in my hand and not thinking anything about it. I think people realized we were just a family working together, trying to make the American dream come true."

Born in September 1943 on Cary Ave. in West Brighton, Roger Pucillo is yet another example of the quintessential Staten Island childhood. In a neighborhood with horse-drawn wagons selling vegetables, watermelons, and biongolene (bleach) in gallon bottles with cork tops," Pucillo grew up to the average middle-class household. His father was a master electrician for the Batlimore & Ohio Railraod (later, the Staten Island Rapid Transit) for forty-five years, before having a stroke and dying on the tracks at the age of sixty-two. Typical neighborhood interactions involved weekly visits from the Metropolitan Insurance man with his foot-thick book, collecting quarters from homes or with Christie DeForest (1911-1986)—the ice and coal deliverer with a grinding machine on his truck to chop up the blocks of ice, as well as a heavy canvas bag to haul coal to basements. "Chincy" (derived from Italian *cenci*, meaning rags), the old Italian ragwoman, would holler her "yoo hoo" and Pucillo's mother would immediately put on the tea pot. Pucillo's grandfather owned a bar/restaurant on Manor Rd. called the Blue Manor during the 1940s-1950s. Pucillo remarked, "My grandfather was an old timer from Italy who had very little sense of humor. My dad worked about fifty hours a week on the B&O Railroad and then every night at the Blue Manor (except Tuesday), and even Saturday night until closing. The only arguments I ever heard between my parents was over him working there. My grandfather paid my father nothing. He said it was his duty to work for his father for nothing. On Saturday morning, I would go with my dad to clean the bar and the bathrooms. All week my father and uncles would drop coins by the cash register which would go under the floor racks. I would take the racks outside and wash/bleach them and I could keep the coins from under the racks, which was usually about a dollar." Pucillo recalled his father having his grandfather's toasted Italian bread with butter, and coffee ready every morning for him. Upon his arrival, Pucillo would be sent to fetch the *Il Progresso* Italian newspaper at the corner store. "My grandfather said I could buy candy with the change from the nickel. Benny, the old Jewish man who owned the store gave me the paper and I stood in front of the penny candy case looking. Benny asked me why I was there, and I said my grandfather told me I could buy candy with the change. He asked me when I would ever learn because the paper cost a nickel so there was no change. He would just laugh and give me a piece of candy anyway." The generosity of local shopkeepers for seemingly miniscule deeds such as offering a free snack to children who stumbled inside their stores was once a common practice on old Staten Island. Natives of Edwin Markham Gardens/West Brighton may recall Henderson Market where a free slice of bologna was offered to children over the counter. Henderson Market located at 697 Henderson Ave. was owned for many years by the Napolitano family, chiefly Joseph (b. 1888) and his sons. The shop can trace its roots back to approx. the 1930s. Michele Gambetta whose uncle (actually an old-time family friend of her father's), Anthony Scalia worked for a short period of time at Henderson Meat Market also had a brother who worked directly across the street at Padavano's Gas Station. Gambetta was the daughter of William Braisted (b.

[The staff of Capitol Market gathered around for a photograph. Bill Braisted and his brother "Rocky Remo" were employed here for a time. Courtesy – Paul Scamardella]

1918)—the owner of Bill's Prime Meats at 957 Post Ave.[20] in Port Richmond. Before operating the meat store for thirty years (late-1950s – late-1980s), Braisted was employed at Capitol Market, owned by Edward Spiro. A photograph from 1951 depicts Brainsted assisting with the store's laborers, which included her uncle "Rocky Remo," in the unloading of a "Rath Packing Co." (a Chicago-based meat packer) freight car at a station in West Brighton. Gambetta recalled, "When my father opened his shop in Port Richmond, he used to keep a room in the back with packs of staple food for tug boats. There was also a meat locker in the back of the property." One tugboat company supplied was the Manhattan-based Moran Towing Corp. In his old neighborhood of West Brighton, Braisted was reared at 131 N. Burger Ave. to parents from Austria-Hungary and the Netherlands respectively. Braisted continued raising his children in the West Brighton tradition with his daughter raised at 11 Davis Ct. Constructed in 1934 with an arched

---

[20] Braisted's first store was at 900 Post Ave., before he bought the propery years later at 957 Post Ave.

doorway, Braisted planted rose bushes and a mimosa tree on the property. The house in the present day has undergone slight modifications, and Davis Ct. has since been separated by a wooden fence from its opposing street, Howard Ct. Adjoining Davis Ct., Davis Ave. boasts the Livingston 1897-constructed Victorian home of Sylvia Prestia—the daughter of the notable West Brighton baker Frank Sorrentino and the matriarch of her numerous descendants. Prestia's father, Sorrentino began his Staten Island baking operation at Henderson Ave. & Campbell Ave. in 1928; in 1931, the bakery swiftly moved to its more recognizable location at 693 Henderson Ave., alongside the meat market of the Napolitano family. Sorrentino, Frank & Sons Bakery was held in special regards by Staten Islanders who witnessed the profound joy proliferated by the establishment's five

[The back of Sorrentino's Bakery. C. early-1930s. Courtesy – Sylvia Prestia]

delivery trucks which carried the borough's only "twenty-five cent pizza." The bakery's specialities included Italian bread, rolls and pastries, fruit pies, cookies, Easter pies, and

[The front of Sorrentino, Frank & Sons Bakery at 693 Henderson Ave. C. early-1930s. Courtesy – Sylvia Prestia]

Struffoli. Frank and his wife Caroline's children—all employed at the bakery—included Marie Mayo, Rose Fruciello, Ralph Sorrentino, Helen Miraglia, Joseph "Pepsi" Sorrentino, Sylvia Prestia, Emily Sorrentino, and Frank "Boopie" Sorrentino, Sr. The business thrived until 1955 when two years after his parents had died, son Joseph "Pepsi" and his wife Katie operated the bakery until the early 1960s and then relocated to Castleton and Oakland Avenue under the name "Daylight Bakery." Though the bakery itself has ceased to exist, the Sorrentino culinary legacy continues to live on in the home of Sylvia Prestia. Prestia—the husband of Domenic [21] for sixty-one years—retains the memory of her family bakery's pizza with the brick-oven fireplace pizza oven built by her husband in 1958. Fired up using wood branches, newspaper scraps, and a little coal, the

---

[21] Domenic Prestia (b. 1921)—born in Manhattan, moved to South Beach, Staten Island at the age of eleven with his parents. During World War II, Prestia served in the 8th Armored Division for three years in France, Germany, and England. Upon his return home, he worked as a "route salesman for his father-in-law's bakery." "Not long after, he went into business for himself. He started Presmar Washing Fluid, a business he owned and would run out of his home in Livingston for twenty years."

177

oven produces among many creations, the family's favorite: Prestia's infamous onion pie. The date of Sylvia and Domenic's move into the house—July 4—is commended annually by an extravagant family feast orchestrated by the woman herself. Attended on average by one-hundred guests, the celebration includes a week's worth of prepared foods consisting of spaghetti with crabs, mussels and clams, spare ribs, London broil, sausage and peppers, macaroni pies, BBQ Chicken, four-five different salads, and roughly ten different homemade desserts. The emotional bonds held dear by the Sorrentino's, reflecting ones so carefully crafted by the community of Staten Islanders, traces back in Sylvia's son's words, Jimmy Prestia's and daughter-in-law Kathy's words, "[to] the founders of the bakery. When Caroline Sorrentino died in 1953, her husband Frank died three weeks

[Albino "Albert" Ciampi in his baker's whites. C. 1940s. Courtesy – Kathy Mittenhuber]

later. It was said that he died of a broken heart. They loved life together and had a very tight family structure."

Of course, at least within West Brighton, bakeries played a fundamental role in shaping everyday dynamics. Asides from Sylvia Sorrentino and her family's establihsment, another example can be observed in Albino "Albert" Ciampi, Sr. (1924-2017). Ciampi was the son of Mary Rasile (b. 1893)—an infamous West Brighton bootlegger who

178

produced and sold tremendous amounts of alcohol, enough to buy the property at 342 Broadway. The family owned the portion of Cary Ave., which ran over to Seneca St. Ciampi's daughter, Kathy Mittenhuber explained, "Back then, all you did was pay one or two dollars on the property per week!" Ciampi, raised at the 130-year-old family household on Cary Ave., would own Ciampi's Bakery at 345 Broadway (currently covered by a fruit-and-vegetable market). For twenty-five years on Broadway, and several years later until the age of eighty in Silver Lake, Ciampi, a professionally-trained German pastry chef, specialized in pastry/bread designs. Mittenhuber remarked, "My father won many awards and made the *Staten Island Advance* numerous times. He made bread into turtles, crafted Easter Baskets, and designed intricate gingerbread homes...He also held a winning title of Featherweight boxing in the Army during World War II. He maintained his physique until my Mom passed! Being only five feet and one-hundred-thirty pounds, they were an inseparable couple...I remember throwing my parents a surprise 50th Anniversary Party. I went to the bakery when mom wasn't working and wrote a bogus order for

[Albino "Albert" Ciampi – always with a smile on his face – prepares to unravel a Christmas present. C. 2002. Courtesy – Kathy Mittenhuber]

wedding cake and left a deposit. Funny - my Mom said 'Oh I know that girl that's getting married.' I had a Rolls Royce pick them up, and still they didn't know. Until my brother told my dad they had to stop at LiGreci's Staaten and the wedding cake he delivered fell. So in goes my dad, and upon seeing his family says to them 'What are you doing here?' With this, he runs out to my Mom in the car with the biggest smile!" Mittenhuber, who worked at the bakery at the age of fourteen, stated, "If there's anything I'll remember about old West Brighton, it's the people that used to come in. We really knew all our customers, and looking back, I realize they were just 'real people'... My family worked long hours for sustaining their children. When I was born, in fact, my godfather had to drop my mother off at the hospital so my dad could finish making dough at the bakery... And Mom not only raised us, but worked long hours in the bakery. So instead of a pacifier, it was a biscuit in our mouth...My dad's greatest gift was to pass his expertise to his son, Al Jr."

Perhaps one of the most recognizable of Italian surnames in West Brighton is Scamardella—most closely associated with the funeral home at 332 Broadway. Matteo Scamardella (Nov. 9, 1889 - Oct. 28, 1968), an immigrant from Bacoli— a comune in the Metropolitan City of Naples—arrived to Staten Island in 1906 under the sponsorship of a Mr. Conti. Before opening his own businesses, Scamardella worked at Zinicola's Bakery on Hooker Pl. (Sherman Ave.) near Port Richmond Ave.; he boarded in the bakery's back room. Following his marriage with his wife Theresa, Scamardella, equipped with the knowledge of bread baking from the Port Richmond establishment, opened Scamardella Bakery on Broadway, near Henderson Ave. After morphing into Queen City Bakery, Scamardella Bakery was purchased by the Santero family—the future owners of Stella D'Oro Biscuit Co. During the time which he owned a bakery, Scamardella operated a gas station and drove for Steers and Steers Funeral Home at Martling Ave. & Manor Rd. When he won the Irish Sweepstakes—a lottery authorized by the Irish government in 1930 to benefit Irish hospitals—Scamardella made a downpayment of three-thousand dollars on his own funeral home (one which would serve the Italian community of Staten Island). His wife, Sophia would become the second female funeral director in the State of New York. The original building on Broadway was constructed by a member of the developer family, the Perosi's—relatives of the West Brighton LiGreci's. Grandson Paul Scamardella, the owner of Louis Florist (founded in 1961 by Louis Scamardella) at 1259 Castleton Ave. from 1977-2000, remarked, "I can remember working at a young age for my family. When my grandfather was being laid out, my cousin and I were shining his shoes in the other room! Some nights at 10:30pm, my grandmother sent us out in the middle of a snow storm or to shovel snow and sweep the cigarettes from the gutters. Visiting hours were over, and it was still snowing! Grandma

[*Matteo and Vincent Scamardella during World War II. This photograph was taken at the funeral home upstairs where they resided. C. 1940s. Courtesy – Paul Scamardella*]

181

would yell out the window, "Don't worry, when you're done, I'll give you a dish of lentils!" And I'd say, "Grandma! It's still snowing!" A few minutes later, she'd yell out, "The lentils will be ready in five minutes!" The Scamardella family continually remains active in community affairs. Robert J. Scamardella (b. 1950)—a managing partner at a high-profile Staten Island law firm—was a previous chairman of the Staten Island Republican Party. Reflecting on the changing Island, Paul Scamardella remarked, "Staten Island once had thousands of small businesses. To see that conformity that comes with suburbanization is sad. I think Ross Perot said it best: 'Most jobs won't come from our biggest employers. They will come from our smallest.' He recognized the importance of small business in the community."

And West Brighton was once the picturesque model of "Small Business America." The block of Casleton Ave. stretching from Broadway to Alaska St.—currently covered by the New York City Housing Authority's Projects—once boasted dozens of business alonge. They included Gootenberg Clothing Store (1067), Wonder Market/Donovan's Market (1930s/1940s – 1107), J. Fochs & Bros. Hardware (1095), Bobrow's Paints (1071), Boston Fish Market (1065), and Del Bove's Deli (1063). Tony Del Bove (b. 1916) was the son of Giuseppe Del Bove (b. 1886) and Giuseppina Figliozzi Del Bove—emigrants from the town of Itri near Caserta, Campania and eastern Sicily respectively. Though he was not originally from Staten Island, Del Bove [Tony] rented out several expansive properties in West New Brighton and opened up his deli at 1063 Castleton Ave. The property was previously another deli, owned by the Zarrella family in the 1930s. According to his nephew, Jim Ogden of Ocracoke, N.C., "[He] could add up numbers faster with his pen on a brown paper bag on the countertop than with using an adding machine." Ogden recalled making regular trips with his uncle to Hunt's Point

Produce Market—currently the largest wholesale produce market in the world—in the Bronx to purchase baccalà. Del Bove's Deli, supplying households with fresh Italian food (Ogden[22] also recalled large barrels of pistachio nuts toward the front of store, as well as dried fish and rolls of salami hanging from the ceiling) was the first on Staten Island to sell Boar's Head cold cuts. Many locals would recall the special spicy ham and bologna sandwiches, Italian cheeses, and remarkably fresh cheeses. "My uncle was exceptionally family-oriented and generous. He used to give figs from his fig tree in the backyard to his neighbors... I can remember my aunt, his wife, Vincenza "Vicky" Verdina making dinner for the entire family very late in the night. Those were great times...And of course, I couldn't forget the 1953 Buick Tony kept for forty entire years!" In 1961, after the city pushed Del Bove out of his property, he moved the store to 289 Broadway. In the late-1970s, Del Bove ended the business entirely. He passed away on May 24, 2018 at his residence in Piney Flats, Tenn. at the age of one-hundred-two. Fellow

[Tony Del Bove [middle] poses for a photograph inside his deli at 1063 Castleton Ave. C. late-1940s. Courtesy – Louis Altadonna]

---

[22] Ogden further described Del Bove having a fruit and vegetable stand set up covering the store's front, and wheeling it in at night."

neighborhood proprietors with Tony Del Bove, Vito Cucuzza Sr. and Filippa Cucuzza owned Boston Fish Market at 1065 Castleton Ave. Boston Fish Market was founded by Cucuzza's mother, Filippa "Fannie" Cucuzza (1903-2001)—an entrepreneur/businesswoman who owned several fish markets on the North Shore of Staten Island, incl. on Broad St., Jersey St., and Broadway. The recipient of barely a sixth-grade education, but who could speak, read, and write excellent English and Italian, Filippa was born to Frank and Domenica Cusumano—owners of a fish market on Court St. in Brooklyn. In the late-1910s, Fannie moved to Staten Island, before opening Boston Fish Market in 1918. Though the fish market was forced to move following the erection of the West Brighton Projects, it relocated to 1001 Castleton Ave., staying in business until its final closure in 2009. F. Cucuzza's granddaughter, Marilyn Cucuzza-Ciaburri explained, "If there was a fish in the ocean, and it was on the East Coast, we basically sold it. We had everything from Lemon sole to butterfish to cod." Cucuzza-Ciaburri, a long-time employee of her family store, dropped out of high school, beginning work at Boston Fish Market immediately. "My dad said to be at the market at eight o'clock the next morning, and begin working...All the recipes we used were mine: clam chowder (New England, Manhattan, and regular varieties), lobster bisque, She-Crab soup, crab cakes, and fish cakes." Though once a treasured family, Boston Fish Market secret, Cucuzza-Ciaburri revealed several ingredients, essential for the making of her special She-Crab soup (a novelty dish in Staten Island, popular mostly in South Carolina/Georgia): crab meat, shallots, dry sherry, and heavy cream. Though Boston Fish Market mainly sold to customers through their store, son Vito Cucuzza, formerly employed for Penn Fruit who took over the market's operations in 1959, also made deliveries across Staten Island. A noted incident involving the delivery service is recalled by Cucuzza-Ciaburri: "I remember my father being asked to deliver a two-hundred-pound sea turtle to Almar-Farm Restaurant[23] in Greenridge! The owner, feeling it was best to leave to leave the turtle in the back of the restaurant, placed it in the garden to wait for his making of turtle soup. The turtle got up on its own, buried into a hole, and was never to be seen again, wandering the swamps of the South Shore!" Other fond memories recalled by Cucuzza-Ciaburri include digging through the dirt patch behind the knocked-out Boston Fish Market (pre-Projects), finding scraps of clam shells from the establishment's early days. "Though I have a lot of phenomenal memories from the time, what I remember most is the level of dedication my family members put toward their life's work and always serving the freshest fish. One Christmas season, we worked three days straight without ever exiting the building!...Many a day did I see my father stand seventeen hours in the same place, slicing countless filets of flounder with a mere two strokes on each side!" Cucuzza-Ciaburri elaborated. "My grandmother was among the most patriotic in our entire family! Her favorite holiday was Flag Day. Today, nobody knows which holiday that is!" Cucuzza-Ciaburri concluded, "Some customers who came in found the store having a fishy smell, but to us that smell just reminded us of home. After your whole life, you actually miss that smell."

Just around the corner at 261 Broadway (now Johnny's Auto Body), alongside the current site of a Kennedy Fried Chicken, was the shop of shoemaker, John Pillarella. Pillarella (1894-1979), like many of his West Brighton counterparts hailed from the region of Molise, but in particular the village of Pietracatella—nine miles east of the capital city of Campobasso. Pillarella's son, Mario—a auto body repairman owner and operator of Mario's Auto Body,

---

[23] Almar – Farm Restaurant, formerly Val's Pizzeria, was located at the corner of Arthur Kill Rd. & Richmond Ave. A large sign above the restaurant read in 1954: "Hamburgers, Barbecue Foods, Steaks, Counter and Table Service, Clams on ½ Shell, Soft Shell Crabs, Steam Clams, and Ice Cream & Soda."

and tractor operator for the N.Y.C. Dept. of Sanitation at Fresh Kills Landfill spray painted bumper cars for The South Beach Rides on Sand Lane- and previously worked for Tony "Post" Pietracatella, the owner of Post Construction. J. Pillarella resided at 57 Seneca St., the two-block roadway, bisected by Broadway. From the 1940s to the 1970s, Pillarella, a watchman during World War II, operated the shoemaking shop. Pillarella's granddaughter, Susan remarked, "Over the years I've spoken to people that remember my grandfather. One MTA bus driver once told me, that my grandfather would never take money from people. He just loved fixing shoes! ... The guy would just put the money on the counter and leave as fast as he could so my grandfather couldn't catch him to give it back. I recall my grandfather got mugged one night on his way home and was robbed. That was one of the reasons he stopped charging people." S. Pillarella further recalled her father always advising caution when using his hammer as his father had lost his eye with it. Due to his accident, J. Pillarella was forced to have one glass eye for the rest of his life. At his home on Seneca St. where he maintained a strictly off-limits workshop in his basement,

[Giovanni "John" Pillarella at work in his shop at 261 Broadway. Pillarella was once a familiar face in the once close-knit community of West Brighton. C. 1940s. Courtesy – Susan Pillarella]

Pillarella lived with his wife Mary (1895-1980)—a seamstress at a factory at the future site of Torrone Signs, 400 Broadway—on a street surrounded by Italian immigrants (many from the same region as the Pillarella's). The families were as follows: 15 [Seneca] – DeSario, 27 – Socci, 32 – Ciaccia, 34 – Martini, 35 – Bolitiere, 37/48 – Mezzacappa, 41 – Capriotti, 50 – LaTorre, 51– Sbarra, 53 – Renzulli, 56 – Canale, 58 – Del Zoppo[24], etc. S. Pillarella stated, "Everybody knew who we were on the street. One time, my father bought me a pony who was nicknamed by neighbors "The Houdini of Seneca St. - the escape artist." The Pillarella legacy is carried on today by the senior Pillarella's grandsons who run the family business— originally owned by Louis and Rudolph, Two Brother's Auto Body Repair Shop at 99 Rector St. Though former customers will often recall the friendliness of the cordial neighborhood Italian cobbler or the fragrant scent of fresh shoe polish, Pillarella's granddaughter concluded, "I'll never forget that silly proverb we used to say in our family, 'The shoemaker's children will always go barefoot': those surrounded by others having certain skillsets will faill to benefit from them."

The Pillarella family was one of the many foundational families of West Brighton, along with others such as fellow countrymen, the Pietracatellas. Tony Pietracatella (b. 1915) was the son of Vincenzo (b. 1882)—an Italian immigrant who moved to the United States at the age of nineteen from the mountain hamlet of Monacilioni. Vincenzo, upon his arrival to Staten Island, would join a community of other Molisani, began a pick-and-shovel business with two-three employees, installing sewers, building roads and walls, and constructing septic tanks predominantly in Todt Hill, but

---

[24] Anthony Del Zoppo (1927-2015), a member of the Italian Club of Staten Island Foundation who moved to Seneca St. from Manhattan at the age of thirteen, was the owner of Lane Deli on New Dorp Lane between 1967-1981, and Campo Deli in Eltingville between 1981-1996.

throughout the Mid-Island. In 1936, after being a hobo riding freely on freight trains crisscrossing the country from 1933-1934, Vincenzo's son Tony returned to Staten Island to take over the business following his father's passing. Tony officially began "Post Construction," which would be one of the chief contractors responsible for the building of Halloran Hospital—an army hospital which would later become into the site of Willowbrook State School for the mentally-disabled—in 1942. "Post Construction" would also see work on the Verrazzano-Narrows Bridge. The distinct Pietracatella-construction style, despite decades of borough transformation, possesses the company's signature custom-made home material—Westchester Granite. Examples can be seen on Stewart Ave., Brenton Pl., and Sanford Pl.: all in Westerleigh/Castleton Corners. Pietracatella, nicknamed "Tony Post" and "Tony Stones" (the *pietra-* in his surname meaning "rock"), was also active within community and religious affairs. A longtime parishioner of Calvary Chapel at 25 West St. which witnessed seventy of its laypeople astoningly survive service during World War II, Pietracatella was heavily involved during the church's relocation to Myrtle Ave. In the late-1960s, following the publicization of the intended sale of the square block enclosed by N. Burgher Ave., Broadway, Myrtle Ave., and Delafield Ave., the pastor from Calvary Chapel, Dr. Joseph S. DeRogatis led his congregation to Borough Hall to place a bid of $26,000 on the property. No other bids were given. The grounds of the new site had previously been occupied by a dairy farm, Browns Farm and a large patch of berry bushes which kids used to pick regularly. On Palm Sunday 1970, Olivet Presbyterian Church, designed by architect James Whitford and constructed by Seneca Construction, opened. Pietracatella was responsible for the construction of the minister's residence (made of Westchester Granite and Fieldstone) at 65 Myrtle Ave. Joe Martino, a parishioner, built a bocce court on the grounds of the Church. Joseph

House, a senior residence, was built next to the Church on property donated by the Church and with the sponsorship of the Sisters of Charity. This facility would come to be recognized as the first senior-living Section 8 housing on Staten Island. The bocce court was reminiscent of the backyard of Pietracatella's childhood neighbor, Dominic Narducci on Cary Ave. On Sunday afternoons after church, the Italian men of the neighborhood would gather at Mr. Narducci's home and play bocce while enjoying homemade wine and eating from the *brahjzoot* hanging overhead on a tree branch. Pietracatella's younger sister Barbara remarked, "Tony was always different than everyone else. At PS18, he couldn't sit still to do his work, so his teachers would have him wash their cars and go to the West Brighton Bank to cash their paychecks. One time, he heard a teacher was intensely harassing a student, so Tony dragged the teacher into the school's cloak room and hanged him on two hooks by his suspenders. He warned him to never harass that student again!" "Religion played a key role in my family's and Tony's upbringing" Barbara continued, "When I was one, my father passed away. Things weren't easy for a large family like ours. But my mother, a woman of great faith, would frequently quote Romans 8:28: 'All things will work together for good for those who love the Lord."

Johnny Latanzio, the charismatic, young Italian fishing equipment salesman at his store The Tackle Box at 497 Jewett Ave., was once a personality rooted deep in the old Staten Island community. Born on December 8, 1911 to parents Paolo and Elizabeth from the town of Tocco Da Casauria, Abruzzo—situated about twenty-five miles west of the Adriatic Sea—who immigrated in 1893, Latanzio grew up first in Westerleigh. The family home, inhabited by twelve members of the Latanzio [25] family, was

---

[25] This spelling of "Latanzio" is most certainly a deviation of the more common last name "Lattanzio," perhaps changed by immigration officials at Ellis Island.

coincidentally located about a block from the future site of The Tackle Box. In the early-1920s, when the City of New York proposed building a subway through Staten Island, the home at the corner of Feltman Ave. & Jewett Ave. was acquired, resulting in the forced removal of the Latanzio's.

[Latanzio alongside a collection of fishing rods for sale at his store. Courtesy – Meg and Peggy Ventrudo]

Despite the relocation—which disappointingly did not even produce a railway or transportation system of any kind—the Latanzio's thrived elsewhere, on Bodine St. in West Brighton. The Latanzio boys—Paolo's sons—engaged in a wide variety of occupations. George worked in the composing room of the *Staten Island Advance* office and was assistant to Samuel Irving "Staten Island" Newhouse Jr., remaining at the publication for life, even after its relocation to Grasmere. Joe, naturally gifted with animals, had kennels on the grounds of the current Staten Island Mall in New Springville. In these, he raised and sold dogs, as well as birds such as parakeets; Joe also owned the property adjacent to the Staten Island Airport and rented the land to the Staten Island Mall. Johnny himself was at once an athlete and an overall sports-enthusiast (whether recreational or professional). At Port Richmond High School, Latanzio, despite his smaller stature, played on the football team; his most notable teammate was William "Bill" Shakespeare (1912-1974), nicknamed "The Bard of Staten Island"—an acclaimed halfback for the Notre Dame Fighting Irish football team. While he resided on Bodine St., he met his future wife—Margaret "Marge"

O'Reilly, a teacher at PS20—who lived directly across the street. Latanzio's first job was at Sears-Roebuck, where he learned the ins-and-outs of retail. He then worked at Ryder's Auto Supply on Castleton Ave., where he sold sporting goods, as well as motor boats. By the mid-1950s, Latanzio had been saving up the money to realize his dream: being the sole proprietor of a store. In 1958, he opened The Tackle Box, a specialist in rods and reels, archery, hunting and sports equipment, and guns and ammunition. In his personal life, he was also a member of the Rod & Gun Club, as well as the Beachcombers. Many would testify to Latanzio's fascination and love for fishing, often recalling the sign which hung above the register reading, "A bad day fishing is better than any good day working!" Latanzio's daughter Margaret (Peggy) Ventrudo explained, "My father would 'give you the shirt off his back,' as the old saying goes. He was the most reassuring person I've ever met in my life! He'd always tell me in bad times, 'This too shall pass.' He was deeply religious, was a member of the Holy Name Society, and was even an usher at his church: Our Lady of Mt. Carmel – Saint Benedicta. And, he could never say 'No!' to anyone. I remember: when I used to get out from the dances at St. Peter's at 11pm, my father, God bless him, who closed up shop at nine, would have to come pick me up. And as soon as I got out, I would say, 'Can my friend get a ride too?' And he would ask, 'Where does she live?' 'Woodrow Road.' And without hesitation, we'd drive all the way down to the South Shore to Woodrow Rd., which at that time was mainly pig farms. By the time we got back, it'd be 1:30am!" "My dad had a soft spot for kids" Ventrudo continued, "If a kid came in and wanted a drop line fishing rig, he'd make it for a quarter, a dime, a penny, and if you had nothing, sometimes for free! The kids would come in with their parents, buy the equipment, and then go to Clove Lakes to fish for a Saturday afternoon. Though my father attempted to teach me how to fish, I was useless! I did, however, like to shoot my bow and arrow with my brother in the backyard! ... In the summertime, my father would go fishing to Seaside Heights and Point Pleasant, N.J, catching Striped Bass and Bluefish. At our summer home at Lake Louise in Lakewood, N.J., we used to catch minnows and use them as bait to catch Pickerel...

[Johnny Latanzio stands outside his shop "The Tackle Box" at 497 Jewett Ave. The front sign advertises various supplies sold at the store. Courtesy – Meg & Peggy Ventrudo]

Although my father spent so much time fishing, I don't think he ever actually ate a fish in his life! He always threw them back or gave them away." The Tackle Box remained in business until 1985, when a new landlord didn't renew his lease. Despite initial resistance, Latanzio was reassured by his wife, Marge who remarked, "That's it, no more store!" "My mother was an Irishwoman!" Ventrudo stated, "I didn't grow up in the typical Italian household. So, my father got quite conditioned to eating meat and potatoes! But she did learn to make a few Italian dishes." Though Latanzio passed away on September 18, 1999, his pioneering legacy was preserved. His son John George Jr. (Jack) who had lost his leg due to Diabetes, was instrumental in providing insight for the design for Ocean Breeze Pier at South Beach. Jack wanted to ensure the pier would be accessible to everyone, including disabled individuals such as himself. "My dad was hard-working and dedicated. He would make custom rods by hand, and do all the threading, coloring, and varnishing himself! And he never said a bad thing about anyone! The only time I can remember when he did was about the Yankees, but that was only when they deserved it!" Ventrudo concluded, "My father saw Staten Island in its best state. He always used to tell us stories of sleigh-riding down Waters Ave. in the wintertime, and watching them harvest ice at Martlings Pond...It was people like my father that truly helped build America!"

~

In part, the conception of modern-day Castleton Corners was shaped by the construction of the Staten Island Expressway. The 1.7 mile-stretch of the Expressway which runs through this North Shore neighborhood goes from approximately Slosson Ave. to Willowbrook Rd. Among those who saw their backyards turned into the several-lane highway was Patricia Borello-Foggin—a native of 122 Windsor Rd. Currently the site of Casey Funeral Home, the old Borello family home (with thirty-six windows and eight rooms) was built in about 1925, before being torn down in 1975. Borello, a longtime Staten Island realtor, was born to a mother of Slovenian descent who escaped an arranged marriage in her hometown of Johnstown, Penn., and a father, Frank (b. 1913) from Greenwich Village. Her parents first lived together on Staten Island on Harbor Rd. in Mariners Harbor. Borello's uncle—a Broadway 1st violinist whose first show was *South Pacific* (1949)—married a member of The Rockettes. Her paternal grandparents (b. 1888), immigrants from Naples and Reggio Calabria respectively, were both entrepreneurs in their own sense. Her grandfather owned a tailoring shop on Sullivan St. in Manhattan, and her grandmother was a skilled real estate investor. She bought and rented bungalows in Midland Beach; for years, she rented the land to Toto's Restaurant on Seaside Ave. Shortly after Borello's parents moved to their Castleton Corners home on Windsor Rd. in 1944, Frank Borello followed in his mother's footsteps and obtained a real estate license in the late-1940s. From the 1950s to the late-1970s, he operated Borello & Borello Real Estate with his brother and partner, Anthony at 1871 Victory Blvd. Prior to the opening of this location, Borello owned "Borello Realty and Insurance" next to the old 120th Precinct station. The Borello household was made of six family members, each of whom grew up in the heyday of Staten Island. Borello, delivered at Sunnsyide Hospital in 1944, recalled her spacious backyard with a wooden garage shed and a chicken coop housing six chickens. Across the street at 115 Windsor Rd. was Mr. D'Alessio who lived in the house now on the property of St. Teresa School (founded in 1955). Borello remarked, "I have

[The Borello family homestead at 122 Windsor Rd. (currently Casey Funeral Home) C. 1940s. Courtesy – Patricia Borello-Foggin]

a distinct recollection of Mr. D'Alessio's property. One time, my friend Margaret was spinning me around on his lawn when I spiraled into the air and landed on top of one of the prongs on his fence! It went right through my chin and knocked my tooth out! Margaret went straight into the confession booth at St. Teresa's and sat there for hours!...It's funny the things we remember in life!" When the Expressway opened in the mid-1960s, six houses on Slosson Ave.

194

were relocated to Little Clove Rd. and the Borello's backyard was half-obliterated.

Just west from the Borello household in Four Corners, around the block from Al's Pizzeria at 2005 Victory Blvd. was another Italian restaurant, Chicken Amore. Founded by Philip Roccaro and Lee (Choida) Roccaro in 1973, Chicken Amore was an Italian variation of Roccaro's franchise of Chicken Delight on New Dorp Lane. Similar to Chicken Delight's jingle, "Don't cook tonight, call Chicken Delight!," Roccaro invented his own rendition: "Cook no more, call Chicken Amore!" It would remain in business until being sold in 1982. Chicken Amore, much like other businesses in Meiers Corner such as the Jewett Deli (renown across Staten Island for its sandwiches) and Victory Cleaners, would fall into several hands in the coming years. Today, Eli Grill & Deli and Rina's Cleaners take their respective places. One establishment on Jewett Avenue that has maintained the charisma of its predecessor—Horst Bakery—is Cake Chef, owned by James Carrozza since 1988. The owner of Cookie Jar on Forest Avenue, Piece-A-Cake in New Dorp, and Cake Chef in Westerleigh, Carrozza fulfills a necessary niche on Staten Island, proven to be existent even in times of economic recession. Carrozza exclaimed, "I've developed a large following on Staten Island because I'm one to put quality before price! In the old days, it wasn't always like that! But, for instance, when I want to make a Macadamia Nut Ring, I completely disregard food cost; when people start tasting it, then I determine the price. Never do I cut corners...It's like my Strawberry Shortcake: I use real strawberries instead of cheap strawberry filling. You know, some bakeries say they sell 'butter cookies,' when in reality, they're making these things with shortening!" Carrozza developed his passion for wholesome baking in Brooklyn— his native borough. He explained, "The way we learned baking back then was completely different than nowadays. In my day, we didn't go to culinary school, and if you weren't a world traveler and just some poor kid from Brooklyn, you weren't exposed to a variety of baking styles or goods. Coming from a poor Brooklyn neighborhood and not having exposure to high quality ingredients, for many years, I thought I hated Lemon Meringue Pie. My local commercial bake shops used canned artificial lemon filling but, when I tasted a home-baker's pie who squeezed real lemon juice and real egg whites, I fell in love with Lemon Meringue Pie!" In the first half of his career at Cakechef, Carrozza developed a tremendous array of cookies. After 20 years of collecting over one-thousand cookie jars, it was time to open his second shop with a theme of just cookies and cookie jars in West Brighton and named it Cakechef's CookieJar. In a recent cupcake craze originating from the television show "Sex and the City's" popularization of the treat, Carrozza has capitalized on the trend by drawing in locals who would otherwise travel to Manhattan bakeries. True to his Italian roots, Carrozza offers a wide variety of Italian cookies such as pignoli and seven-layer rainbows at his shops. In 2012, he opened Piece A Cake Bakery Cafe serving breakfast, lunch, coffees, soups as well as something to satisfy anyone's sweet tooth. He also creates a focaccia-of-the-day that has become popular with the locals. The New Dorp location expanded in 2016 with a second adjoining Cookiejar location. When he is not baking, Carrozza enjoys "feeding his addiction: collecting vintage items." With the help of his childhood friend Stephen Squires, Carrozza opened "Objects of Interest" on Victory Blvd. in 2016. The novelty, antique, vintage store sells items bought exclusively from Staten Island households.

Meiers Corners is also home to the renown Staten Island bakery—Alfonso's Pastry Shoppe—located at 1899 Victory Blvd. Serving the Island since 1970, Alfonso's was founded by Alfonso Campitello—a dedicated, young Neopolitan immigrant who had begun honing his baking skills in Salerno and Naples. Initially a coffee server at the Plaza

Hotel in Manhattan, Campitiello would work his way to assistant pastry chef at both the Plaza Hotel and Hampshire House; he would also work at the no-longer-existent Angelo's Pastry Shop on 86th Street in Brooklyn. In 1970, Campitello opened up shop at 943 Manor Road (previously Jessie's Cake Box), and later purchased the current Meiers Corners location. The business, having now expanded to Cranford, NJ and Eltingville, is run by Alfonso's sons Anthony and Vincent who were given the choice to either "pay [their] way through college" or "work at the pastry shop." Anthony Campitiello recalled, "I remember when we used to get into trouble as kids, my father would punish Vincent and I by having us stand on milk crates and wash pots and pans. Either that or go and fill donuts." Despite adapting to changing times and offering an array of elegant French-Italian pastries (in contrast to the coffee and crumb buns of the 1970s), the family recipes have remained unchanged since Alfonso's days of ownership. Anthony notes, "He could come in any day and begin working like nothing ever happened." Running the business is a family affair; Anthony's daughters Cristina—general manager, Dianna—manager, and Angela—head cake decorator, all ensure the operation runs successfully. Alfonso's Pastry Shoppe gained notoriety when it was featured in James Signorelli's 1983 comedy film *Easy Money*, in the scene where Montgomery "Monty" Capuletti (Rodney Dangerfield) and Nicholas "Nicky" Cerone (Joe Pesci) carry out a wedding cake from the bakery[26]; the bakery's sign, however, was adjusted so as to also include "Scungilli."Additionally, not only is Alfonso's Staten Island's largest purveyor of occasion cakes, but the dominant maker of cannoli, going through five to six hundred pounds of cannoli dough each week. On average, Anthony estimates, the pastry shop

---

[26] Campitiello recalls having been forced to go to school on the day of filming, while all of his classmates were absent, standing outside the bakery.

requires forty new aluminum [empty] garbage cans— important containers for the safe storage of cannoli shells— each year. Baking aside, Anthony is actively involved with the Staten Island community; in 2001 and 2002, he served as president of the Gateway Rotary Club, and is the current chairman of the Victory Boulevard Merchants Association. The association hosts four annual, family-friendly events, and through Anthony's leadership, is working toward making the segment of Victory Blvd. a Business Improvement District (BID).

Alfonso's is only one contemporary example of the rich Italian heritage steeped in a century of Meiers Corners tradition. Though the area was named for distinguished 18th-century Dutch resident Joachim Meier who resided at the pre-Revolutionary-built Martling-Cozine House (demolished in 1981), Meiers Corners received its secondary name "Nanny Goat Hill" due to the large amount of Italians who raised goats in that area. There were also several Italian businesses, including the Ettore School of Music (later, Al's Pizzeria), owned by Tony Ettore, the former president of the American Accordionists Association, in the 1950s, 60s, and 70s. Ettore offered musical training and specialized accordion lessons which produced superstars such as Sandra Gargaloni and Vinnie Zummo. Zummo—a native of Meiers Corners—over the course of his career has played three world tours and on six albums (most notably, Body and Soul) with Joe Jackson, subbed for Eric Clapton on the Paul Carrack album "Groove Approved", and has had his work featured in the movies *Iron Man III*, *Must Love Dogs*, *The Weather Man*, and the American television crime drama series *Ray Donovan*. His time at Tony Ettore's School of Music on Staten Island, however, was one of the foundational aspects of his career. Zummo remarked, "Uncle Tony ('Unk') as we used to call him, was closer than any blood relative to us because he was my father's best friend and often spent weekends at our home. He used to take us to accordion competitions all over the country, from upstate New York to Washington. We even won the world accordion competition one year, which was a huge deal! But when the Beatles became popular in the 1960s in America, the accordion went flying into the closet. Nevertheless, when I would go on tour years later, I found Tony Ettore had prepared me for a professional musician's lifestyle." Zummo was raised in a traditional, Staten Island, Italian setting—the kind where a summer treat was jumping on the old Italian man, Gorobello's vegetable truck with Zummo's grandfather and hand-selecting a fresh pea in a pod. Zummo's sister, Sandra—a columnist for the *Advance*—offered an intimate portrait of Nanny Goat Hill, writing: "When they weren't playing pinochle down at the Bradley Avenue Republican

Club, the old men of the neighborhood could be found in my grandfather's apartment, playing the Italian card game Briscola (Brisk), comparing homemade wines and smoking putrid-smelling DiNobili cigars...If we weren't playing, we were picking blackberries from a patch across the street, trailing behind my grandmother as she foraged for mushrooms in the woods or filling glass jars with icy-cold water from the well at the bottom of Livingston Avenue." Vinnie even

[Tony Ettore melodically plays his accordion on a sunny afternoon in Nanny Goat Hill. Courtesy – Tony Orazio Troiano]

199

recalled picking mint from the garden to add to the tomato sauce simmering in the old, Italian kitchen. The Zummo household (made entirely of cement) on 210 Holden Blvd. was constructed by Vinnie's grandfather, Vincenzo Rappa. Rappa lived in Hell's Kitchen, Manhattan, and spent the weekends on Staten Island with a loaf of Italian bread, some provolone cheese, and a salami, and worked on the house piece-by-piece at a time. For Vinnie, many everlasting memories would be made on Staten Island, whether they be at his uncle's place Benny's Luncheonette in old Nanny Goat Hill, or at the bar The Shoals (formerly Sauer's) in Great Kills where as a kid, he played the only song he knew by heart "Guitar Boogie" with his dad's well-known Staten Island band 'The Mellow Tones.' The Staten Island of the 1950s has since dissipated into the heart of suburbia.

[*Vinnie Zummo Jr. plays along on the accordion in a jam session sometime in the early-1960s with (from left to right): Vinnie Zummo Sr., Tony Ettore, Sal Rappa, Vinnie Rappa, and his sister. Courtesy – Vinnie Zummo*]

Another testimony of mid-20th century, Italian Meiers Corners/Nannygoat Hill is given by Donna Comis—a retired Nursing Clinical Instructor who graduated from St.

[Comis' uncle, Vincent Anzalone Jr.—a former Eagle Scout at St. Rita's who returned home to 177 Holden Blvd. in 1968. Courtesy – Donna Comis]

Vincent's Hospital School of Nursing. Comis grew up at 177 Holden Blvd., down the street from Vinnie Zummo. Comis' mother, Carmella Iaizzo-Anzalone was born in 1936 on Hendricks Ave. in New Brighton; a hair stylist, she owned a salon, Mel's, at 1652 Richmond Rd. in Dongan Hills for thirty-eight years. That location was purchased by Emily's after its closure. Comis' father, Rosario "John" Anzalone, a native of Market St. in Little Italy, moved to Bradley Ave. in 1939. The couple met at the Tompkinsville Pool on Victory Blvd., and married at the Church of the Assumption in May 1955. Anzalone was a fervent racer of homing pigeons, domesticated birds, which unlike feral pigeons typically found in urban areas, were not returned to the wild. Anzalone engaged in the for-profit-racing along with other neighborhood Italian men such as Joe Dolce—the body-and-fender man who maintained the pipe of spring water on the edge of his property. Anzalone purchased the pigeon feed from Joe Bonamo—a resident of Orange Ave. in Port Richmond who had one of the largest coops on Staten Island. Carmella Anzalone was a devoted member of the St. Bernardino Society (men and women's auxiliaries)—headed at that time by Sam Pirozzolo Sr.—a fraternal organization which met at St. Mary of the

Assumption Church whose members hail from the town of Molisano town of Vinchiaturo. Comis explained, "The neighborhood was predominantly Italian and African-American. Many of those Blacks who resided in Nannygoat Hill were employed at Seaview Hospital, treating Tuberculosis in patients. Since fresh air at that time was the only cure for the disease, Staten Island was where most diagnosed patients ended up." "We weren't like the Irish households. The walls weren't allowed to have any holes, fingerprints. No fun! But we did have a fig tree in the garden, and of course, tomatoes!" Comis elaborated, "We used to see the nannygoats after getting off at the R-111 bus stop!" Comis' memories of old Staten Island consisted of trips to Fazzino's Superette on Manor Rd., mass at St Rita's on Bradley Ave. (where her grandmother was among the first parishioners), and playing accordion at Ettore's School of Music. Comis remarked, "In 1964, Sandra Gargaloni walked into my second grade classroom and changed my life forever by putting an accordion in my hand!"

One community which evolved around one certain industry was Rosebank (formerly Peterstown): a district in the north-east portion of the island, bordering Arrochar to the south. Around 1850, the Louis De Jonge Paper Works moved to Staten Island to Austin Place & Victory Boulevard, and in 1918 to 330 Tompkins Avenue—an exquisite paper manufacturing company notable for its production of the blue "Tiffany" gift-wrapping paper. An October 17, 1975 edition of the *Staten Island Advance* described its products as being used for "gift wrappings, box coverings, wallpaper, lamp shades, and food wrappers." A trade card for the company displayed at the Centennial Exhibition in Philadelphia in 1876 read, "Louis De Jonge & Co.: Manufacturers of Fancy Papers. Importers of Fancy Paper, Leather, and Engl. Book Cloth." The company at its peak (prior to World War II) would employ more than four-hundred Rosebank residents. Its pricing for the time period would be relatively expensive, charging $8.50 for 5 reams of German medium brown marble paper, dull finish 20 by 25 inches, in reams of 480 sheets. The company's paper would become a gigantic success all over the United States, having been transported in freight cars by the Baltimore & Ohio Railroad Company. A testimony to De Jonge's (also a trustee of the Staten Island Savings Bank) superior quality of paper read, "it appears that De Jonge and his descendants have built up a thriving business in specialty high grade paper stock of the coated, decorative variety which places it in a class by itself with an assured market for its output which is said not to be exceeded in quality." Louis De Jonge & Co. would maintain a spectacular reputation until long after the mid-point of the 20th century—demonstrating the Staten Island standard of quality presented to the public at the "lowest market rates" with the "highest degree of confidence." The manufacturing of "scrap book-reliefs, genuine moroccos, Russia hides, English calf, [and] marble papers" would continue until the factory's unfortunate close and filing of Chapter 11 Bankruptcy in the mid-1970s, following several changes in ownership and an employee strike in 1947 after supposed "violations of union agreements." Although Louis DeJonge Jr. passed away in 1913 (in San Remo, Italy), his pioneering legacy lives on. The area surrounding the site of his former production plant would be referred to for decades later as "Paper Factory Hill."

De Jong's factory was built by the hands of Rosebank Italian laborers, many of whom originated in small villages in Campania, Apulia, and Calabria (as well as from the first Italian settlement "Little Palermo" in the lower French Quarter in New Orleans), who helped form the island's earliest most populous Italian enclave; the area's earliest Italians were longshoremen and agricultural workers. Their prevailing religious beliefs enabled them to form benevolent societies and organize festivals, much like the Germans had done in Stapleton. Italians from Contursi Terme and

Auletta—both villages in the province of Salerno, Campania—celebrated the Feast of Saint Donatus of Arezzo, a martyr, each in Tompkinsville and Rosebank on August 7th and 17th. The Society of San Donatus (San Donato) was marked by the founding of San Donato Hall at 207 St. Marys Ave., alongside the former Marino Foods. On February 28, 1903, the Italian immigrants from Campania incorporated the Society of Our Lady of Mount Carmel—a mutual-aid society which provided unemployment and burial insurance whose commencement would coincide with that of the OLMC society of the Nolani in Williamsburg, Brooklyn. The society, an organization intended to foster the traditions which abounded in the Mezzogiorno region, honors the patroness of the brown scapular-wearing Carmelite Order: established in the Crusader States on January 30, 1226. In 1920, a meeting

[Thomas Tedesco – one of the three main builders of the Our Lady of Mt. Carmel Shrine on Amity Pl. – drives a float through the streets of Rosebank. C. 1950s. Courtesy – Joyce Burns]

hall (finished with wooden paneling in the 1950s) complete with a kitchen and bar for the society was established: functioning as an exclusively-male social club and women's auxiliary. The Italian members, including founders Andrew J. Palma (father of the future borough president) and Vito Louis Russo, saddened by the pneumonia-induced death of his 5-year old son, Vito Jr., would construct an elegant shrine/grotto at the dead-end of Amity Street. Born in 1885 in the 6,000-person village of Sala Consilina, Russo was orphaned at a young age; after having lived in the Lower East Side, he moved to Rosebank in 1895. His culminating feelings and sudden loss would produce a 30-foot high shrine adorned with glass marble shells, plastic flowers, figurines of St. Anthony of Padua, St. Anne, St. Lucy, etc., thousands of pebbles and rocks from Buono Beach, and other sacramentals. The shrine, previously maintained by World War II veteran, director of housekeeping for the State of New York, and lifelong Rosebank resident, Anthony Fontaino, "consists of a central chamber built with fieldstones, flanked by two adjoining sections stretching out in serpentine fashion. The central apse contains a linen-draped altar with a padded kneeler and an alcove housing a statue of Our Lady of Mount Carmel holding the infant Jesus. Rising from the grotto are a series of towers and crown-like protrusions, many topped by crosses." The shrine, based on an aluminum foil, cardboard, and paper model constructed by president-for-life Vito Russo, completed in 1938, is the largest of its denomination in the United States, making it the epicenter of pilgrimage for American Roman Catholics, as well as for the annual feast of Our Lady of Mount Carmel held between July 14-16. During the festival, attended by many of Rosebank's 4,100 Italian residents, mourners light candles for their lost loved-ones, the statue of Our Lady of Mount Carmel holding the baby Jesus is paraded through the streets, street vendors sell the traditional zeppole (Italian donuts commonly served during the Feast of San Gennaro) and sausage with grilled peppers, the reminiscent songs of Frank Sinatra are blared through the speakers, and a mass is held at St. Joseph's Church on 171 St. Mary's Avenue. Established in 1902 by Reverend Paolo Iacomino, St. Joseph's is the oldest Italian parish on Staten Island; although, in recent years, it has catered to the large Irish population, holding St. Patrick's Day festivities. Its longest serving pastor was the venerated-Monsignor Anthony Catoggio who remained at St. Joseph's between 1905-1959. In his book *Italian Staten Island*, acclaimed author Andrew Paul Mele writes, "The Reverend... was born in Armento, [Basilicata] Italy in 1876 and ordained in Rome in 1899. He arrived in America in 1905 after submitting his name as a volunteer to help Italian immigrants in the new land." During his tenure, St. Joseph's, in 1912, also added a "six-ton cast-iron bell from Vickers Foundry of Sheffield, England." Catoggio was energetic, devout, and determined. Locals frequently spotted him riding on his bicycle through the unpaved streets of Rosebank on his way to administer communion to one of his homebound parishioners. On August 30, 1914, having collected a large amount of donations from beachfront businesses and wealthy summer residents of Staten Island, he established a small wooden chapel on Sand Lane as a mission of St. Joseph's on the former grounds of a silent-movie production center—Fred Scott's Movie Ranch: "the birthplace of Westerns." Rosebank's transformation was to be one of hundreds of development booms on Staten Island prior to the opening of the Verrazzano-Narrows Bridge. The short, one-block gravel roads down which children used to play were lined with quaint wooden cottages, housing the earliest Italian immigrants to America who enjoyed spacious yards with dilapidated wooden fences (sometimes failing to separate neighboring yards) and even three to four goats which grazed on the untrimmed, dry grass. In fact, according to New York City historian Peggy Gavan, "[i]n 1900, members of the new Fox Hills Golf Club overlooking the Narrows began complaining to authorities about the goats that were running at large and interfering with their game. They claimed that the goats came from 'Goatville,' a settlement near Rosebank inhabited primarily by Italian immigrants who held tightly to the old country customs and religion."

The Italian population of the northeastern corner of Staten Island (Rosebank, Clifton, and South Beach) saw an upsurge of 2,000 during Word War II wherein Italian prisoners of war were imported from Tunisia and Libya to Fort Wadsworth. Members of the Italian Service Unit (ISU) were placed under the command of Brigadier General John M. Eager, former attaché at the American Embassy in Rome under Ambassador Robert Underwood Johnson, who observed the prisoners' high morale and cooperation under the instruction of the Ordnance Department. They were certainly as the documentary film by Camilla Calamandrei's title suggests, "Prisoners in Paradise." The local Italian community treated the POW's like true *paesani*, especially some intrigued women who slaved away in their kitchens preparing home-cooked meals for the prisoners. St. John's Villa Academy on Cleveland Place treated the men to dinner every Sunday, even arranging for excursions; a local church drove the men for a relaxing daytrip to Palisades Park and then Union City for dinner; Our Lady of Pity in Bulls Head hosted dinner-dances for the POWs. One of B.G. John Eager's "least desirable jobs was to was to answer complaints by citizens who believed the prisoners received preferential treatment while American boys fought overseas." By the time the end of the war came, and consequentially—the time for the ISUs to depart—Italian–American women wrote President Franklin Roosevelt, his wife Eleanor, and Secretary of War Henry Stimson pleading to exempt their fiancés who in some instances had fathered a child. Author Dominic W. Moreo writes in his book *Riot at Fort Lawton, 1944*, "Twenty-five Italian officers commuted daily to their jobs by ferry from Fort Wadsworth in Staten Island to Manhattan. Another fifteen went to work for the Office of War Information in mid-Manhattan writing radio scripts to be performed and beamed by short waves to Italy." The POWs who remained following the end of World War II settled in the homes surrounding Paper Factory Hill in the quiet Italian neighborhood populated by residents who were beginning to notice a dramatic modernization and unprecedented development. Paul Mattiola, the owner of Rosebank Pharmacy from 1964 till his daughter, Florence Levine took control of operations, still recalled silent film stars from Fox Hills's days as a studio staying at his grandfather's bed-and-breakfast. Founded in 1890 by a Mr. Goldschmitt—a German immigrant in 1890 alongside St. Marys Church on Bay St., Rosebank Pharmacy was later purchased by Herbert Lens who moved it across the street. Following Frank Coscia's ownership, Paul Mattiola finally moved it to 500 Tompkins Ave. in 1977. Born and raised till marriage at 130-132 Lyman Ave., Mattiola resided in the house used by his grandfather (a merchant marine, sea captain from Palermo, Sicily who first came to Little Italy in Manhattan) starting in approx. 1900 as a bed and breakfast. The face of Lyman Ave., as regarded by Paul Mattiola, has been one significant case study in Rosebank's development. In fact, the 50-foot wide street's gradient is also historically intriguing. The Staten Island Rapid Transit Railway's South Beach Branch's Fort Wadsworth Station, in operation from 1886-1953, stood at the very top of Lyman Ave. at Tompkins. A lone, diagonal piece of rail track is the sole reminder of the train service to South Beach. Directly across from the Mattiola residence at 137 Lyman Ave. was once the Burnswell Coal Co. which was later transformed into a lumber yard by Joseph Lamattina (b. 1887) who resided at 192 Garfield Ave. Marie Dudley, a native of neighborhing High St., recalled sleigh riding at Cubs Field, adjacent to Burnswell. When Mattiola married and later moved from Lyman Ave., he, having had uncles in the pharmaceutical industry (though they never owned a physical business), took over Rosebank Pharmacy. He had "slowly worked his way up...before earn[ing] his white pharmacist jacket, by delivering goods to Rosebank residents by bicycle." When Rosebank pharmacy opened its door on Tompkins Ave. in

1977, a "ribbon cutting" ceremony was lead by Msgr. John Villani and Councilman Frank Biondolillo. Among the few success stories, Rosebank Pharmacy has withstood a daunting challenge from the market-giant Walgreen's in which the final result was the closure of its newly-opened store. Despite claims from the corporation that its expansion allowed nevertheless for friendly competition, Karen O'Shea wrote in her *Staten Island Advance* article "Cozy neighborhood pharmacy on Staten Island faces 'Goliath,'" "Mattiola can recount former owners of the Rosebank Pharmacy, and he remembers other drug store owners. As a former president of the Staten Island Pharmaceutical Society, he recalls a time when the society had seventy-two members. The group long ago disbanded and Mattiola estimates just a handful of those smaller pharmacies exist on the Island today. He said some doctors are even surprised to learn he's still in business when they call in prescriptions." Walgreen's decision to open a store at 570 Tompkins Ave. triggered a community backlash. Signs posted on street corners and storefront windows, written in the colors of the Italian flag gallantly proclaimed, "Rosebank Unite – No Walgreens." When in 2016, Walgreens determined it needed to cut five-hundred million in costs, despite the initial failure of the Rosebank community's effort, its Rosebank store was chosen as one of several to go. Mattiola remarked, "It was tremendous! It was proof that the community was there supporting my pharmacy and had my back." When the perceived victory was achieved, new signs commended it: "Rosebank United – Thank You."

The sense of community was embodied by many a Rosebank family which boasted long lineages of children, aligned with the certain respected surname. Fraternal organizations were common among them—the most notable of which was the Rosebank Boys, headquartered for many years at an old barber shop at 513 Tompkins Ave. One of the founders was Mr. Alan Magnotti—a relative of Louie, Frankie, and Funzi who operated Magnotti's Bakery at 214 St. Marys Ave. (later, Sophia & Son Bakery). The bakery could trace its roots to the early-1910s, shortly after the family arrived to the United States in 1912. Among the other respected families included the DeRosa's who resided at 320 Clifton Ave. David DeRosa emigrated from Auletta, Italy to Staten Island—specifically, to live with his sister on Virginia Ave.—in 1907. David's children included six girls and two sons. The two-story family propery at 320 Clifton Ave., still intact today, was constructed in 1895, though the brick porch was added later in 1925. It is among the more unusual buildings in the immediate area as the dwelling is essentially divded into two distinct pieces, each with radically different styles of architecture and coloration. George DeRosa (b. 1927)—a formed U.S. Navy servicemember from Jan. 1945 to Sept. 1949—detailed his father's life on old Staten Island. A streetsweeper for the N.Y.C. Dept. of Sanitation, David DeRosa drove a horse-and-wagon to fulfill his daily tasks. A noted family photograph depicts DeRosa holding the reins of the horses pulling the junk-filled wagon in front of the home and photography studio of Mr. John V. Malnati (b. 1879) and his son Richard (b. 1899) at 641 Tompkins Ave. near the corner of Maryland Ave. "Most of those sanitation men were devout Catholics and members of the Holy Name Society" George explained, "I can recall one time in the 1930s they held a parade in Manhattan toward St. Patrick's Cathedral. Afterward, they had breakfast at the Waldorf-Astoria Hotel." George recalled other memories such as his mother cooking in the traditional Italian basement kitchen at their home; the growing of peppers in his small three by six feet dirt hole at DeMatti's playground; roller skating on the

[Mr. Malnati and DeRosa - C. 1910s. Courtesy – George DeRosa]

DeMatti handball courts; and celebrating the feasts of San Donato and Our Lady of Mt. Carmel. One duty consisted of walking east on Hylan Blvd. and then all the way north on Edgewater St. to collect driftwood for the purpose of burning in the home furnace (the Environmental Protection Agency has since addressed the toxicity of this practice). Weekend outings were trips with his mother to Angelo's Produce Store on Tompkins Ave. or the live Chicken Market at the corner of Fletcher St. & Virginia Ave. Among the more outstanding moments from childhood was being brought to the roof of P.S. 13 by his teacher, Ms. Granato to witness the crossing of the RMS Queen Elizabeth through the Narrows. Before entering the U.S. Navy, DeRosa in 1943 was a volunteer Air Raid Warden who had his post first at the former photography studio of Mr. Malnati and then at 246 Hylan Blvd. next to the FDNY Battalion 21 & Engine 152. Lorraine Guerrera, who grew up in Rosebank in her grandfather's house on Hylan Blvd and graduated from New Dorp High School in 1965 when the family moved to Dongan Hills, provides more insight into Rosebank during World War II. "My father, John J. Guerrera (b. 1913) was serving with Patton's 3rd Army in the vicinity of Alsace-Lorraine in

[The Guerrera family gathers around the dinner table. C. 1944. Courtesy – Lorraine Guerrera—Maciejowski]

France. [He] was a member of the Railroad Battalion, living in railway freight cars and surviving on K-rations in 1944. His parents Catherine and Giuseppe Guerrera rallied the family together and prepared monthly Italian food packages of pasta, dried salami, and even wine. The wine was camouflaged inside a big loaf of Italian bread! The local Italian baker would bake an oversized loaf and the Guerrera's would hollow out the bread, placing the wine bottle inside and taping it back up for shipment. As far as we know, not one bottle broke! The Italian dinners were scheduled when they were in a local French village for several days, so that the army cooks could make the sauce for the pasta. At one point, there was so much pasta, they invited the entire village to have dinner with them. The French village people were so grateful, they dug out their hidden bottles of Cognac to toast their Italian-American friends and the family in

[Anthony Cavallo (left) as the New Year's Baby, with Nino Guerrera (right) as Father Time. C. New Year's Eve, 1951. Courtesy – Lorraine Guerrera-Maciejowski]

Rosebank, Staten Island for sending the food!" Lorraine (named after this region of France) also recalled a Staten Island in which eternal memories were made and traditions were established. Of those she recalled "The Guerrera and Cavallo families celebrated New Year's Eve at the home of Marie and Anthony Cavallo on Tompkins Ave every year. Marie Guerrera- Cavallo (102 yrs old - 2018) was the first daughter of Catherine and Giuseppe Guerrera of Hylan Blvd. Nino Guerrera (the first son of Giuseppe) would dress up as Father Time and Anthony Cavallo would be dressed in his diaper as the New Year's baby! They were like a comedy team and always was the life of the party"

Just approximately four blocks from the Guerrera family home, on the other side of Hylan Blvd., on Maryland Ave. is the childhood home of Aldea Simon—the granddaughter of Lucrezia Nuzzolo (nee Mazzone). Nuzzolo, an emigrant from South Campanella in the Metropolitan City of Naples, was brought to the United States by her [future] husband, Carmine. Carmine Nuzzolo (b. 1900), a sewer maintenance worker in Manhattan respected by many children for his recovering of balls from New York City's underground, originally from the Italian region of Tuscany, saved a sufficient sum of money to pay for his bride's ship fare to America[27]. "Like many Italian immigrants of his time, my grandfather was approached by the Black Hand every single payday. He had to pay them a certain amount of money to avoid getting beat up. They'd take ten cents from him every two weeks…It was disturbing to know that these poor Italian vendors who made pennies were being forced to output "protection money" for the sake of maintaining their existences." Simon explained. Much to Nuzzolo's benefit, the family managed to fulfill their dietary needs through the vast vegetable garden behind their Rosebank property—a typical characteristic of most neighborhood households. The

---

[27] Lucrezia Nuzzolo's stepmother also assisted in paying for the voyage.

garden included plum and cherry trees, as well as a large collection of rosemary/sage bushes and Italian greens. Lucrezia Nuzzolo, the daughter of a baker in Naples, often baked struffoli (deep fried balls with sweet dough) with sprinkles on top during Christmas time. "Rosebank really was a community then" Simon elaborated, "I can remember when I was sixteen, my father enforcing his strict nine p.m. curfew by when the minute it rolled around, putting a Blue patent suitcase out on the porch. He would say to my mom, 'If she likes it so much out there, then she can stay there.' One time, I was through with his disciplinary rituals, so I took my bike through the streets of Rosebank. The entire night, I remember chatting with different firemen, policemen, and friends who I ran into. It was a different time…" Grandma Lucrezia Nuzzolo, a resident of Maryland Ave. for her entire existence on Staten Island, would eventually pass away while heading back from visiting her family in Naples on the SS Michelangelo during a terrific accident on the morning of April 12, 1966. "My grandmother had a stroke on the ship and didn't have the means to to get shipped to a medical facility. While her deceased body lay on a slab, the employees of the cruise ship stole her watches and rings. She was identified as an 'illiterate Italian immigrant.' When we picked my poor lost grandfather up in Manhattan, he was holding a large porcelain doll. It was for me! The family in Italy I never met gave up a treasured joy for me!... I knew I would never see [my grandmother] again the morning we dropped her off" Simon confessed, "I cried that whole day of her departure in my room, feeling as though I had lost my mother."

~

By the time the Our Lady of Mount Carmel shrine on Amity Street reached completion in 1938, Rosebank still had even managed to preserve a fairly rural sense. Across from the shrine were a collection of horse stables along with a carriage house that echoed a decade liberated from the increasing presence of telephone lines which towered above the 19th century alleyways of Rosebank. Though the horses have long vanished into the abyss of time, the stables remain, serving the purpose of garages. The 1930s were indeed a transmogrification for the areas of Old Town, Rosebank, South Beach, and Dongan Hills, particularly for the Italian sectors. In 1932, for instance, Villa Tocci—a mansion named for the original owner, Mr. Felice Tocci (though some speculate it is named for a region in northern Calabria)—became the Academy of St. Dorothy at 1305 Hylan Blvd. Villa Tocci was inhabited by the Goggi brothers, winemakers who had purchased their former place of employment—Luigi Bosca & Figli (Sons)—located at 754 Van Duzer St, in 1917. Luigi Bosca's winemaking tradition can be traced back to 1831 to his father Pietro, who first began selling Moscato d'Asti Canelli—a distinct Piemontese wine—outside of his native country. Bosca's wine won him the *Grand Prix* title at the Brussels International in 1910, and the Panama-Pacific International Exposition in San Francisco in 1915; not to mention, widespread popularity in Argentina, France, and Germany. "The strong work developed in 1905 made known the necessity of having true wine cellars like in... Piedmont. It was chosen Staten Island, suburb of New York, on the highest and driest point, on the hill overlooking the sea. In the living rock were dug various lines of cellars that go into the ground for a depth of several hundred feet." The hillside provided an advantageous place to store the wine as the insulation prevented against water infiltration and external temperatures. The Goggi brothers— Pio and Charles—both were employed at the winemaking operation (Pio served as "direttore enotecnico" – director of "enotecnic" (related to wine) affairs). They later bought the operation, but were ultimately put of out of business by the ratification of the 18th Amendment—Prohibition—in 1919.

Among the Goggi brothers' most notable products were their fermented-in-the-bottle sparkling Burgundy and champagne, which was enjoyed once by Italian operatic tenor Enrico Caruso. By 1972, not only was the wine business long gone, but the mansion sold, and the entire property demolished to clear way for a new convent. Concerning the mansion, it was once written, "Villa Tocci on Staten Island gives to Southern Richmond a touch of Southern Italy. Mr. Felice Tocci, the owner, has developed his six acres of irregular surface into a charming setting for an attractive residence ... the commodious house is of brick, stone and terracotta, and is designed on a ground plan of unusual convenience and attractiveness... The passer-by on the Old Town Road near Grasmere lifts his eyes to the peaceful Villa Tocci, crowning its grassy slope, and instinctively feels a desire to have just such a home on just such a site." Other historic buildings however, have been met with the same fate. In 2017, Bayview Partners proposed constructing a 72-unit complex on an empty, grass lot at the end of Scarboro Avenue. In the same year, a developer purchased the grounds of the original Holy Rosary Church and the Dominic Epifanio Parish Center intending to construct residential housing. Many of Staten Island's parishes/churches would suffer under Cardinal Timothy Dolan's re-organization initiative "Making All Things New"—a program designed to save the Archdiocese of New York money by consolidating, merging, or even closing parishes. Victims of the plan included the Church of St. Roch and St. Mary of the Assumption in Port Richmond, Church of the Assumption in New Brighton, and the Church of St. Mary in Rosebank (which merged with neighboring St. Joseph's). St. Mary's, Staten Island's second-oldest Roman Catholic church, was constructed in 1857 in the North Italian Romanesque Style at 1101 Bay Street. Its first pastor was Rev. John Lewis, a native of Alsace-Lorraine, France, who arrived on the shores on Staten Island on October 2, 1852. The church is credited with establishing the first parish school in Richmond County in 1864; in 1867, the Sisters of Charity administered education at St. Mary's School located at 1124 Bay Street, and helped run the church's orphanage. The Sisters of Charity also founded St. Vincent's Hospital in West New Brighton, Bayley Seaton Hospital in Stapleton, and St. Joseph's by-the-Sea School in Annadale.

Extraordinary Italian residents of Rosebank/Clifton (excluding actor Gianni Russo who played Carlo Rizzi in *The Godfather*) whose actions would have far-reaching ramifications in the engineering and socio-political fields are also certainly to be mentioned—Antonio Meucci, the inventor of the telephone, and Giuseppe Garibaldi, the nationalist unifier of Italy. In April of 1850, Florentine Antonio Santi Giuseppe Meucci arrived on the shores of Staten Island along with his wife, Esther, and an ingenious mindset that would propel his application of fourteen U.S. patents and hundreds of revolutionary breakthroughs in the candle, culinary, telecommunications, filtration, ammunition, and energy industries. Beginning in 1860, Meucci established the New York Paraffin Candle Co.—a small enterprise, but nonetheless first of its kind, based on his previous filings of patents establishing the procedure of the manufacture of a sufficiently smooth and polished candle and a non-metallic mold. In his patent officially granted on January 25, 1859, Meucci states, "My invention consists in the method of forming mold candles by means of candle molds of a porous material saturated with a lubricating material, in contradistinction to the method now in general use of forming mold candles by means of candle molds of metal or other impervious material." For a brief period of time, before declaring bankruptcy only years later, the candle company produced over one-thousand candles per day, employing several Italian exiles including Giuseppe Garibaldi and Colonel Paolo Bovi Campeggi (an 1852-expatriated, armless engineer and military officer). Other employees included an Irishman, Pat Fitzpatrick, and Giovanni P. Morosini—cadet in the Austrian Navy, volunteer in the patriotic army when Italian rose in 1848, refugee after the fall of Venice, common sailor, resident of Riverdale, Bronx, Erie Railroad official, confidential secretary of railroad developer, Jay Gould, father of the 'best dressed woman in New York,' and foremost Italian in New York. The factory preserved a unique originality in Richmond County because of its manufacture of improved kerosene lamps, containing cognate oils rich in carbon, which did not emit any smoke. Later, in May of 1863, Meucci would also invent a new and improved procedure for the preparation of hydrocarbon liquids for paints. An 1864 advertisement from Rider & Clark Co. on 51 Broad Street in Manhattan for "Meucci's Patented Oil" would entail its recommendation as a "substitute for boiled oil…linseed oil for painting the outside of buildings, roofs, iron works, ships, etc., costing only half the price."

Giuseppe Garibaldi, rheumatism-ridden, found his job bringing barrels of tallow from Vanderbilt's Landing to the boiling vat at Meucci's factory to be extremely boring, disgusting, and useless. In his book *Garibaldi: Hero of Unification*, biographer Christopher Hibbert gives an account of Garibaldi's health and psychological condition while on Staten Island, writing, "he would sit in a corner of a room, almost forgotten, rarely speaking. Sometimes in the evenings he would go out for a game of bowls or to play dominoes at Ventura's café near the Park Theatre, but more often he stayed home." Hibbert also notes Garibaldi's travel from ship to ship at the Staten Island docks asking to find work. Even requesting to be brought on without pay as a sailor, Garibaldi was met with replies of silence and apathy. Finally, after a futile search, in April of 1951, Garibaldi embarked for Central America, having tired of his monotonous lifestyle—leaving Meucci to the confines of his Gothic-revival house and cornucopia of inventions. Only years earlier in 1849, administering a treatment to a patient suffering with a migraine in Havana, Cuba, Meucci experimented with the use of oral electrodes, connected to a power source, a Bunsen battery, observing an electrophonic effect. The groundbreaking discovery prompted Meucci to develop (thirty models of) the "Telettrofono," assembled with copper wire and paper. Trapped in his second-floor bedroom by his "invalid" wife suffering from rheumatism, Meucci had the opportunity to operate his new system; he did so by extending a link from the bedroom to his laboratory. By and large, Meucci's greatest invention would be that of the telephone; he was officially recognized as the inventor of the telephone in 2002 by the passing of House Resolution 269 by the 107th U.S. Congress proposed by Staten Island Representative, Vito Fossella (R-NY-13). Backed only by minimal finances, as well as an incredibly miniature legal team compared to industry giants such as Alexander Graham Bell, Antonio Meucci suffered countless defeats, closures, and enduring hardships. In 1860, his former candle factory, now owned by Matthew Carroll, would be destroyed by a horrific fire along with several adjoining buildings. On July 30, 1871, aboard the passenger ship *The Westfield* (termed the "The Vessel of Death"), designed to assist the Staten Island Ferry in accommodating afternoon traffic, Meucci suffered severe burns during a boiler explosion which would become known as the worst disaster in Staten Island Ferry history, injuring two-hundred and resulting in the death of 126 people. Meucci's and Garibaldi's contributions to Staten Island, particularly concerning industry, would be the first of their kind. In 1851, they opened Clifton Brewery—the first lager beer factory in the United States. Clifton Brewery would later be taken over by Bachmann's Brewery by Frederick Bachmann whose employees' transportation needs would propel the opening of Staten Island Railway station, "Bachmann," in 1886.

By 1884, all that remained of Meucci's once fairly-successful paraffin company was a mere furnace and caldron. On July 19, 1887, Judge William J. Wallace, Judge of the United States Circuit Court for the Second Circuit, appointed by President Chester Arthur in 1882, would render his opinion against Antonio Meucci in awarding the plaintiff in American Bell Telephone Co. vs. Globe Telephone Co.— dismantling Meucci's claim of having invented the telephone first. On October 18, 1889, after having suffered through a dangerous illness, Meucci would pass away as the most unrecognized genius in American history. His home of nearly forty years would be preserved by the Garibaldi Society until 1919, when it would be transferred to the Order of the Sons of Italy in America. In 1980, the site's first chairperson Vincent Polimeni—Treasurer of the Richmond County Republicans, member of the Giuseppe Mazzini Lodge No. 137, and member of the Staten Island Chapter of Cooley's Anemia Foundation—would, with the assistance of Senator John Marchi help get the Garibaldi-Meucci Museum on the U.S. National Register of Historic Places. During his tenure, Polimeni would host several Italian presidents and prime ministers at the museum, including 1983-1987-serving P.M. Bettino Craxi, 1978-1985-serving President Sandro Pertini, and 1981-1982-serving P.M. Giovanni Spadolini. For his "commitment to the community and for disseminating the Italian language and culture in [the United States]," Polimeni would be awarded the Leonardo Covello Education Award from the American Association of Teachers of Italian in New York in July of 1985. He would also officially receive the title of a "Cavaliere" (a knight) by the Italian Government in December of 1984. The officers of the Order of Sons of Italy in America today seek to preserve Garibaldi and Meucci's legacy, and educate Staten

Island residents in the Italian language and Italian traditions. The site would also be the gathering place of the Italian Rifle Society (many members of which would be brutally pummeled and clubbed while celebrating Garibaldi's birthday in 1930 by a gang of "Industrial Workers of the World" members).

Other organizations on Staten Island continue to cultivate

[Vincent Polimeni mows the lawn of the Garibaldi-Meucci Museum on a summer afternoon. C. 1980s. Courtesy – Maria Marchiano]

and maintain Italian culture in the United States such as The Italian-American Women of Staten Island, as well as the Italian Club of Staten Island Foundation Incorporated. The former club is derived from the American Committee on Italian Migration, but focuses solely on matters concerning Staten Island; the club has implemented several beneficial programs, and hosts events highlighting inspirational speakers such as Matilda Cuomo—the wife of the former New York State governor Mario Cuomo. Paula

Caglianone—former president of the Italian-American Women (IAW) and board member of the I.A.W. of Staten Island—explained, "The group gives people a chance to talk about the culture, educate other people, and figure out ways to make it more prominent in the lives of Italian-Americans. Some of these traditions include going to dinner every Sunday at 2pm, celebrating 'La Befana' (an Italian folk tale that tells story of an old women who delivers gifts to children while looking for the Baby Jesus) and keeping recipe books with dishes made from past 'nonnas' (Italian grandmothers)." The Italian Club of Staten Island Foundation Inc. serves a similar purpose: to raise money to improve the quality of life for residents of the community. The club was formed in 1950 by a group of Staten Island business and professional men of Italian origin lead by Daniel Santoro, and had an initial focus of that of a fraternal/civic organization; the "club" since became the Foundation in 1985, and is now a 501C3 organization and member of the Staten Island Not for Profit Association. The foundation's members, many of whom for well-over twenty years, are truly well-respected and recognized on Staten Island due to their response to an individual or family in need of financial aid or counsel. The foundation has two main projects: the Annual Food Drive Project (since 1984 – delivers food cartons between Thanksgiving and Christmas to Staten Island families in need; besides raising the necessary funds ranging from $8,000-$10,000, members do the shipping, packing, and delivery of the goods) and the Annual Scholarship Awards Project (since 1991 – gives qualified students scholarships upon their submission of both scholastic and personal information; approximate funds needed range between $8,000-$10,000 and are raised through annual membership dues, event donations, and net profit from the organization's main fundraiser 'The Annual Honorees Dinner Dance'). In addition to these projects, the foundation also supports the Staten Island Save a Heart Foundation, Staten Island

Leukemia Foundation, and countless other programs which support the well-being of both New York and American citizens; furthermore, the foundation has shown its support for the cultivation of Italian culture in America by supporting the Aurora program which teaches Italian culture and language to grammar school-age children. The earliest Italian culture-promoting organizations on Staten Island, however, can be traced back to the days of the Italian-American Civil Rights League which rented space on the ground floor of 116 St. Marys Ave. The property was owned by Peter Castelli (b. Jun. 1916)—the owner of Pioneer Radio & TV on Bay St. (described by his grandson, lawyer Howard F. Murphy of Pittsburgh, Penn. as "a one-man welcoming committee for any Italian immigrant who relocated into [Rosebank]... who'd fix your TV whether you could pay or not"). The IACRL began as the Italian-American Anti-Defamation League in the late-1960s with the goal of "[preventing] Italian-Americans as a group from being stigmatized by negative stereotypes linking them to criminal organizations such as the Mafia." Among its accomplishments included its campaigning to have Italian taught in the New York City school system. A prominent figure within the organization was Joseph Colombo Sr.—the head of the Colombo Family who created the IACRL in spring of 1970. The IACRL Staten Island location held annual summer camps for neighborhood children and helped promote community among residents. The space was later rented out by Rosebank Youth & Parents.

The inconspicuous streets of Rosebank once boasted dozens of Italian family-owned businesses (e.g. Magnotti's, Marino Foods, DeSantis Candy, DeCataldo's, Scaramuzzo's, V. Moschella's, Romolo's), in addition to a plethora of Italian households whose remnants were transformed into reconfigured apartments and single-family residences. To a certain degree, the term "native Staten Islander" calls to mind a set of early to mid-20th century decades in which charity and diligence reigned supreme. Among the strict, disciplined Italian households of the 1920s-1930s was the Tucciarone family who resided at several locations across Rosebank: Hylan Blvd., Tompkins Ave., and St. Marys Ave. John Tucciarone and his wife Josephine Brocato settled in Rosebank in 1920, one year before getting married. Tucciarone hailed from the town of Latina, Lazio (south of Rome), while Brocato (a relative of Angelo Brocato's with the Italian Ice Cream and Pastry shop in New Orleans) was from Cefalù, Palermo, Sicily. When Tucciarone's brother sent for John, and Brocato's sister sent for her in the United States, the two families lived next door to each other on Maryland Ave. The couple married in 1921 and had nine children. Daughter Theresa Csorba recalled, "My father was a hard, hard worker! He was a concrete worker by trade and helped construct the George Washington Bridge across the Hudson. When the Depression hit in the 1930s, he helped build the original New Dorp High School! And in those days, you couldn't afford to be lazy; they had a social worker checking to see if you were doing your job!...Later on, my father would work at the Richmond Gas Co.[28] He would get himself up at three in the morning to make gas for the Island. When my father worked at the New York City Farm Colony, the patients there used to make and would give him handmade wooden ladles, cutting knives, and cooking spoons!" Around 1928-1929, Tucciarone and his wife owned and operated a small vegetable and produce store on Hylan Blvd.; despite leaving the business, Tucciarone maintained a vast garden behind his home, growing corn, Swiss chard, tomatoes, etc. Csorba continued, "My parents were immensely generous. They would pick and give some of our crops to the neighbors who came by. They especially loved when my mother made 'American Bread'—white

---

[28] In 1957, the Richmond Gas Co., which served all of Staten Island, was acquired by the Brooklyn Union Gas Co. by CEO John Heyke.

bread...People helped each other back then! It was a different time...My father made sure to keep all of us in line at all times, however! When we lived over on Tompkins Ave., we lived in a four-family dwelling with strictly girls on one side of the building, and boys on the other. Whenever they were in the front or back we weren't allowed, or vice-versa. We did manage though sometimes to meet in the hallways! And you had to go to Mass every single Sunday; if you were a perpetual absentee, you couldn't go downstairs to dinner. You could only come down to help clean up, and then were sent back up! We never were hungry or filthy. Before dinners, my father would have us put our hands in the air to make sure we had thoroughly washed both sides." The Tucciarone family lived at 103 St. Marys, and then at 99, by the old railroad tracks. The house at 99 St. Marys Ave. before their move-in was occupied by Rosario Marrusso (later known as "Sonny Mars")—the music teacher at PS 18, but more notably, the piano player in *The Godfather*. Theresa's sister Viola described, "hearing him practicing playing the piano at midnight!" Across the street from the house at number 100 was Ignazio Rosso's dress manufacturing company (at which two of the Tucciarone sisters worked, making better-grade dresses), formerly the Staten Island Macaroni Corp.[29] Among the Tuccarione sisters' fondest memories of growing up in old Italian Rosebank were going to Sparandera's Bakery on Bay St. in Clifton, getting either a birthday cake or the whipped cream cake with peaches and bananas; a favorite of Viola's was going to the bakery in the afternoon and buying a large bag of stale morning buns for just ten cents. Other memories include pooling the pennies from all the poor neighborhood kids and going to Magnotti's bakery to purchase bread, as well as parading the statue of Our Lady of Mount Carmel during the Feast. Viola reminisced, "During Christmas time in Rosebank, my mother would go to the rectory at St. Joseph's Church and make zeppole! My mother was a great cook...She used to make escarole, lentils, spinach with potatoes, macaroni, pasta e fagioli, *pupo* (octopus), and fried

[The set of buildings on the one-hundred block of St. Marys Ave. owned by Ignazio Rosso. C. early-1900s. Courtesy – Phil Rosso]

dough balls stuffed with anchovies or baccala." While Viola remained in Rosebank, Theresa moved first to Auburn Ave. and then to Gansevoort Blvd. in Manor Heights. Theresa recalled, "In the early 1950s, we

---

[29] Ignazio Rosso (b. 1871) was a relative of Jack Rosso's who owned Jack's Italian-American Self Service Grocery at 415 Jersey Street. Ignazio Rosso was the owner of the Staten Island Macaroni Corp. at 100 St. Marys Ave. (building constructed in 1917) as well as an Italian bread bakery "Panetteria Italiana" at 108 St. Marys Ave. The building where the dress factory was located also housed Randazzo's Printing & Gun Store on the first floor.

had policemen mounted on horses, not in patrol cars. The policeman would come on his horse daily and hitch it across the street from my home so he could go make his rounds. He'd usually go to The Gay Manor bar and get drunk! At 5pm, the horse would just leave by itself and head back to Moore's Stables on Clove Rd. It was so funny seeing that horse walk by our house everyday." Reflecting on the bygone days, Theresa concluded, "I distinctly remember after midnight mass at St. Joseph's, everyone we knew would walk directly to our home. Of course, none of our doors were locked...if there's one thing that I miss most about old Rosebank, it's that freedom of not having to lock your doors. You don't have that anymore..." Similar to the ritiuals of the Tucciarone family, Rose Nazzaro-Paterno (b. 1923) was raised enjoying life's simple pleasures in old Rosebank. Her parents, Rose and Edward Nazzaro both emigrated from Italy, and "provided a happy home for [their] children." One of Nazarro's brothers worked for Merritt, Chapman, & Scott off Hylan Blvd. as a diver's tender, while her other brother worked for the Staten Island Rapid Transit in their offices in Tompkinsville (another brother also worked in construction). Growing up, before being employed at an artificial flower factory in Manhattan with her sister, Nazzaro-Paterno enjoyed going to the playground on Tompkins Ave. and playing jacks (a competitive activity at the time), getting taught to make items from raffia from the teachers at PS 13, and going to the Quarantine to fish. "We would have a bamboo stick fishing pole, and our bait would be a paste of flour and water" Rose exclaimed, "You would be surprised how many fish were caught with that bait! My brothers would also cast crab pots and catch a lot of crabs! It seems as if my mother was always cooking either fish or crabs."

"The day they changed the zoning laws, replaced all my childhood treasures with strip malls, and put three homes where there should've only been one, Staten Island was

[Gati's aunt and a fellow employee pose in front of Sparandera's Bakery at 979 Bay St. in Clifton. C. 1940s. Courtesy – Peter Gati]

ruined. And it will never be able to go back to the way it was." Peter Gati—a native of Rosebank—was born and raised till the age of six on 50 Fletcher St., before moving to Fox Hills in 1948. Gati's grandparents Peter and the former, Josephine Inzerillo emigrated from the outskirts of Palermo and Naples, respectively. Gati elaborated, "My grandmother and her sister came to the United States from Naples in the early-1900s unaccompanied. There's a story that either my great-aunt or my grandmother killed the man who had raped them in Italy, and then they fled." Inzerillo and Gati settled initially in East Harlem, near Pleasant Ave. During this period, Gati worked on the tunnels stretching across the Hudson, installing tile. Staten Island, however, was not the couple's initial, ideal destination. Gati had purchased property in Metuchen, N.J., alongside the train tracks, where he cultivated an apple orchard, harvesting the apples during their propitious season. Due to state taxes which made retaining possession of the property difficult, Gati ultimately came to Rosebank, obtaining the deed to 50 and 54 Fletcher St. The family lived in tight quarters: 50 Fletcher—a once entirely white stucco dwelling—housed seven people, while the smaller home next door housed six. At 48 Fletcher, Volpe the Italian ragman resided. His cries could be heard throughout the year: "Rags! Rags! Any rags?" At 54 Fletcher, the Sparanderas (the proprietors of the bakery on Bay St.) lived. And at 62 Fletcher, Fusco's Bakery and grocery carved out an existence in a quaintly small storefront, identified by its large display window. The Gati household accomdated various aunts, uncles, children, and of course Peter Gati's father, Carlo. Carlo held several titles over the course of his life: baker at Sparandera's, longshoreman, and master sergeant. He was also a part-owner of Veterans Taxi of Stapleton, and had before going into baking, worked at a farm on Rossville Ave. on the South Shore. Gati explained, "In the army, my father—a baker—was in charge of a divisional bakery, a mess hall which was responsible for the nutrition of thousands of servicemen. Before he was sent to Calcutta, India to fight in the China/Burma/India Theatre in East Asia, my father, stationed in Boston, was requested by the General to bake his wedding cake. My father baked him a Boston Cream Pie. When the war concluded and returned to his employment at Sparandera's, my father baked the first Boston Cream Pie on Staten Island! And the bakery became famous for it...In fact, I also had another family member, Aunt Gustie, who worked at Sparandera's, behind the counter. She was a German war bride who married my uncle Sammy in 1946!" In fact, the Gati family has a substantial connection with the armed forces. Gati continued, "My uncle Vincent "Jimmy" Gatti was stationed in the 49-51 years in Panama with Joe Scaramuzzo—the owner of Scaramuzzo's Funeral Home on St. Marys Ave. I remember the day they came back home from the war very fondly. My father and I were waiting in the car at the corner of Vanderbilt Ave. and Tompkins Ave. As soon as we saw the bus, we pulled forward and kept honking the horn to alert the bus driver. We picked Joe and Jimmy up, and took them back home to Rosebank. They were lifelong friends...In fact, Scaramuzzo and my uncle often went to Fort Lauderdale to go fishing!...I remember having occasional sleep-overs at the funeral parlor, as well. I distinctly remember, one night when I was

[Laura and Josephine DeSantis in their establishment, DeSantis Candy Store at 172 St. Marys Ave. C. Oct. 1984. Courtesy – Peter Gati]

maybe seven or eight, I wanted to go use the bathroom downstairs. Someone had left the casket open! It scared the living daylights out of me!" "The center of the neighborhood was the Rosebank Cardinals Club (the site of the original Labetti Post), a social/fraternal association on the corner of Fletcher and St. Marys" Gati explained, "I never remember going in there and not seeing those guys playing cards! One time, I actually got to sit next to my uncle and hold his money. Even at home, playing cards was how we entertained ourselves. I remember always playing twenty-one. My uncles used to quibble over pennies and dimes! Besides playing cards, on Saturday mornings, everyone in Rosebank would watch cowboy movies! That's how my uncle Frank got his nickname "Hoppy," after Hopalong Cassidy." Among Gati's memories of growing up in the Italian heyday were walking to DeSantis Candy Store, buying penny candy and candied wax bottles, as well as sneaking into the garden of the house behind the Garibaldi-Meucci Museum and stealing tomatoes. Mr. Harry Singer, the Jewish traveling salesman, would come by homes in the springtime with two

230

to three suitcases, convincing residents to purchase a set of curtains. As he came by each house, Italian women would prepare a fresh-brew of coffee, conversing as they scanned his products. Throughout the year, Gati recalled taking shots of his uncle's homemade anisette liquor, in addition to drinking wine aged in barrels beneath the ground. Gati remarked, "If the wine went bad, it just became wine vinegar. We'd put that on our salads! And we never ate our salads before the meal, always after...My grandmother was an extremely talented cook. She'd make sausage, meatballs, and pork ribs with tomato sauce. Sometimes, she'd cook eggplant or go to Magnotti's Bakery and buy some pizza dough to make the Sicilian Square Pie. I have a distinct image of her always hunched over the stove!...You couldn't walk into any house in Rosebank without some lady shouting *Mangia! Mangia!* (Eat, Eat!). On the other hand, if you did something stupid, you couldn't go anywhere without some person calling you a *stunad* (an idiot). The old Italian ladies in Rosebank were difficult to evade; there was always one widow peering inconspicuously out of the window." Through time, the neighborhood has faced several changes, for better or for worse. Gati recalled at 54 Fletcher St.—the property adjacent to his childhood home, owned by his family—putting wood into the cast iron stove, and witnessing the operation of a kerosene heater. At nighttime, the three cats possessed by Gati's Aunt Rose would hide behind the cast iron stove to keep warm; one cat, Aunt Rose trained to use the toilet. Asides from cats, Gati's uncle kept a turkey in a cage in the alleyway which separated the two properties. Gati stated, "The turkey became my personal pet. It used to chase me around...we had a lot of fun. Thanksgiving of 1948, I walked into the dining room for the feast and my entire family was looking at me. I asked, 'Where's Gobble Gobble?' Nobody ate the turkey that evening.' That year, my family had moved to Fox Hills. As a master sergeant, my father didn't have to sleep in the

231

barracks, but had a private residence in which we all lived. Even after I moved, I would still walk over the old wooden bridge on Chestnut Ave. which connected Fox Hills to White Plains Ave. It's the little things like that I miss. I could talk and talk all day, but it would still be impossible to comprehend what a wonderful upbringing I had."

"There's really something special to be said about these men that got together, simply out of friendship, and wanted to do a wonderful thing for their community." Joyce Burns, a lifelong Rosebank resident, was the granddaughter of Thomas Tedesco—one of the four main builders of the Our Lady of Mount Carmel Shrine: Umberto Somma, Angelo Madrazzo "Mr. Maderantes," and Vito "Freedman" Russo (Vincent Lupoli also painted figures on the apse's walls, which no longer exist). Thomas played not only a key role in the prominent shrine's design and construction, but also the Grotto of Our Lady of Fatima and the crucifix on the side of the main shrine; Tedesco is credited with bringing back the fountain, located in the forefront of the Our Lady of Mount Carmel Grotto today. Burns noted, "My grandfather also did a mini version of the grotto in our backyard!" Tedesco was born on 15 Fletcher St. across the street from the Rosebank Cardinals Club, on Sept. 15, 1907. His parents Giuseppe J. Tedesco and Elvira J. Scala were natives of Salerno, and were among few who immigrated directly to Staten Island. Upon exiting the Rosebank Quarantine,[30] the couple "liked what they saw," and settled down. They had brought with them two children to the United States, and then later bore ten more—Thomas among them. At the age of twenty-three, Tedesco married his wife Gertrude

---

[30] The Rosebank Quarantine Hospital, located on Bay St. & Nautilus St., was established in 1873, acquired by the U.S. government in 1921, and was ultimately evacuated in 1971. The history of quarantining on Staten Island goes back to 1799, when the N.Y. State Legislature relocated the Quarantine Establishment of the Port of New York from Governor's Island to St. George/Tompkinsville.

Greffrath—a sixteen-year old escapee from the Bethlehem Home in Grasmere—who he met while she was playing softball. Tedesco's first employment was at the Fox Hills Golf Course in the 1900s, as a caddie; he was among those privileged with witnessing the golf course's transformation into a silent movie studio, and later a U.S. Army Base. While in the Works Progress Administration (WPA), Tedesco assisted in the landfill of once-separate islands to create Battery Park in lower Manhattan. Burns also recalled discovering large wrenches in the basement years after her grandfather's passing; she learned her grandfather had also taken part in the installation of steam pipes in the N.Y.C. steam system. In keeping with the labor-centric spirit, Tedesco also drove ice trucks for the Silver Lake Ice Co. and movd to Long Island to continue driving ice trucks for companies out there. Upon his marriage, Tedesco eventually began a forty-two-year career as a building engineer at Louis DeJonge & Co.[31] where he ensured Number 6 Fuel Oil was baked properly to prevent the boilers from exploding. Burns explained, "We still have 19th century wash basin pottery, which used to hold acid, my grandfather used from Louis DeJonge & Co....The whole neighborhood used to have such a rich cultural, industrial heritage. In fact, on Chestnut Ave. at White Plains Ave., was the site of the original Bachmann's Brewery fermentation tunnels. All those homes currently seen on the property have dirt, and entryways into the cobblestone tunnels which contain hooks on the ceiling used to hang beer barrels; to date, the underground cobblestone tunnels still remain." Burns described in vivid detail the personalities and establishments which once defined Rosebank's very existence: DeSimone's Butcher Shop, Johnny Rumolo (the "mayor" who knew everyone and everything happening on the block), D. Fontana & Sons

---

[31] Remnants of the paper mill today are found in the bathroom of Our Lady of Mount Carmel Hall on Amity St. where the black wallpaper teems with swans.

Scrap Metal, and V. Moschella's Market. "As the youngest child in my household, I used to have to go Vicenz' [Moschella] down the street to buy my Aunt Carol a six-pack of Schaeffer beer, and a pack of cigarettes. What kid today would ever be sold a six pack and cigarettes?" Burns continued, "I'll always remember the first time I got intoxicated in my teens. The morning after, at 7am on Sunday, my grandpa came over to my bedside and hit his hand smack hard against my bed board, instantly awakening me. He said, "So, you're a big person now? Grandma told me you came home drunk! ... My punishment was to make the gravy and roll the meatballs. It lasted all day. I was so green I wanted to vomit everywhere! 'You want to drink again?' my grandpa told me at the end of the night." Her reply was simply "no." Among Burns' fondest memories of old, Italian Rosebank were of the Italian ice cream man, various humorous incidents involving the construction of the shrine, and hearing stories from her grandfather. Tedesco kept a 125 lb. Alaskan Malamute in his front yard on White Plains Ave. at which adults often crossed to the other side of the street simply to avoid. The ice cream man, "Butchie" Pucciarelli would fill up a double-scoop, broken ice cream cone in the back of his truck, and throw the ice cream in the air. Burns remarked, "No matter how he threw it, our dog would jump into the air and eat it whole every time...My grandfather was the funniest man. When he was telling us stories of building the shrine on Amity St., a co-laborer brought in some homemade wine which my grandfather found to be on the rancid side. Just to make it palatable, he had to add several spoons of sugar. Without realizing its potency, my grandfather and everyone else got wasted, so much so that they could barely stand. Upon attempting to create a cement piece on top of which would be inscribed, "St. Anthony Bless Us," the men broke the mold three times. And when they finally got it right, they had written the S's backward. Their mistake is entirely visible today!... Asides from getting in a good laugh, my grandfather loved telling ghost stories. He always told one of walking home late at night back from the shrine with Vito "Freedman" Russo[32] and saying hello to an old Italian lady on her porch. This one evening, they were walking home and said hello to the woman when they realized she had already passed away, in my grandfather's language, 'Freedman went flying across the street from one sidewalk to the other sidewalk!' And it's from my grandpa that I got my love for horror today." Tedesco learned the art of scrollwork used on the shrine from Vito Russo, and helped build the shrine made of cinderblock, exteriorly covered by cement. Naturally, Tedesco and Vito Russo's son Mickey also designed a multitude of floats paraded down the streets during the annual feast. Burns concluded, "The neighborhood used to be so warm, yet at times strict. I can recall a time where Msgr. Villani slapped someone across the face for not answering the confirmation questions correctly. He left his fingerprints on his cheeks! ... It was great in Rosebank when I was a kid. I also can't recall a day when I wasn't sent out to play. Even in the wintertime, my grandma told me, 'Go get your cheeks rosy!' But what I'll always remember most was those traveling salesmen that used to come around the neighborhood. I'd be doing my homework and my grandmother would be enjoying some Holtermann's coffee cake and coffee with Mr. Singer or Mr. Joseph at the table. I never understood how these guys made any money! They just talked all day to all the women in Rosebank!"

---

[32] Uniquely enough, most individuals in Rosebank had various nicknames. Vito "Freedman" Russo, had bore a son—James, nicknamed "Dick Tracy." Thomad Tedesco was also called Marsie or Mazzie.

The first of the Scaramuzzo's—Antonio Scaramuzzo and his wife Philomina Pomargo—came to Rosebank in 1880; the family's lineage can be traced back to the town of Auletta, Campania. For about six generations, the family has made its roots deep into the area's culture, businesses, and society. Joseph F. Scaramuzzo[33] (1907-1960), president of the Holy Name Society and resident of 223 Clifton Ave., started Scaramuzzo's Funeral Home, located originally at 119 St. Marys Ave., in April of 1928. The funeral home (having already relocated to 160 St. Marys Ave. at the corner of Tompkins Ave.), characterized by the two white crosses on each entryway window on either side of the front door, existed in an era when the current St. Joseph's Church building at 171 St. Marys Ave. was simply an empty, gravel lot, covered by dried grass, and bordered by a rustic, wooden picket fence on its west side. The burgundy brick, three-story building constructed in 1931, for roughly twenty years housed the funeral parlor which was the center of neighborhood congregation. Rosebank native Cathy Pucciarelli recalled, "Scaramuzzo's had the only TV in the entire neighborhood! In the late-1940s and early-1950s, Joe would invite all the kids from the area in to watch an episode of Howdy Doody. He was also quite wealthy,

[Joseph L. Scaramuzzo (left) and Joseph F. Scarmuzzo (right). C. About 1940. Courtesy – Shay La Scalla]

---

[33] Though Joseph F. ran the home mostly by himself, his wife Christina Cosozello (m. Oct. 21, 1928) contributed by applying make-up to the deceased females.

so he would also occasionally take the Rosebank kids to a Yankees game!" Joe, though his last name would forever come to be associated with funeral arrangements in the decades to come, in reality, was initially employed at Bethlehem Steel in Port Richmond. After having grown tired of the manual labor required for to fulfill his tasks, Scaramuzzo craved "something different." In the early-1920s, he attended American Academy McAllister Institute—a top mortuary school—on 54th St. in Manhattan. In paying his way through school, Scaramuzzo retained in mind his desire to establish something which would be beneficial to the community—one where he could assist the grieving and suffering by providing excellent and often, discounted service. Scaramuzzo's grandson Michael explained, "My father knew that if someone couldn't afford the necessary funeral preparations, he would do the best he could anyway. After all, death confronted everyone, even the poorest in Rosebank. In those days, due to tradition, the women stayed at home while the men worked; if no work was to be found, then debt and misery infested every aspect of a household's existence. When the elders were ill or near-death, Monsignors John Villani and Anthony Catoggio came to each home to perform the Anointing of the Sick. Before departing, they placed a small sum of money on the family's kitchen countertop as alms to assist in the purchasing of groceries or other necessities. I remember: my father in Scaramuzzo's basement used to keep several long, three-inch, black leather books filled with hundreds of yellow pages. In each page were dozens of names, listed alphabetically, written in the finest cursive handwriting; the names were those embalmed by Scaramuzzo's, alongside cemetery plot listings. Scattered throughout, some names had a "+5" or "+10" scribbled next to them. Those were indicative of the money my father received from that deceased person's family after the embalmed had already been laid into the ground. If the family could not afford the arrangements, sometimes in the future, they would come by and hand my father a five or ten-dollar bill. He'd open up the book and write the money collected in that sitting." A noted "client" of the home was Mickey Cangro (1903-1929), a local boxing hero, who had passed "after contracting an infection from giving blood to his ailing sister." An article from the *Staten Island Advance* described a procession of "twenty limousines, politicians, and friends of the boxer." Scaramuzzo's was at the time of Joseph's death, taken over by his son Joseph L (1930-1998). Joseph L, nicknamed "Scoots," shortly after the change-of-ownership, went to a restaurant supply outlet on Canal St. in the City, and turned the funeral home into Tompkins Luncheonette; the establishment offered chips, candy, newspapers[34], lottery tickets, chocolate egg creams, ice cream floats, a soda bar, and a deli. Among its unique features was the large, expansive countertop atop which patrons enjoyed the store's specialties, in particular the bacon, egg, and cheese sandwich with coffee which some customers referred to as

[Joseph L. Scaramuzzo (left) rings up a customer, Bonnie DeFilippo (right) at his luncheonette in Rosebank. Courtesy – Shay La Scalla]

Bonnie DeFilippo hopes it's her lucky day as she purchases a lottery ticket from Joseph Scaramuzzo, proprietor of Scoot's Luncheonette, Rosebank.

---

34 Newspapers sold ranged from local publications (e.g. The New York Times, The New York Post) to Italian newspapers such as Il Progresso Italo-Americano (in circulation from 1880-1988), to serve Rosebank's substantial Italian community.

"the best sandwich in town." *Staten Island Advance* journalist Geoffrey Mohan paints a nostalgic picture of old Rosebank, particularly with regards to Tompkins Luncheonette: asides from the shrine dedicated to Our Lady of Mount Carmel, "there [were] the less impressive, but equally interesting "landmarks." Mr. Bundo's cows. Carmine Lenzo's rooster. Everyone's pigeons. "Old man" Pellegrini coming in to the luncheonette to get his Italian military pension forms notarized, verifying he was still alive (Tell 'em I'm still here, Joe"). Luncheonette grew to be a neighborhood hangout—a vibrant corner spot—in which a kid could go in at anytime of day and recognize everyone inside. During this period, "Scoots" continued his funeral practice at A. Azzara Funeral Home at 183 Sand Lane in Arrochar where he had his license. Though Scaramuzzo's food-service operation was ultimately dismantled in 1994 ("Scoots" having retired at the age of sixty-four), the current store, Corner Stop, which fills its place, still carries on in a similar line of work. Describing the nostalgia for the old St. Marys Ave. and vanished traditions of antique America, Mike Scaramuzzo stated, "The whole neighborhood was different. On St. Joseph's Day, I remember parading a gigantic flag of the Holy Family through the streets of Rosebank. The Italian ladies used to pin money to it; by the time the procession had finished, the entire flag was covered from end-to-end with bills. And in Catholic school, it felt more like a military academy. I have a specific recollection of Monsignor Villani at St. Joseph's reading over each student's report card; he never paid attention to our marks in math, English, spelling, etc., but in *conduct*." "Rosebank was a very small, but quaint community," Scaramuzzo continued. "As a delivery boy for the *Staten Island Advance*, where each copy (excluding the higher-priced Sunday paper) sold for ten cents and weekly subscriptions for a dollar-ten, I remember going into people's homes and smelling the sweet scents of

239

peppers, onions, and tomato sauce. The Torricelli [35] household, I distinctly recall smelling like a restaurant. During the holiday season, I would receive $10 in a sealed envelope; the money I earned I applied toward a car...My family—the Scaramuzzo's—was blessed with a relatively good income. But the earnings didn't come without labor. On Saturday mornings, I would have to get up with my father at three-thirty a.m. to put the inserts into the newspapers. When I finally grew up, my father looked at me and said, 'Mike: get yourself a city job, get a pension, and get a life." Scaramuzzo's granddaughter Shay La Scalla remarked, "Having a life of my own now, I often think of how [my grandfather] was able to own a home, keep it together all the time, six children, up at four or five to open the luncheonette, home at 11pm, still have time to keep the house and pool clean and running smooth, *and* direct funerals. One man, a hundred jobs, yet he never complained. He always taught us when and how to do things without being frustrated...He was the only father I ever knew, and I am who I am because he was a father to me, in Rosebank!"

Carlo Sorrentino (1877-1941), Italian immigrant and entrepreneur of old Rosebank, was recognized by his friends, neighbors, and associates as among the most influential people in pre-1940 Rosebank society. Sorrentino was the chief force behind the building of the first St. Joseph's Church, Rosebank, in 1901; he owned the properties of 162-166 St. Marys Ave and several others east of Tompkins Ave. He even operated his hardware store "C. Sorrentino General Supply Store – Hardware & Auto Accessories" at 488 Tompkins Ave. (the green-painted building immediately south of the old Scaramuzzo's Funeral Home). Carlo's sister

---

[35] The Torricelli family of Rosebank boasts ancestry to Evangelista Torricelli (1608-1647)—the Italian-born inventor of the mercury barometer. Family member Donato "Dennis" Torricelli Sr. (1920-2007) was commemorated for his involvement with the East Shore Little League by the renaming of Summer St. which runs perpendicular to Lyman Ave.

Concetta, nineteen years his senior, along with her husband Antonio Rolando, owned a property at 60 St. Marys Ave. constructed in 1910. Though the property today has seen some needed renovation, it was once a brown shingle shack, inhabited by eight people on the second floor, with an old-fashioned heater and an architectural design in which later years the floors tilted downward when walking into the kitchen. Hot water came from boiling water on the coal stove

and poured into a basin for washing and showering. The Sorrentino's hailed from Cava de' Tirreni in Sorrento (hence, their surname – a demonym for those in the region), while the Rolando's came from Salerno. In the late-1890s, Carlo Sorrentino immigrated to the United States. From the mid to late-1920s, he operated his hardware store. The store sold dry goods, toys, dolls, model cars, chandeliers, antiques, auto accessories, rocking chairs, and more. Some alive during those days would have also recalled vats of kerosene for sale outside. An antiquated photograph depicts the middle-aged Carlo in his black, button-up suit, tie, and fedora leaning against the side of the display window. A series of chandeliers line the ceiling, and knick-knacks displayed are quite typical of this intriguing era in New York history. According to the photograph's caption, the store was

[The store of Carlo Sorrentino at 488 Tompkins Ave. C. 1933. Courtesy – Carmen Sorrentino-Higgins]

241

sold on Saturday, Sept. 3, 1933 to a gentleman by the name of William J. Orlando. Financially-ruined during the days of the Great Depression and Prohibition, Sorrentino found himself gambling more and womanizing, and possibly bootlegging. Though his intentions remain unclear, jugs of liquor discovered past a trap door at 60 St. Marys Ave (where Carlo resided downstairs) hint at a scandalous past. Joan Priola, a native of Oxford, North Carolina who later moved to Rosebank, further described an incident which occurred in 1924 in which her grandfather was stabbed during a card game outside the household, and her uncle, who had a gun in his pocket, shot the perpetrator. Her uncle was released on "self-defense." Furthermore, Sorrentino's nephew, Anthony also detailed an incident in which at the age of nine, he was asked to bring some food for Carlo to his apartment downstairs and found his uncle with a non-fatal bullet wound in his chest. Carlo's grief stemmed from bank failure and loan defaults, which resulted from his tenents inability to pay their rent due to the recessive circumstances and possibly having been jilted by a woman he loved. It is believed his incident with a bullet in his chest may have possibly been a suicide attempt; years later in 1941, Sorrentino asphyxiated himself by inserting his head into the oven. The family had always struggled to make ends meet. In the 1930s, Carlo's sister Concetta sold apple pies and bread from a window on her porch. Before her death in 1945, possibly from dementia, neighbors in the late-1930s recalled her throwing feral kittens into pots of boiling water when they annoyed her. In the late-1930s, the household underwent a generation change, and Thomas Sorrentino, along with his wife Madeline Rolando assumed "control." Thomas—a tailor by trade—owned a small shop in the 1930s and 40s at 17 St. Marys Ave. At a young age, his son Anthony frequently worked alongside his father until starting his fifty-eight year career at Fort Wadsworth as a civilian government worker. Anthony's daughter Carmen S.

Higgins remarked, "My grandparents were the kindest people I knew. I remember bringing food to an elderly Black lady, presumably named "Mabel," who lived in a shack in the backyard at the house at 60 St. Marys Ave. We knew nothing about her, who she was...there wasn't even running water in the shed! I could only imagine how she got in there. My grandmother welcomed everyone with open arms! ... I'll never forget her Easter Grain Pie, Sunday sauce, or homemade raviolis. She used to lay them down on a big white sheet on the bed to dry. We poked them with our fingers, knowing little about how much work she had put in to make them. Sometimes I wish I could just walk the streets of Rosebank in the 1920s, just to see the world in which my grandparents lived!"

That world, as fondly described by Sorrentino, is further illustrated by Mr. Frank Martucci (b. 1950)—a longtime Rosebank business owner and native of the neighborhood."I can remember The Elegants (lead by Vito Picone) rehearsing in the empty lot[36] at the corner of Clifton Ave. & Tompkins Ave.!" Martucci reminiscned. Martucci was born the grandson of a stonemason Sicilian immigrant; his great-uncle operated Martucci Carting in Bay Ridge, Brooklyn. His grandfather grew up at the corner of Clifton Ave. & Fox Hills Terr., and had nine children. Martucci, who grew up directly across the street from Paul Parlamenti's Candy Store, is remembered by many Rosebankers for his owning of "Rosebank Bakery" [1978] at 511 Tompkins Ave., which later became "Martucci's Deli" the next year. "I bought the store from the Italian owner of the fish store which used to be right next to the bakery. All the other deli owners told me I would have to make everything fresh – the potato salads, the prepared foods, the roast beef, etc. So, that's what I did"

---

[36] This empty lot (529 Tompkins Ave.), currently occupied by Pizza Mia Restaurant, was once the site of J. Russo General Blacksmith in thr 1920s/30s. The blacksmith was owned by John Russo (b. 1875), a resident of 219 Clifton Ave., who described his profession in the 1920 Census as a "Wagon Maker."

Asides from serving delightful sandwiches, Martucci's Deli would raffle off an "Easter Basket" annually, filled with an assorted array of Italian products. A 1983 edition of the *Staten Island Advance* depicts "Michael Parisi" as the winner "as chosen by Frank Martucci's son, Michael." In 1986, Martucci sold the business to three individuals, two of whom were Bobby DeSantis and Eddy Porto (employed beforehand at Montalbano's on Bay St.). Martucci had been interested in joining the food business at an extremely early age. "At the age of twelve" Martucci stated, "I worked at Sophia & Son Bakery sweeping the floors for twenty-five cents. At the age of thirteen, I worked on the truck twelve-hour days, making seven bucks. And by the time, I was seventeen, I was driving the trucks! ... I have so many phenomenal memories of the bakery. I used to put a stick of butter in the baking bread in the hot oven, and then go out and eat it on the porch on St. Marys Ave.!" Other memories Martucci holds near and dear to his heart include Scara's Hardware on Tompkins Ave.'s selling of nails by the pound and Msgr. Villani from St. Joseph's Church's corralling of the children outside of Scoots' Luncheonette to go to church. "But I'll remember this one 4th of July night in 1961. The neighborhood kids, include my brother Anthony "Snookie," knocked down a telephone pole across Tompkins Ave. and set it on fire. They threw all these fireworks into it, and shot Roman Candles at each other! Suddenly, there was a car coming the street. And upon seeing the fire, the driver sped up (oblivious to the fact that beneath the fire was a telephone pole), and floored his car directly into the conflagration! The car went up high into the air, and landed a few feet away. The guy just kept driving, and took off toward Hylan Blvd.!"

The original Montalbano's Pork Store was founded at 1130 Bay St. in Rosebank in 1926 by Domenico "Dominic" Montalbano (b. 1897), an immigrant from the small town of Corleone, Palermo, Sicily. In December of 1902, Montalbano immigrated with only $1.50 in his pockets on the SS Sicilian Prince to be with his brother-in-law, Filippo Costantino. The original establishment, the three-story, tannish brick building now occupied by Memento Beauty Salon, was before its evolution, simply the quintessential pork store. Montalbano's in its original state offered an array of canned goods, dried peppers, pork products (e.g. dried sausages hanging from the ceiling), chestnuts, baccala, and baskets of beans and *babbalucci* (live snails) outside; through the decades, Montalbano's had become such a part of the property that the smell which the dried cheeses that hung from the ceiling emitted were absorbed into the walls. Through a few changes of ownership (one of the workers having purchased the store, and later becoming landlord), the Parrelli family acquired Montalbano's in 2001; the current store thrives next door from its original location at 1140 Bay St. In the present day, Montalbano's is run by Cosimo Parrelli and his sons Vincenzo, Pasquale, and Cosimo Jr. The store has since expanded by adding a second location at 1 Gunton Pl. in Rossville on the South Shore. Cosimo Parrelli Sr. himself is forty-five years involved in the pork store business, having first owned Gioiosa Pork Store & Meat Market Inc. at 422 Avenue P in Midwood, Brooklyn between 1979-1992. The store took its name from Parrelli's hometown, Gioiosa Ionica, in the province of Reggio Calabria, Calabria. Parrelli was born and raised in Gioiosa until immigrating to the United States at the age of seventeen in 1974. Cosimo Jr., a native of Bulls Head, explained, "I knew this is what I wanted to do since I was a little kid. Every Sunday, my father would take me to his pork store, so by the time I got out of Moore H.S., it was clear to me I'd go into his business...Montalbano's isn't your everyday pork store. At most others, you buy what you need, and the guy at the counter says, 'Here you go, have a good day!' We do things a little differently. We treat everyone like family, and try to know most of our customers on a first name basis...So much of our clientele consists of old Italians, so in many cases, we like to hire people who can speak or have some knowledge of the Italian language. But even for those customers who don't speak Italian, they still enjoy authentic Italian food! That's why we have all our cheeses and other products imported straight from Italy; even the gelato comes in from Palermo! ...We've really expanded the store from its humble beginnings. We've become a full-fledged caterer, Italian grocery store, and butcher, offering ribeye, T-bone, and the latest all-the-rage steak: the Tomahawk. I'll never forget, the week of 4th of July, we sold twenty-two Tomahawks in one day!"

Constance Rosenblum wrote in her book *More New York Stories: The Best of the City Section of The New York Times*, "De Luca's General Store is little more than a square vestibule, intruded upon all sides by dangling merchandise, and a small countertop cleared off for conducing transactions...Mr. De Luca, a glassblower by trade before he left his native Sicily, gives the impression of a daydreaming tinkerer who one day happened to find himself running a hardware and house-wares store." De Luca General Store, one of the many curiosities in Italian Rosebank, projects a uniqueness in all aspects of its existence. 1253 Bay St., a three-story brick edifice whose coloration teeters on the brink of greyish-white, stands distinctively in prominence amongst other dwellings with its carefully-designed moldings, faded copper-tone cornices, and its Italianate pediment. The business was founded in 1977 by the individual from which it derives its namesake: John De Luca. Born in 1930 in the comune of Aci Castello in the metropolitan city of Catania, Sicily, De Luca by the age of fifteen "was working in a glassblowing shop and as the projectionist at his town's cinema. He fell in love with the America he saw on the screen", and immigrated to New York in 1958 on the SS Cristoforo Colombo. The next year, De Luca found employment as a glassblower at the laboratory glassware manufacturer Eck & Krebs Inc. at 27-

09 40ᵗʰ Ave. in Long Island City. In 1967, De Luca settled in Rosebank and opened De Luca's Deli on Bay St; in 1977, he opened his neighborhood-renown hardware store. The establishment sells an eccentric array of oddball parts, standard home-ware supplies, and nuts-and-bolts. Though a clear, concise meaning cannot possibly be attributed to the overall structure of De Luca's, one phrase can certainly be applied to the displayed, engineered creations and varied building, home-improvement supplies: a collection of emotions. *Staten Island Advance* journalist Bill Lyons wrote in 2015, "On a recent visit to the store he reached up to a shelf in the back of the store and pulled down a large model ship he built out of wood. He said it was like ones he saw as a youngster in the harbor of the Italian city of Catania...he built it from memory...There is a galleon made of Silver Thunder cans displayed on a wooden base with the title 'Malt Liquor' attached and a replica of the Pathfinder on a nearby shelf constructed of lamp parts, wheels, and gears with a proper coat of silver paint...Not using patterns or kits, De Luca gets his ideas when he is sleeping. He says, pointing to his head. 'They come from my cucuzza' he said, using the Italian word for squash." As consistent with previous themes in this work of literature, De Luca's is an ever-growing rarity in contemporary commercial culture; in favor of replacement with big-box outlets, extinction as a future for the "Keys Made While-you-Wait"-type stores (as advertised on the store's awning) is becoming more likely. The charming slightly-rusted white metal paneling with the words "De Luca General Store" written in between two "Enjoy Coca-Cola" accessories may not necessarily withstand the test of time.

The fabric of Italian Rosebank as implicated in previous sections, and frankly in many other texts concerning various cities in America, was composed of the rugged individualism that drove immigrants in a non-big-box period to rely on themselves, their skillset, and their establishments.

The quintessential manifestation of this vision for early-mid-20th century America was executed accordingly at 206 St. Marys Ave.: the site of V. Moschella's Market. Born Vincenzo Moschella on October 8, 1894 in Savoca, Messina, Sicily (the same town in which certain scenes of *The Godfather* were filmed) in a farmhouse on the slopes of Mt. Etna, the young man immigrated to the United States first in 1912, working as a laborer, before returning to Italy and serving in the military during World War I. After having traveled back to the U.S. in 1923, he returned to Italy in 1927 and married nineteen-year-old-Vincenza Riccardi of Limina, Sicily (less than four miles from his hometown of Savoca). The couple moved permanently to America via second-class sailing on the passenger ship SS President Wilson, finding their way to Rosebank, and had their first and only child Joseph Moschella (b. March 30, 1928). They settled at 206 St. Marys Ave., where Vincenzo renovated the property and converted it into a grocery store with a rental apartment in the back. Vincenzo later purchased the duplex next door. The couple's grandson, Vince wrote, "Grandma and Grandpa ran Moschella's Market together until his death on October 1, 1963. She minded the store while he drove a fruit and vegetable truck through the Italian neighborhoods providing fresh produce to the neighbors who knew he would pass through on a regular schedule and waited for him. In order to do this, he had to get

[The Moschella storefront, known to many as simply "Vicenz"at 206 St. Marys Ave. C. 1930s. Courtesy – Vincent Moschella]

up every morning and drive his truck via the Staten Island Ferry to the Washington Street Market in lower Manhattan, later the site of the World Trade Center. Grandpa and Grandma also gave advance credit to people who could not afford to pay until they got their welfare checks later in the month. Years later people still commented on their generosity in that regard and I can never recall hearing about anyone not finally paying back their debts – most of which were written on the back of a paper bag and tacked up alongside the register. Grandpa could not read or write at all in English and very little in Italian, though he knew his numbers well in both languages. Grandma could read and write in both languages. Her mathematical skills were legendary. She would add up the cost of a customer's groceries in her head unfailingly. When the cash register broke, she never got it fixed; she would just add it up in her head or sometimes in pencil on a paper bag..." Until his death, Vincenzo Moschella—a sufferer of arthritis—would sit behind in the store, and silently observe the front of the market. Among grandson Vince's fondest memories of the store were taking turns with his siblings sleeping over at Grandma's house during the summer and holiday breaks to help out the store, in addition to going to Sophia & Son Bakery (the site of the former-Magnotti's) to get the fresh bread, rolls, and doughnuts every morning. Until Vincenza's suffering from several mini-strokes in 1984, the store remained opened six-and-a-half days a week; on Sunday afternoon, Vincenza would go to mass at St. Joseph's Church and prepare the traditional Sunday, Italian meal. Vincenza was known to be a strong-willed woman; asides from her aforementioned attributes, Vincenza was also known to carry a hatchet under the cash register. Whenever young, neighborhood kids would come in and make trouble, she would chase them out with the weapon. *Staten Island Advance* journalist Matthew Monahan wrote in 1982, "[quoting Vincenza] 'Years ago, all you needed was some onions, potatoes and fruit and you could go,' she said. 'Today, it's much harder. And some people like the big supermarkets, so business is not like it used to be.' But young customers in a supermarket will not be asked if they finished their homework – and if not, why not...Owners of supermarkets are not seen watering azalea and spider plants, and two plants of unknown species found by the front window and telling visitors the plant that looks like garlic is garlic...Moschella's Market is not going to drive any of the local supermarket giants out of business. But neither will they force her to close." Though Vincenza later passed away on December 12, 1992, and the family store converted to private residences, Moschella's, for those who remember it, remains a symbol of Staten Island in its golden years.

The era of simple fruit-and-vegetable markets on Staten Island, as described by Ms. Moschella, is indeed a vanishing one. Charlie Perrino—a retired educator, statistician for the New Dorp H.S. football team, and descendant of the Stapleton grocery titans, the Messina family—provides brilliant testimony attesting to this fact. Founded by Alfio Messina (b. 1887), an emigrant of Sicily who opened his first vegetable market in Brooklyn before 1920, Messina's Market (first called Stapleton Market) had its initial location at 560 Bay St. The market would supply restaurants and maritime pilots. From 1923-1929, the family resided on Union Pl. (directly behind the store) in the Vanderbilt Cottage—the boyhood home of railroad magnate and philanthropist, Cornelius Vanderbilt. Perrino's aunt, Candelora Paolercio stated, "[w]e had the whole house to ourselves, a beautiful front porch, the width of the house, a pantry, two floors – up and down. We had so many rooms that my father raised canarys for pleasure in two of the rooms upstairs. Rent, it was stated was $10 a month for six or seven rooms, and cottages upward to $25 - $30 and $40 per month. In 1930, the property was sold to the developers of the Paramount Theater, the Netco Theatre Corp.—a subsidiary of the Publix Theatres Theatres Corp., and moved to 632 Bay St. By Paramount Theatre's opening day, Oct. 28, 1930, "all that remained of the Vanderbilt Mansion was a few scattered timbers and laths, and masonry walls of the cellar. The timbers, more than a century old, plainly showed the marks of the axes that had hewn them. They were neatly mortised together, and fastened with wooden pins." At its time of

opening, Paramount Theatre seated 1,808 persons on the main floor, and 494 on the balcony. At the original location, Perrino recalled the milkman next door, Mr. Durkin who had been forced to quit his job after his company

[Grace Messina (Perrino's mother) and her father Alfio Messina stand in front of their own Stapleton Market – later known as Messina's Market at 560 Bay St. C. 1923 Courtesy – Charlie Perrino]

discontinued the use of the horse-and-wagon delivery mode. Shortly after, however, Mr. Durkin received his driver's license and resumed his occupation. After a short stint at 632 Bay St., Messina's Market moved to 179 Broad St. Perrino, who grew up nearby at 46 Coursen Pl., recalled, "Everyone lived and worked on that one block. My grandparents, aunt, uncle, and cousins resided at 173. At 179, my grandfather and his son Charlie had their store. At 183, my father's cousin Philomena Polizzano Siclari had a toy store (formerly Graef Toys). At 189, my cousins had Polizzano's Pizzeria[37]

---

[37]Philomena was a Polizzano who married Nick Siclari—they worked the toy store at 183 Broad St. together. Philomena was the daughter of Mrs. Rose Polizzano. Other Polizzano's on Broad St. included Antonio Polizzano (b.

(later, Mauro's Restaurant which moved to New Dorp Beach in 1976)." In the early-1940s, Messina's Market opened its final location at 1590 Hylan Blvd., currently 1690-1700 Hylan occupied by Chase Bank and an Urgent Care center. Perrino remembered, "Grandpa Messina used to have a fish pond and a grazing area for sheep in the back of the market. The fish pond was eventually filled in after a young child fell into the pond and had to be rescued...It's funny, to get me to eat lamb, my mother always had to say it was one of grandpa's sheep. Usually it's the opposite for other children!" On his paternal side, Perrino's father Anthony (b. 1912)—an emigrant from Caserta—was a barber in Stapleton. Among his notable clients included Elmer Kenneth "Ken" Strong—a halfback for the Staten Island Stapletons "Stapes" which played in the National Football League between 1929-1932. A. Perrino, when his father died, was forced to drop out of school after the eigth grade to work two jobs as a schoolbus driver and barber to support his mother and two sisters.

[Grace, Charlie, and Anthony Perrino sit alongside the fish pond in the rear of Messina's Market at 1690-1700 Hylan Blvd. Courtesy – Charlie Perrino]

1892) who operated a shoemaker's shop at 227 Broad St. sometime from the 1910s through the 1920/30s.

In 1954, Perrino purchased "The Strand" Tonsorial Parlor from Vito Maio at 19 Nelson Ave. in Great Kills, operating it until 1971.

Bay St., the home of the former Messina's Market, once hosted a wide array of Italian businesses; examples include: J. D'Albero Delicatessan (1084-6 Bay St.), Napoli Pizzeria (1140 Bay St.), A. Gargiulo Bakery (1169 Bay St.), V. Immiti's Grocery Store (1248 Bay St.), Sparandera's (979 Bay St.), and Gilardi's Produce Market (1256 Bay St.). A bakery just north of the intersection of St. Marys Ave. & Bay St., owned by Tony DeSalvatore and his wife Gertrude Navarino was just among the many storefronts that defined the area's decadence. Getrude Navarino was the daughter of Anna Santarella Navarino who resided on the land sold by the Santarella Family for the Church of the Assumption on Webster Ave. Gertrude and her husband operated the Rosebank bakery from the late-1940 to the 1960s, before he went to work inside Borough Hall. During World War II, DeSalvatore was a chef in the army; it was here he honed his culinary skills. The bakery offered Italian pastries, wedding cakes, and other baked goods. DeSalvatore's niece Ann Baglio, a native of Port Richmond, remarked, "My uncle was always a generous man! He would send pastries down to Mr. Black, an older man, who owned a penny candy shop. For us he'd make little baker hats, have

[Anthony DeSalvatore. C. 1948. Courtesy – Ann Baglio]

us pretend to wait on customers, and have us paint butter on top of the pastries." Baglio's father, Michael (Mike) owned the Richmond County Ambulance Service in 1964. A former driver for Staten Island Hospital, and husband of the hospital's operating room's supervisor, Navarino in the early-1960s had a Chrysler station wagon converted into an ambulance, and began his service at the east end of Victory Blvd. For roughly twenty years until the 1980s, Navarino would be patient's alternative to 911 in times of business. Baglio recalled her father driving patients back from Staten Island all the way to Texas. It is also of interest to note that Michael's grandfather Ralph, was the original composer of the song "Who's Sorry Now?," popularized by Connie Francis in 1957. Ralph, a vaudeville performer, sold the music for $100 in the early-1920s; the original sheet music is no longer in possession of the Navarino family.

~

Just bordering the west edge of the Italian community, surrounding Cameron Lake, another enormous, largely previously uninhabited area in Rosebank, underwent significant changes. The 300-acre estate "the last of the 'English Parks' in Modern Babylon" was once used by Canadian-American Sir Roderick Cameron (1823-1900)— the co-founder of R.W. Cameron & Co. (a shipping line based in New York City) and founding member of the American Jockey Club—to breed imported horses for racing competitions. Previously even, the grounds were known as "Camp Scott," an encampment for the Sickles Brigade, and functioned as one of Staten Island's Civil War troop-recruiting stations; the camp housed at one point 5,000 soldiers. Cameron was responsible for the importation of the thoroughbred racehorse, Leamington (1853-1878) which would go on to win against the first winner of the Kentucky Derby, Aristides, and against Iroquois, the first American-bred horse to win the Epsom Derby; Cameron would also breed Warminster, Hampton Court, and Glenelg: the four-time leading sire in North America and 1869 Travers Stakes winner. During his time breeding horses, Sir Cameron resided at his large mansion, "Clifton Berley," until his death in October of 1900. He is credited with the naming of the neighborhood "Grasmere" after Grasmere, Cumbria in the English Lake District. The once-influential stud ranch would morph into New York City's premier garden which contained a rose garden, vegetable garden, croquet lawn, apple orchard, several cow stables, a rhododendron patch, and a vineyard. Offering a portrait of the estate in the wintertime, Helena Livingston wrote, "The leafless trees seemed clothed in fairy garments of silver, while the dark green of the fir trees shows in splendid contrast with their mantles of snow. Here and there are found the tracks of a rabbit, a squirrel or chipmunk, but these are the only marks that break the dazzling surface of the snow, and, as one gazes around the world of enchanted whiteness …it is indeed hard to realize that 'Clifton Berley' may call itself 'New York.'" Although a certain segment of Sir Cameron's former land would remain for the garden, much of the northern part would be sold to Philip Brady in the 1880s. Brady was a founder of the Master Plumbers' Association, and even operated a plumbing and heating business at 863 Sixth Avenue in Manhattan; he used the freshwater pond on his portion of land to harvest and sell ice. To his dismay, children and adults used the pond for ice skating in the winter, and consequently against his warning, many fell through the cracks and reached their deaths. Today, Brady's Pond remains the only pond in all five boroughs that has a beach for swimming; it is maintained by the Cameron Lake Club. In the 1920s and 1930s, however, as has been observed in nearly every historical concept presented in this work, the Cameron Estate would fall victim to major developers seeking to urbanize the borough, and unintentionally demolish treasured aspects of Richmond County history. Shortly after Philip Brady sold the property to Heinrich Feith in 1909, and then to Charles Durkee in 1911, Cameron Lake saw its final moments of the "bucolic" Staten Island era; Durkee had constructed a mansion "Durkee Manor" for himself and even cared for the vegetation and wildlife. Unfortunately, by 1927, real estate developers began to subdivide his property which had already been split due to the extension of Southfield Blvd. (later Hylan Blvd.), and commenced the realization of their vision for a suburban community. Nearly fifty years later, in the 1970s, the stone foundation for Cameron's mansion would be used to construct Tudor homes on Radcliff Road, designed by Beaux-Arts style architect Ernest Flagg. Flagg's Staten Island works include the fieldstone water tower on Flagg Court (named in his honor) in Todt Hill, the St. Charles Seminary, and several stone homes and cottages. In many respects, the landscape transformation covering the former Cameron Estate can be described as a microcosm of the development of the entire Island. Though decades have since passed, the areas of Rosebank, Grasmere, and Todt Hill remain strongly neighborhood-friendly areas which exhibit an element of close-knitness and pride.

A native of the forgotten borough through-and-through, Richard Barbato was among the few thousands privileged with observing those distinctions separating "old" from "new" Staten Island. Born in Staten Island Hospital, raised in New Brighton until the age of seven, Barbato spent his formative years on Spring Street in Concord (referred to as "Emerson Valley") in what was still an untouched area inhabited by predominantly Italians. Descended from grandparents who emigrated from Avellino, Campania, Barbato saw those traditions from the old country spring alive in a neighborhood thousands of miles away. His father—an employee at Con Edison, and his mother—a seamstress, had three children: two boys, and a girl.

Combined with an eccentric array of aunts and uncles, the family radiated Italian culture. Barbato remarked, "I didn't even realize till decades later that I never really knew my relatives' names. My aunt 'Assunta' was nicknamed 'Sue.' My aunt 'Grace' was called 'Tessie.' My uncle 'Salvatore's' name was changed to 'Sonny.' I happened to find this out when I came up empty-handed doing genealogical searches years later." Among his fondest memories of growing up was watching his father, Frank, make homemade cavatelli (small semolina pasta shells) during 'poverty time.' Barbato explained, "Whenever my parents were making macaroni, we knew the funds were low! My dad worked so hard at Con Edison, so as kids we were always told to entertain ourselves outside while my father slept. We had to be inventive! We used to play punchball and stickball on the foundations of homes being constructed in the neighborhood between about 1965-1970. Sometimes we'd go sliding down the dirt mounds across the street on a piece of cardboard!" Food was also a major part of Barbato's upbringing; items which made frequent occurrences at holiday dinners included ginette cookies, kruschicki, and handmade ravioli which were cut using a drinking glass. Barbato recalled, "The only thing we never really ate was chicken because my father—a native of Staten Island—had to kill them when he was little. He was a real character! He'd always tell us a story about meeting a werewolf when he served in the war in Italy. He stabbed the guy with a fork, and

[Frank Barbato prepares homemade cavatelli during "poverty time" C. 1950s. Courtesy – Richard Barbato]

the guy begged him to not tell anyone his secret...Concord had so many personalities back then! My father among them. There was a household with three generations which lived alongside us; the old lady used to wear a shawl on her head, and would sit on the back porch with her hand in front of her face because she didn't like the wind. She would always jokingly yell to me, "Ti ammazzo!" (I'm gonna kill you!). My entire family lived within blocks of us. Before you got home, your parents already knew you were in trouble! One time, I drove my bicycle into a telephone pole in front of my uncle's house; when I got home, my parents promptly took away my bicycle. My uncles co-owned a business together in which they converted school buses into campers. We used to vacation a lot to Lake George in Upstate on one of those campers. I never really understood how it was a vacation for my mother. Instead of doing it in her kitchen, she would just be boiling macaroni all day in the woods...We had some strange vacations. One time, the entire family did the three-day drive to Miami, and when we got there, my aunt yelled, 'Oh no! The buildings are too big here! We have to go back!' My father wasn't too pleased, needless to say...But we also had lots of fun! On Sundays, my father would sing to Mario Lanza and Jimmy Roselli. His favorite song was 'Mala Femmena' which he'd sing to with the widows open, loud! He was actually a frustrated opera singer who used to tell a story that he was supposed to be on *Ted Mack and the Original Amateur Hour*... A landmark of every one of my relative's households was the album rack which always had Pat Cooper's 1967 album "You Don't Have to Be Italian to Like Pat Cooper" with him in between two pieces of bread, in front. We made the best of what we could for the circumstances. Because my parents couldn't afford to buy a color TV, and the knob on our black-and-white TV broke off, we had to use a pair of pliers to change the channel!" Despite growing up Italian on Staten Island, Barbato never learned the language. He said, "the only time my parents ever spoke

Italian was when they didn't want us to understand what they were saying. But I knew they were talking about me for some reason when they said, 'gistocca.'" Barbato concluded, "Staten Island back then was so different! I'll forever remember stuff like going to Robin Hood Market or going to Sear's and getting a Hires Root Beer from the lady in the white uniform. But something I'll never forget was when my dog 'Sunshine' passed away, and my brother and father dug a hole the garden and made a cement pit for the burial. In the 1980s, when my sister and I were walking through the garden, she would say "'we're walking on sunshine.'"

~

Not far from the home of Richard Barbato, Joseph Primiano (b. 1896), the patriotic stonemason responsible in a significant part for the erection of the Museum of Tibetan Art in Lighthouse Hill, saw a piece of his homeland of Molise in the bucolic Mid-Island. Like many in New Brighton and New Dorp, Primiano hailed from the central Italian village of Vinchiaturo; at the ripe age of fifteen, Primiano followed his brother, Cosmo[38] over to the United States. In 1911, Primiano found employment in the mines outside of Spokane, W.A. which emerged from the discovery of silver, gold, and lead in the Coeur d'Alene, I.D. region. Shortly after, he migrated to Mexico where he encountered an old Italian man who taught him the craft of masonry. In the early-1920s, Primiano settled at 1356 Richmond Rd. Primiano poured the first concrete foundations in Dongan Hills Colony. In 1928, under the leadership of a Mr. Latino—a builder of custom houses—

---

[38] Cosmo Primiano (1890-1971), older brother to Joseph, is known for his founding and operating of the restaurant Cosmo's Drive-In "Food and Fun for The Entire Family" at 1300 Hylan Blvd. from Jun. 1951 to 1968. The hamburger, seafood, and pizza establishment, famous for its rides in the back, would later become The Cosmopolitan Lounge.

Primiano laid the foundations for twelve Dutch Colonial homes on the right side (looking northeast) of Norden St. between Dalemere Rd. & Richmond Rd. He later worked for Tony Pietracatella (whose namesake derives from the sparsely-populated municipality of Pietracatella in Molise), a builder. At Pietracatella's firm, Primiano built homes on Stewart Ave. in Graniteville, Flagg Pl., Slosson Ave., and Ocean Terrace. At his future residence, 20 8th St. in New Dorp, Primiano installed the gray stones visible on the property today; other marks of his craftsmanship can be seen at 100 and 86 Chapin Ave. Perhaps his most notable project, however, was that at the future Museum of Tibetan Art on Lighthouse Ave. In the late-1930s, early 1940s, Jacqueline Klauber (known by her professional name "Jacques Marchais") sought out a stonemason to construct a museum on her private property to commemorate her favorite variety of art—relating to Tibetan culture. Primiano's daughter Mary Iammatteo explained, "Together, my father (working concurrently at the shipyards) and Jacqueline would go search for Flagstone in the hills of Staten Island. The remaining stones needed for construction were purchased by Primiano at the quarry located in Yonkers. They constructed the museum the old-

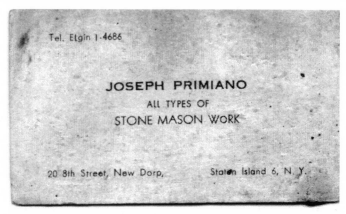

Tel. Elgin 1-4686

JOSEPH PRIMIANO
ALL TYPES OF
STONE MASON WORK

20 8th Street, New Dorp,   Staten Island 6, N. Y.

fashioned way. On a certain rock behind the front gate, I recall my father lighting a fire under it, cracking it right in the vein with his trowel at just the precise moment!" The museum's construction officially began in 1941 and ended in 1945; the building was initially used a research library before becoming the actual museum in 1947. In 2009, the museum received official status on the state and national Historic Register of Historic

Places." Though Primiano passed away in the late-1960s, his legacy is still strong today. His son, John P. Primiano who

was lost at sea during World World II, also, is memorialized at Miller Field. Iammatteo concluded, "At the age of five, my older brother passed away of leukemia. In the 1940s, my other brother was never to be seen again. I don't think if it wasn't for religion, my parents would've made it. I give them a lot of credit for that. My mother would tell us, 'If you've fallen into something difficult in your life, in ten years, you'll realize you were put on a path for a certain reason, and that God had done you a favor.'"

Integrated into all aspects of hardware and home supply, as well as dining, real estate, and industrials on Staten Island, the DiLeo family has been an influential, dynamic clan in Richmond County, particularly the East Shore, for over a century. Vito DiLeo (~1860s-1959), the husband of Caterina "Catherine" Catanese, immigrated to the United States from Sciacca, Agrigento, Sicily around the turn of the century. The couple settled with their two-three children first on Chrystie St. in Little Italy in Manhattan; by the late-1900s, the family had expanded to seven total offspring. In 1915, Vito DiLeo moved the family to the block of Hylan Blvd. between Reid Ave. & Bath Ave in Dongan Hills. It was here that DiLeo constructed by-hand a solid brick house—a style of architecture considered refined for the times. In fact, when Catherine DiLeo was asked about her place-of-residence, she would proudly reply, "The Brick House on Hylan Blvd." Vito's son Gus (m. 1931 with Ms. Frances Governale) would have three children: Victor, John, and

[From left to right: Victor, Gus Sr., and Gus Jr. stand in front of the family store at 1413 Hylan Blvd. in the early-1960s. Courtesy – Gus DiLeo, Jr.]

Gus Jr. Gus and his wife would settle at the old brick house shortly after their marriage. It was through the instrumentality of Governale that the DiLeo family acquired the property on the corner of Hylan Blvd. & Reid Ave—the future sight of DiLeo's Hardware at 1413 Hylan Blvd. (located diagonally across the street from Joe Fricano's establishment "Ciro's Italian Restaurant & Pizzeria") in 1960. Gus DiLeo, Vito's grandson, who attended PS46 in South Beach and McKee H.S. in St. George, explained, "In 1956, my brother John and William Vaccaro formed Hylan Electric (an electrical contracting co.) which is still operating today. Four years later, my brothers and father (I was only seventeen at that time) established DiLeo's Hardware, which later became DiLeo's Home Center). The store operated until 2006, when we entered into a land lease with HSBC Bank...From the 1980s to early-2000s, we operated three home centers on Staten Island: DiLeo's, Handyman Hardware & Paint Store in the Oakwood Shopping Center, and True Value Home Center in the Forest Ave. Shopping Center." DiLeo's supplied traditional homewares, paint, building supplies, tools, plumbing parts, but also Hot Wheels, Wiffle bats and balls, Street Hockey sticks and pucks, "Spaldeens"[39] and black tape to increase the longevity of Hockey sticks. In era without 1978-founded Home Depot, DiLeo's was the destination for home repair-related issues. With the changing times, personality has been swapped in favor of standardized, corporate practices. The character of Gus Dileo Sr., remembered by many for his organization-centric, strict demeanor, will be missed by those who frequented the old store. Reminiscing on the simpler days, Gus Sr.'s daughter-in-law Deanna Durso DiLeo, stated, "My whole family worked at Handyman Hardware in Oakwood: my daughter and two sons, at all different times of the day,

---

[39] "Spaldeen" in N.Y.C. terminology refers to typically pink "Spaulding Hi-Bounce Balls" once manufactured at the southwest corner of Pacific St. & 6th Ave. in Brooklyn.

but mostly after school. They would take over the register and close up shop...The store was open from 8am to 9pm, so we had many regular customers all the time. Because we had two lottery machines, we had so many locals that used to come in who really spent lots of money on these crazy games! But we never got a big winner! ... As the bookkeeper, I really did enjoy balancing the prior day's receipts and depositing the money!" In the present day, the DiLeo's control a wide variety of Staten Island business interests: real estate, cuisine (John DiLeo opened the Perkins Restaurant & Bakery just up the street from DiLeo's Hardware in 1970; Michael DiLeo, a graudate of the Culinary Institute of America, opened Chef Mike's Rodizio Grill in Bloomfield in 2017), and industry (Arthur DiLeo owns Cardinal Electrical Supply Co.). Though DiLeo's Home Center is no longer existence, the DiLeo legacy is stronger than ever.

~

Moving east toward South Beach, we discuss first the history of among the neighborhood's oldest landmarks. The most intriguing of which was Fred Scott's Movie Ranch. Fred Scott's, "a colorful character whose farm stood on Olympia Boulevard, South Beach, then part of Old Town Road, had assembled over many years a wonderful collection of carriages, stagecoaches, buckboards and the like" Movie Ranch produced over one-hundred silent films between the 1890s-1914. His theatre was one of three nickelodeons located on Staten Island. Some of the film's most-widely recognized productions include: film pioneer, Edwin S. Porter's movie starring "Broncho Billy" Anderson, "The Life of an American Cowboy" (1909); "Russia, the Land of Oppression," (1910) depicting the persecution of Jews in Kiev, Ukraine and Chişinău, Moldova; and a segment of the melodrama film serial "Perils of Pauline" (1914). William B. Heinrich writes in his book *The New York Nobody Knows:*

Walking 6,000 Miles in the City, "Many film stars of the silent era got their start here, people like actress Lillian Gish and director D.W. Griffith." Lillian Gish would star in Griffith's 1915 controversial, silent drama film *The Birth of a Nation*, which was partially filmed at Eibs Pond Park—a mere eight blocks from Scott's movie ranch. Other actors/actresses who saw their careers expand here were Irish-born Cyril Scott who debuted at a production of "The Girl I Love" in 1883 in Paterson, New Jersey; as well as the "Queen of the Serials" Pearl White. Fred Scott even drove his stagecoaches in "The Great Train Robbery" (1903) and the Buffalo Bill's Wild West Show which came to Mariner's Harbor in 1886; they were also exhibited during the 1939 New York World's Fair in Flushing Meadows-Corona Park. It was on the property of Fred Scott's Movie Ranch that Fr. Catoggio, as previously mentioned, would bring his mission. The erection of Father Catoggio's chapel on Scott's property would be short lived, however. On September 23, 1927, upon the signing of decree by Archbishop of New York, Patrick Cardinal Hayes, an entire parish—Holy Rosary Church—would replace the small chapel. The church's construction could be attributed to the growing number of Italians, many of whom helped build the white-stucco, wood-frame institution and adjacent rectory. The parish's first pastor, Reverend Dominic Epifanio, a native of Italy, for whom the parish center is named, originally served at St. Patrick's under the leadership of Irish, Father Kearney. Prior to the rectory's opening, Rev. Epifanio boarded at DeMaso's Inn which helped feed the movie crews from Scott's ranch, run by Mary and Jenny DeMaso. He would celebrate mass within the confines of the inn until the completion of Holy Rosary Church. A stained-glass window would be dedicated to the DeMaso sisters' father—John. Those who would attend Sunday mass at Holy Rosary in the years to come would forever remember the delightful, contrasting smells of the Church's wooden interior and the aroma of meatballs frying, sausages, and sauce cooking from the rectory and surrounding homes. On April 26, 1956, nine years after newly-appointed Rev. Harry Forrester began exploring the possibilities of providing an education to South Beach residents in the Catholic tradition, the former Sixth Archbishop of New York, Cardinal Francis Joseph Spellman dedicated Holy Rosary School on the corner of Jerome & McLean Avenues. Education would be administered by the Sisters of Notre Dame. In the present day, all facets of the Holy Rosary Parish cater to a wide variety of nationalities (offering mass in Italian, Spanish, Polish, and English), but particularly to Italians who comprise about 30% of South Beach's 85,000+ residents. In fact, Holy Rosary Church was for a great duration between 1951-1999 a gathering place on Sundays for the Staten Island Chapter of the Manhattan-based American Committee on Italian Migration (ACIM)—an organization intended to support Italian immigrants throughout New York. From the Italian community of South Beach would emerge celebrities such as rock musician Frankie LaRocka (originally, LaRocca), rock drummer Sandy Gennaro, former Mr. Universe Larry "Powers" Ciancetta, Staten Island's first professional hockey player Nick Fotiu, and entertainer Vito Picone. Picone was and still remains the lead singer and founder of the Doo-Wop group "The Elegants." The original group consisted of Picone, Arthur Venosa, Frank Tardogno, Carman Romano, and Jimmy Moschello; the present group, retaining only Picone and Moschello, has since included Nino Amato and Bruce "Sonny" Copp. Formed in 1956 in South Beach by fifteen-year-old-Picone, as well as Carman Romano, The Elegants gained international notoriety for their number-one hit song "Little Star" released in 1958. Picone explained, "The song was actually created entirely by accident. We were rehearsing at my friend's girlfriend's family's apartment, when we got tired toward the end of the night, and began fooling around with nursery rhymes. Then the guys began singing 'Twinkle, Twinkle, Little Star.' The next day, Arthur Venosa and I went back to my place and wrote the song. When the song was finally released and became number one in 1958, it managed to remain at its peak for the whole summer, fending off Perry Como, Bobby Darin, and even Nat King Cole and Elvis Presley. 'Little Star' was only beat by Domenico Modugno's 'Volare.'" The record sold over two-and-a-half million copies and gained The Elegants stardom; they would later tour with Buddy Holly, Chuck Berry, Jerry Lee Lewis, etc. in the United States, Canada, and Mexico. "Little Star's" opening line "Where are you little star?" would also be the inspiration for Gene Roddenberry's science fiction television series *Star Trek*. On the 35th anniversary of the song, Picone returned to South Beach and requested a celebration with the group on the F.D.R. Boardwalk. Despite resistance from politicians, Picone persisted, received a donated flatbed trailer, and rode on stage on a candy apple red '57 Chevy. Picone stated, "We had our friends who were employees at Con Edison feeding us power cables...the local catering hall down the street sent some food down! We drew a crowd of about 20,000 people! It brought me back to the time where we had a record signing at Earl's Records in Stapleton in 1958, and all of Tappen Park across the street was packed. There were even kids pushing up against the windows of the shop! We eventually had to escape upstairs through the rear window, and were escorted to the precinct station by the police!" Picone would go on to have his own talent booking agency "Headline Talent Inc." Though he would later shut down his Manhattan office of twenty-six years located at 1650 Broadway, Picone still runs in semi-retirement the Staten Island segment of his operation. Although his fame would push Picone beyond the shores of Staten Island, he still recalls his humble origins in the old Italian neighborhood of South Beach. Picone reminisced,

"There used to be the old junkman who we called 'Zio Niccolo' who used to come around his horse-and-buggy with cowbells hanging off of it. He'd look for any scrap, metal, or any other valuable material. My task everyday after school before I went out to play was to grab my bushel and shovel, wait for Zio Niccolo's horse to crap in the middle of the street, pick it up and go deposit it on my grandfather's tomato plants...South Beach was a different place back then. We all just had good, clean fun. If anybody tried to sell us any drugs, we'd usually beat them up! Some of my fondest memories include parking in the gas station down the street from Licastri's Bakery with some friends and getting the fresh, baked bread at 2am in the morning. Boy, when you smelled that stuff in the air in bed, you really went crazy! We'd go in and bring the bread back into the car; meanwhile, we had some olive oil, salt, pepper and oregano waiting so we could douse the fresh bread! Other memories I have are of Louie's Salameria owned by Louie Iacobelli who would hang his baccala (salted cod) both asciutt' (dry) and bagnat'

[Mr. Frank Marrone stands outside his shop – F. Marrone Hardware on Sand Lane. A scene witnessed many a day by Islanders such as Picone. C. 1930s. Courtesy – Mike Cancemi]

(wet) outside his shop. You could smell that putrid stuff from about a block away! When we were kids, we'd always have to cross the street and walk on the other side, just to avoid the stench...Then

268

there was Marrone's Hardware which had two locations five blocks apart, and were each owned by two cousins who didn't speak with each other! I particularly remember walking into old man Marrone's shop. He'd greet every person, depending on whether they were a male or female, with 'Eh, Goombah'da bell(o)/a!' And, if you came in looking for a certain nail or screw, he would just stay in his chair and give you directions without ever having to get up! ... One more neighborhood Italian guy was Tony Giordano who we called 'Tony Grapes.' Every year during *la vendemmia* (grape harvest in September), Tony would come around to all our homes and sell grapes so that households could make homemade Italian wine. After everyone was through making the wine, you'd see nothing but wine crates stacked outside people's homes for days. Tony would also go to Florida once a year and come back with a truck full of about a thousand watermelons!" The old Italian South Beach as witnessed by Vito Picone was the one which brimmed with authenticity and warmth. Former food distributor Sal Marino exclaimed, "I mean...you want to talk about 'Little Italy', hell! South Beach in the 1940s and 1950s *was* Italy!" Marino's grandfather, who came from 14th Street in Manhattan, established a wholesale and retail Italian bakery on 209 St Marys Avenue in Rosebank after having purchased the building in 1915. His son would then in 1930 convert the operation in a full-fledged grocer supplying nearly every single pizzeria on Staten Island with cheese, olives from Spain, San Marzano tomatoes, artichokes, flour—everything "except the 'mut'zadel.'" Marino Foods, until its closure in the late 1970s, would be one of the biggest suppliers to Ronzoni, Star Fine Foods, and Del Monte; Marino Foods would also supply countless numbers of bakeries and delis on Staten Island, such as Jack Rosso's on Jersey Street, and Conte's Deli. Marino went on, "In South Beach alone, there were around twenty pizzerias! The one that sticks out in my memory the most is Cataldo's... It was a complete coincidence that the opening of Marino Foods coincided with the increasing popularity of pizza in the United States. Everything was so different back then! I even remember going to the railroad station in Manhattan where the Highline in Tribeca currently is, and picking up Stockfish (unsalted fish) from Newfoundland, and baccala! ... South Beach is a completely different ball game nowadays; I can barely recognize it! I knew the neighborhood back in the day when the priest from Holy Rosary Church would buy a car, ride around all year with a sign attached to the car reading 'Take a chance on the car!,' and then raffle it off at the festival. That went on annually." After leaving the food industry, Marino would apply Marino Foods' "low profit, high volume" strategy to the model train business; after starting a mail order company specializing in model trains, Marino would open SMC Model Railroad Center in 1974, after purchasing part of the old Stapleton Service Laundry. In the mid-1980s, Marino would then move Wallich's Camera Shop & Photo Lab (originally founded in 1940 by German immigrant Alphonse Wallich on Castleton Avenue) into his train business; Wallich's is the only current custom lab left on Staten Island. Regarding the former property of Marino Foods in Rosebank, Marino stated, "Today the original store stands but has been converted to an apartment. The warehouse was demolished and houses built on the land. I wonder if that huge brick oven is still built into the ground behind the building!"

Though Sal has since transcended the realm of food to photography, Marino Foods carries an enormous legacy in South Beach. Many local businesses relied on Sal Marino to provide them with the quality products necessary for the enjoyment of Staten Islanders. One such bakery was LaRosa's Bakery, owned by Salvatore "Tuttie" and his wife, Antoinette "Sadie." Salvatore LaRosa Sr.—an ambitious baker from San Giuseppe, Palermo, Sicily—immigrated to America in 1901 at the age of twenty-nine with his six

270

[Sal and Nancy LaRosa pose alongside each other with a finished wedding cake. C. 1970s. Courtesy – Annette LaRosa]

children; he began his career selling cannolis out of a push cart on Elizabeth Street in Manhattan's Little Italy for two cents a piece. In 1918, LaRosa moved to South Beach, and opened up shop at 11 Olympia Blvd. [40], at the intersection of Lansing St. LaRosa's over the next several decades would gain widespread notoriety due to its superb cannolis, sfogliatelles, napoleons, tortoni, spumoni, and gelato; not to mention, LaRosa's signature lemon ice which soothed any Islander on a hot, summer day. Though Salvatore's (Tuttie's) children would take over the South Beach operation until 1976, the old man often sat outside the bakery in his brim, black leather chair; he resided directly above the business in an apartment. Sal would be remembered for his outgoing, charismatic personality; he began everyday with a toast "Cent'anni" (one-hundred years) as he drank his breakfast of a raw egg with espresso. LaRosa was a devoted parishioner of Holy Rosary R.C. Church; "[e]very August, he organized a one-week feast in honor of Maria S.S. Della Providenza (Our Lady of Providence), the patron saint of his home town." Tuttie's granddaughter and former employee at LaRosa's Bakery, Annette LaRosa recalled, "If you came into the store, on the right side were cold cuts, bread, cheese,

---

[40] Next door from the bakery at 13 Olympia Blvd., "Sadie" LaRosa's mother Ms. Sardone, owned and operated a small dry goods (initially), grocery store, F. Sardone.

and provisions, while on the left side, were the pastries, cakes, etc. But if you walked directly to the back, there was a gigantic, twelve by eight portrait of the Madonna sitting on a table, surrounded by lit candles! That was the portrait my grandfather paraded around during the festival; it was so heavy, you'd need about four guys to lift it! ... I remember every night at the table where the portrait was, we'd all eat a nice, big Italian dinner. On St. Joseph's Day, my grandmother would make macaroni with sardines and fennel, and Sfinge (deep-fried dough balls) with a demitasse. Some nights, we'd eat Linguine with clam sauce; other nights— gnocchi or ravioli with salad. On holidays, my mother Nancy would make her famous spinach pizza with Italian sweet sausage, or her mozzarella pizza ... On Christmas Eve, she would make the seven fishes. I can still smell the crab sauce cooking on the stove! But we'd always finish the evening with a homemade dessert and black espresso coffee! That's why I always tell people: 'Some kids are born with a silver spoon in their mouth, but I was born with a sugar spoon!'" "I have so many great memories of LaRosa's" Annette went on, "on Sundays, if you came too late, my grandmother Sadie would kick you out! ... Another time, a customer came in and asked, 'Is the cake fresh?' and I said, 'No, it's very polite and well-mannered.' The most embarrassing thing I experienced was when I was still learning to write on the cakes. A customer came in and wanted 'Happy Birthday Brian!' to be written on a cake, and I accidentally wrote, 'Happy Birthday Brain!'" "I also got my dirty mouth from my grandmother" Annette continued, "I remember this one time I told my teacher off at New Dorp High School in Italian. They sent for my father, and oh boy! I was in big trouble!" Though many everlasting memories would be made at LaRosa's, the most poignant include the bakery's assembling of the cookie tray used in the film *The Godfather* and the lines which wrapped around the corner. Annette tearfully exclaimed, "But what I'll always remember the most about my father,

Salvatore LaRosa, was when he got to see my fiancé and I get engaged on Christmas morning, 2013—the last Christmas he would ever live."

Like LaRosa's Bakery, numerous Italian institutions have closed throughout the years – creating an image of South Beach entirely different than in the first half of the nineteenth century. On the corner of Sand Lane and Robin Rd. a large sign atop a public meat market in the 1920s read, "Frigeria e Capozzelle a Forno"—Cooling units and Sheep's Heads baked in the Oven. The exotic delicacies were a curious sight in Italian delis' windows, and centerpieces during holiday dinners. This market would later transform into the famed Club Trio, owned by brothers Thomas, James, and Joseph Bilotti. Born to parents Anthony Bilotti of Rome, and Lillian Gheraldi of Milan, the Bilotti brothers "came up in the Staten Island-based crew of Gambino crime family capo Michael D'Alessio...[Thomas] Bilotti had a reputation for being a 'tough guy,' feared by street level thugs on both sides of the Verrazzano-Narrows Bridge." Thomas Bilotti grew to be a protégé of Paul Castellano, and performed numerous tasks, taking various positions under Castellano's guidance. Those positions included being an aide-de-camp, chauffeur, bodyguard, and vice-president at Castellano's concrete supplying company Scara-Mix at 2537 Richmond Terrace which supplied concrete to New York City. "What Castellano liked best about Bilotti was his toughness; he was known to smash opponents over the head with a baseball bat as a way of ending disputes." In a mafia power struggle with Bilotti in line to replace Aniello Dellacroce as underboss, and Thomas Gambino to replace Castellano as head of the Gambino family, John Gotti's assassins fatally shot Castellano and Bilotti outside Sparks Steakhouse on East 46th Street in Manhattan in 1985. Bilotti over the course of his life was married twice, first to Catherine Crocitto whose family owned Crocitto's directly across the street from Club Trio at 165 Robin Road. Crocitto's was started by Frank

Crocitto—an immigrant from Bari, Puglia who first had owned a pool hall in the early-1900s at the site which would become the Sullivan Street Playhouse in Greenwich Village where Harvey Schmidt's 1960 musical *The Fantasticks* premiered. In 1919, Crocitto moved to Staten Island to a more spacious, healthier environment where he could raise his ten children. It was there in South Beach that he purchased St. Cuthbert-by-the-Sea Roman Catholic Church—a church which had been built in 1901 on the estate of Cuthbert Mills. Crocitto made the church into a pizzeria and nightclub where many present and future celebrities would perform. Performers featured included Ruth Brown, Hank Garrett, the Tear Drops, Bernie Allen, Phil Sanchez, The Pantomaniacs, and actress Patti Paget (not to be confused with Patti Page). Hollywood composer and arranger Nick Perito remarked, "Dolph Traymon, a very good pianist, and I traded off playing piano in our jazz band. He managed to get a job for five of us every Saturday and

[A talent showcase brochure from Crocitto's. "Just a Hand Full of Great Entertainers who have appeared in '64 and will be back in '65. Courtesy – Sal Marino]

Sunday night at a local pizzeria in South Beach, Staten Island, called 'Crocitto's'...Unfortunately, a large bar and pizza kitchen was right next to the dance floor and the night club area. The chef was an angry old Italian man who didn't give a damn about anything or anybody other than to loudly inform the *entire world* when a pizza order was ready. No matter what was going on the restaurant, we regulars soon became accustomed to hearing him yell out at the top of his voice, 'PORRRRTA VEEEYAH' (Porta Via)—which meant *take it away!"* Richard Crocitto, grandson of Frank Crocitto, who grew up on 31 Neal Dow Ave. in Westerleigh recalled, "Every Tuesday and Sunday, Crocitto's hosted 'Twist Night.' On those nights, there was a band that played composed of Carmine Giovinazzo—the accordion "quarter box" player, Billy Masiello—the drummer, Carmine's cousin Gary—the saxophone player, and my brother Dominick "Don Corey"—the singer. Whenever anybody dancing got involved in a fight, I remember, all the waiters would surround the persons and throw them out! ... My family lived and breathed pizza! In fact, my grandmother even had a stroke and died in front of the pizza oven!" In 1978, a 35-year-old-Richard Crocitto moved to Reno, Nevada and carried on Crocitto's legacy in the west coast by opening Nu Yalk Pizza; Crocitto's in South Beach closed down in 1976. "Growing up, my father never wanted me to go into the pizza business. That's why we almost never went to Crocitto's! My father really didn't want to get us involved with mob. But when I moved out west and told him I wanted the original family recipes, he just gave them to me and said, 'Good Luck!' Crocitto's closed down shortly after my Uncle Mario borrowed money from the Bilotti brothers in an attempt to make the pizzeria/nightclub into a disco. The plan failed!" Richard explained, "But you can still get a piece of Crocitto's in Nevada. So many people ask me, 'Why does your pizza taste so good?' and I always tell them, 'The Crocitto's have million dollar tastebuds!'" What remains of the original Crocitto's Pizzeria, now a

Mediterranean restaurant, Chinar on the Island, is a steeple and baptismal hall.

Crocitto's was the epicenter and showcase of South Beach, Staten Island's diverse talent during the 1950s and 60s. South and Midland Beach welcomed icons such as Benny Goodman, Bobby Darin, and Johnny Maestro. Born John Peter Mastrangelo on May 7, 1939 to parents Salvatore and Grace in Manhattan's Lower East Side, Johnny "Maestro" moved with his family to Staten Island in the late-1950s (though the Mastrangelos had spent many a summer at their bungalow along the Island's east shore). In his later years, Maestro was a frequent visitor to his parents' and brother, Ronald's Staten Island homes; he would also perform at many fundraising events on Staten Island such as the Borough President's "Back to the Beach" concert. Maestro had begun his career in Manhattan at the age of seventeen as the lead singer of the interracial doo-wop group *The Crests*, known for their 1958 hit, "Sixteen Candles." Maestro would go on to in 1968 form *Johnny Maestro & The Brooklyn Bridge*—a merger of Johnny Maestro, *The Del-Satins*, and *The Rhythm Method*. The band's name originated during an office conversation concerning how to brand the musical group; someone remarked, "This is going to be difficult. We have eleven people. That's hard to sell. It's easier to sell the Brooklyn Bridge." The band gained notoriety for its recording of Jimmy Webb's "The Worst That Could Happen." After residing on Staten Island for over a decade, Maestro moved to East Islip, Long Island in 1971, and then to Cape Coral, Florida where he passed away on March 24, 2010 of cancer. Less than a year later, the City of New York honored him by renaming the intersection of Mason Ave. and Midland Ave. as "Johnny Maestro Way." During his summer holidaying on Staten Island, Maestro encountered other future-celebrities; the most noted of these was Bobby Darin. Born Walden Robert Cassotto in 1936 in East Harlem, Darin moved to the Bronx but vacationed annually at his family's rented summer bungalow in South Beach in the late 1940s and early 1950s. South Beach had been where years earlier, Darin's maternal grandfather Saverio Antonio "Big Sam Curly" Cassotto, financially unsuccessful, had gone to sell orange Popsicles. The Staten Island bungalow was indeed a great accomplishment for the Cassotto family. It served as proof for Gary Walden—the singer's brother—to dispute Darin's "version of a poverty-stricken" childhood. Darin would rise to stardom after releasing several, enormously successful hit singles: "Splish Splash" in 1958, "Beyond the Sea" in 1959, and the number one hit in the United States and England in 1959, "Mack the Knife." "In later years," writes *Staten Island Advance* journalist Rob Bailey, "Darin's hit song 'Mack the Knife' was played on jukeboxes at Ocean Breeze establishments like The Tower's, Rocky's, Enquist's, and Dement's."

Before the era of Bobby Darin, however, the earliest vacationers to the East Shore of Staten Island stayed mostly in dozens of family-owned lodges, awaiting the construction of their bungalows. This is significant considering Staten Island only possesses a handful of hotels today, mainly of the corporate variety. Among the earliest ornate jewels of Arrochar was a quaint Italianate hotel on 250 Richmond Ave. (McClean Ave.)., 150 feet from the street, overlooking the sea. Rigali's Hotel, as it was known in 1917, having been known years earlier as Rigali's Arrochar Park Hotel, was the European-style centerpiece of eastern Staten Island. Its courtyard entrance was marked by trimmed hedges, a water foundation, and an expansive greenery which vanished under the brick homes constructed on the property in 1970. The hotel proprietor was Italian immigrant, Pietro Rigali (b. October 4, 1846). Historian Richard Simpson notes, "At the age of twelve, [Rigali] lived in France for thirteen years where he learned the trade of painting highly decorative fresco wall murals. He moved back to Italy where for three years he painted. In about 1874, he sailed for America landing in New York and for the next ten years worked as a painter. He accumulated the necessary capital and moved to Staten Island where he opened a restaurant in Rosebank ... [He] needed larger quarters and moved his restaurant to 250 Richmond Avenue...The facility held five-hundred guests and frequently hosted large banquets to groups from Manhattan." The hotel's dining room had a five-hundred guest capacity, providing a refined dining experience with high ceilings and large windows; flower pedestal stands, in addition, were placed around the room for decoration. Some of the hotel's memorable guests included members of the Giuseppe Mazzini Lodge on Staten Island, about which their 1902 celebration was written, "[t]he banquet was held on Staten Island – the green island of which cannot be explained the enchanting seductions of the landscape – in the elegant Arrochar Park Hotel of Mr. Rigali." A surprise, 11-course dinner party in 1915 was also held at the hotel, honoring designer Franz F. Deiner of Wetzel Tailors, located at 2 East 44th St. in Manhattan. After Mr. Deiner was presented with a silver loving cup as a token of his achievement, the celebration went on with athletic contests and dancing into the night.

Just several blocks east of the hotel at 45 McClean Ave.— once housing the Staten Island Family Physicians—was the former home of Dr. Francis "Frank" J. Romano (b. 1921). Built in 1868 by architect Henry Hobson Richardson—one the three great architects of America—the home's gardens were designed by Frederick Law Olmsted. The "Queen Anne-style house with a mansard roof and a widow's walk" was purchased in 1940 by Dr. Romano's parents, owners of the former Vesuvio Restaurant in Manhattan's Little Italy. The couple had spent summers at a home on Lily Pond Ave. In 1947, Romano began his private practice as a doctor, which would last until 1997. Carol Ann Benanti wrote in a *Staten Island Advance* article, "On his first day, a snowstorm walloped the Island, making streets impassable, and especially in hard-hit South Beach and Arrochar. But that didn't stop [Romano]. With the help of a sled, and medical supplies in hand, he made it to the home of a patient on Lamport Blvd." Romano's achievements include bringing the first cardiac life-support ambulance to the former Staten Island Hospital in 1969. Romano, who would come to be known as the "King of South Beach," was recognized for his outstanding humanitarian actions, particularly the house calls he made whose prices were patient-negotiable.

Debated to be the oldest surviving restaurant in South Beach, Arrochar and Staten Island, Basilio Inn maintains a rusticity from its founding period, relating each dining experience to a summer outing in the rural countryside. The modern edifice took shape on the grounds of a former estate, on which a carriage house—constructed in 1850—would become the famed Italian eatery. The upstairs portion of the carriage house, once used as lodging for hired help, was employed by owner Basilio Giovannini as a true "inn" until 1961, at which point the dining room downstairs had been serving patrons and guests since 1921. Giovannini—a cooper (repairer of wine barrels and casks) from the Piedmont region of Italy—immigrated to the United States in 1911, and in 1918 took over the inn at the end of Galesville Ct., tucked away from Lily Pond Ave., which previously had been the carriage house. Through the generations, Basilio's has served multiple purposes, from that of a speakeasy to the winemaking mecca of Arrochar. Those vinous traditions are recalled in the current day by the presence of a grape arbor behind the restaurant. Other homegrown practices include/(d) crowning annually "Miss Basilio," playing bocce ball, and harvesting herbs/vegetables from the pristine garden whose offerings include fresh tomatoes and basil. The produce is applied to the Italian staples on the menu which include Ossobuco, zucchini blossoms, and a vast array of daily-homemade pasta. Basilio Inn's seasonal hours, and consequently its menu, revolve around its former clientele who were summer vacationers who resided at their bungalows along the water; for this reason, Basilio Inn was formerly only open from Memorial Day to Labor Day. The restaurant has since undergone a change of ownership in the 1970s where the Neapolitan Giovanni Asperti, and later, his son Maurizio, took control of operations.

A recognizable face on New York television, Mickey Burns—a lifelong Staten Islander—stood witness to the change which overwhelmed the borough in the mid-20th century. Raised in the South Beach Projects—city housing next to Pier 46—Burns came up in the post-World War II community, inundated with hundreds of gleeful children playing in the streets. The tight neighborhood entailed a two-minute walk to elementary school, and an opportunity to enjoy the simplicities of old South Beach. The nephew of a Sandy Hook Pilot, and relative of the owners of the Staten Island, 19th-century bakery in Concord "Muller's," Burns time-and-time-again observed those labor-centric values tying together the fabric of South Beach. Burns' grandfather was in charge of tugboats at the waterfront of the Quarantine Station at Hoffman Island, coordinating with doctors to help them reach vessels. After graduating from New Dorp High School, Burns attended Missouri Valley College on an athletic scholarship, and went on to earn a master's degree at Central Missouri State University in Education and Communications. New Yorkers know Burns today as the host of *Profiles*, a television program in which celebrities discuss their careers in an interview format; notable guests—derived from distinct backgrounds and professions—have included Helen Reddy, Tony Orlando, Joe Montana, Maya Angelou, Joan Rivers, and George Foreman (among many). Burns also serves as the President of Quest Media Entertainment Inc. Despite rising to national stardom, Burns still recounts his middle-class childhood and adolescence in fond terms, with special regard for the lost "Staten Island."

Burns recalled, "Back in those days, getting to go to a place like Al Deppe's was a very, very special treat. Our way of celebrating a sixteenth birthday party wasn't to go the Staaten and enjoy a DJ, three-course meal, dancing, etc...we'd go to Cosmo's Drive-In on Hylan Blvd. and maybe get a hamburger. That was about it!" "If there's one story that captures the essence of my childhood on Staten Island, it's this one" Burns continued, "when I was between the ages of 10-13, I played baseball in the Vacation Playground League. One year there was a tournament, and my team beat all four other boroughs! That was a huge deal in those days! For our victory, we were taken to Yankee Stadium, and the members of the 1961 Yankees signed to each of us a baseball. That team would come to be unofficially known in MLB history as the greatest team of all time! That team included Mickey Mantle, Yogi Berra, and several other outstanding players. When we got back from the stadium, a few weeks later, I was playing baseball outside with my friends, when we needed a baseball. Thinking nothing of it, I grabbed the only ball I could find—the signed Yankees baseball—and took it out to play! Within weeks, the ball was hardly recognizable and had been nearly torn apart. To think nowadays the ball would be worth in the millions! But that was Staten Island back then..."

Licastri's Bakery—a once-worshipped institution in Italian South Beach—was the epitome of quality bread manufacturing. In fact, an accurate portrait of South Beach in the early to mid-20th century cannot be drawn without the infectious smell of bread pumping life into an entire civilization. The establishment began as the dream of Philip Licastri (b. November 25, 1887)—a native of a *paesello* (small village) in the Madonie mountain range in the Palermo province of Sicily. Licastri entered into the craft of bread-baking at a bakery in Manhattan. As oral tradition has it, he would get on the Staten Island Ferry at the end of each day with his horse-and-buggy, and deliver the product on his self-formed delivery route. As he slowly built his business in the most authentic, entrepreneurial fashion, Licastri finally realized his dream. In 1919, Philip Licastri & Sons bakery was opened at 33 Olympia Blvd. at the corner of Piave Ave. The bakery—a strictly wholesale enterprise—offered Sicilian and French style-bread, though corn muffins, dinner, club, and Kaiser rolls were later added to its repertoire in the 1970s. As a courtesy, walk-in orders from the street were accepted solely on a circumstantial basis. It is estimated that Licastri's supplied approximately seventy-five percent of Staten Island's food businesses with their bread. Philip's son Ciro recalled, "We used to buy our flour from Olivieri & Sons. And we weren't buying it in pounds or bags. We'd measure how much flour we needed in 'carloads!' We were baking with brick ovens until the 1960s. You could fit about four-hundred loaves in those!... The bread we made could be smelt all over South Beach! I'll never forget seeing the biggest smiles on customer's faces who had followed the smell of the bread and had come into the bakery." Ciro's son Stephen, who was born in a small house owned by Nick DeMaso behind Rosemary's Dance Studio rented by his parents for fifty dollars a month, further elaborated, "Working at Licastri's was at times a dangerous environment. Sometimes, workers would get their fingers caught in the machine that would flatten the dough out and mold it into a roll! My grandfather's solution to this issue was stick their hand first in a raw bucket of rice, and then bring them to the hospital! ... I'll never forget, this one time we had an employee who received a phone call in the middle of baking bread and said, 'I'll be back in fifteen minutes.' Although we asked him, 'Where are you going?' he replied, 'Don't worry about it.' Fifteen minutes later, he came back with blood all over his apron, but he just continued working like nothing had ever happened. Twenty minutes later, the cops came into the bakery and dragged him out! We were eventually informed that his daughter had called him and told him that her fiancé wasn't treating her right. Consequently, the man left work to go stab his future son-in-law!" "We worked tirelessly at Licastri's Bakery" Steve explained, "When the phone rang in the middle of the night, we always knew there was a problem. We lived our entire lives on pins and needles, awaiting that 'dreaded' phone call. But we never stopped working. Even the day my grandfather was being laid into the ground, we went to work at the bakery first to make the day's orders, and then we went to the cemetery." Growing up, Stephen Licastri switched between working at Licastri's Bakery and his maternal grandfather, Joe Fricano's restaurant at 1400 Hylan Blvd.—the original Ciro's Pizzeria. Founded in 1956, Ciro's lasted until the mid-1970s; it re-opened in 1983, and lasted until 1986; it re-opened once more down the road from its original location at 900 Hylan Blvd. in 1988, before being sold in 1993. Stephen Licastri reminisced, "I remember one time in the 1960s, Ciro's was fully-booked for Eastern Sunary dinner. All of us were there working early to prepare for that busy day,

[Ciro's Restaurant & Pizzeria, owned by Joe Fricano, at 1400 Hylan Blvd. C. late-1960s. Courtesy – Stephen Licastri]

when we noticed it started to snow. It snowed about a foot! That day, not one single person showed up for their dinner reservation!... It was a trip being related to both Licastri's and Ciro's! Needless to say, I was garnered a significant amount of attention in school. Out of the eight-hundred-fifty kids in my graduating class at New Dorp H.S., everyone knew me!" Among Licastri's fondest memories of growing up in South Beach were going over to LaRosa's Bakery and wreaking havoc on Sadie—"Tuttie" Salvatore's wife. Licastri recalled going into the bakery with his friends, hearing Sadie exclaim obscenities. Licastri continued, "When you're young, you like to hear old people swear. When we went into LaRosa's, the cookies were on one side and the Italian ice was on the other. Sadie would say, 'What do you kids want?' And she'd point at us individually. 'What do *you* want?' My friend would say, 'A cookie.' Then she'd point to my next friend, 'Ok, how about you?' He'd say, 'Italian ice!' Then Sadie would reply, 'Oh shit! Now I need to go over to the other side.' Then she'd point to me, and I'd say, 'I want a cookie' And Sadie would say, 'Why! You little bastard! Now, I gotta go back to the other side!' And we'd drive her nuts making her go back and forth...My father once told me a story of Sadie when she used to go to weddings. She obtained her entire glass and silverware and China collection, because when she went to weddings, she'd bring a big bag and steal everything off the table. One time, when she went to a wedding, her husband Tuttie told her, 'Ok, Sadie. Don't steal anything off the table, this is a good friend of mine whose getting married!' Sadie agreed to Tuttie, but nonetheless, filled her bag with a dozen crystal glasses. At the end of the night, Tuttie looked at his wife and said, 'You didn't steal anything did you?' And she said, 'Nope, nothing!' And Tuttie said, 'Are you sure?' 'I swear to God' Sadie replied. And as Tuttie keeping repeating, 'Are you sure?' he smashed his fist into Sadie's bag and broke all the crystal glasses inside!"[41] Witnessing his fair share of incidents on old Italian Staten Island, Stephen Licastri nevertheless moved forward and exceled in the culinary arts. On Dec. 5th, 2016, Licastri opened "Dough by Licastri" at 1456 Richmond Rd. in Dongan Hills. "After observing, learning, and creating OLD WORLD dough recipes, [Licastri] has now combined that knowledge with today's techniques to produce artisan pizza and breads to satisfy the most sophisticated palate and toughest food critic." Licastri concluded, "My grandfather, Philip Licastri. He was the most well-respected guy you'd ever met. He had a five o'clock shadow five minutes after shaving! And let me tell'ya something: my grandfather was one tough son-of-a-bitch!"

The southern end of South Beach, just around the corner from Licastri's and LaRosa's bakeries, was once a world in its own. George Anastasio who grew up at 61 Pearsall St. recalled many a day wandering the marshes at the end of McLaughlin St., walking across the dated wooden bridge that connected the neighborhood to Seaview Ave. 61 Pearsall St. according to city tax records is written to have been built in approx. 1935. Anastasio supplemented this claim by recalling finding a silver dime dated 1937 just under the stairway. The

[The following three photographs depict an old trunk (and stickers attached to it) belonging to Anastasio's home's previous owner (presumably from Italy), rumored to have been in Anastasio's father's closet. Courtesy – George Anastasio]

---

[41] These stories are told with permission of the LaRosa family.

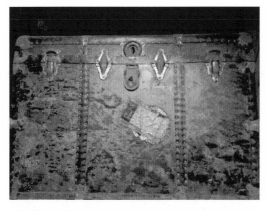

home—a modest dwelling whose stairs crossed from the right to the left—was built as a summer bungalow, but was converted to a year-round residence in the 1950s. The first of the Anastasios to immigrate was George's great-grandfather Giosue from Conca dei Marini on the Amalfi Coast; at the age of twenty, Giosue—the ship's Second mate—jumped into the water off the coast of Florida, and took the train to New York. Giosue's grandchild, born and raised on McDonald Ave. in Brooklyn, moved to the South Beach Homes—a middle-class housing project. A postman, he moved to Pearsall. St. in the early-1970s. Anastasio recalled catching killifish the South Beach swamps. The swamp engulfed the area so much so that Anastasio recalledhearing the sounds of squashed toads as cars drove through the streets. Other memories consisted of going to Antler Archery—an odd taxidermy establishment alongside Licastri's, and buying his mother a pack of Palrliament 100

cigarettes at Dimino's on Olympia Blvd. "There's something to be said about that little old man behind a local grocery store's counter. For me, it was Pat Dimino.

It's really a sin what happened to the Staten Island of today. Children wil never know the joys of a true childhood today in South Beach."

Among those children who enjoyed the "joys" of a South Beach childhood included Mario Alfredo Ariemma (b. 1956)—the owner of Ariemma's Italian Deli at 1791 Hylan Blvd. Born in the old Staten Island Hospital, and raised till the age of nine at 14 Vulcan St. in the western edge of South Beach, Ariemma was the grandson of Alfredo Ariemma—a skilled home painter from Campobasso, Molise who arrived to Manhattan from Italy in 1910. A. Ariemma, working alongside his partner Pietro Biondo from Switzerland, painted numerous structures across Staten Island. Extraordinary examples include the train bridge parallel to the Goethals Bridge, as well as a significant amount of the Victorian dwellings in St. George. When World War I erupted in Italy, A. Ariemma returned to serve as a Master Sergeant in the Italian Army. Finally, in 1920, A. Ariemma returned to Staten Island, never to leave again. In 1946, after being employed making fruit-and-vegetable deliveries for Joe Messina of Messina's Market in 1938, his son Mario Richard Ariemma, born at 253 Sand Lane, would begin a delivery business, peddling Italian groceries, produce, but predominantly eggs. "Ary's Eggs" as the business was termed, derived its eggs fresh from farms in Heightstown, Mercer County, N.J. "Every Monday when I didn't have school, I'd go with my father to the farms!" Mario A. Ariemma remarked, "We'd pick up about thirty crates of eggs to deliver fresh across Staten Island. In fact, due to my father's intense determination and hardwork, other egg peddlers soon sold him their routes, as well!" The first motorized delivery truck to be used was a 1935 International truck—purchased for thirty-five dollars at the scrap yard of Charles Pippiano. Italian households across South Beach would use Ariemma's eggs to make *fritad'* (frittata)—the Italian variation of quiche prepared in the Staten Island

[Ruth Kuczera, the wife of Mario Richard Ariemma, delivers eggs in Tottenville in appropriate attire. C. 1950. Courtesy – The Ariemma Family]

method using potatoes, onions, and Romano cheese. With that one simple dish, one could feed their entire family for three dollars. As time progressed, at the ages of eighteen and twenty-eight, Ariemma contracted rheumatic fever. This prompted an order from his doctor's mandating him to work indoors, away from the excruciating weather. Consequently, in 1956, he opened Ariemma's Italian Deli in Dongan Hills. Ariemma's Deli in the present day, run by chiefly by Mario A. Ariemma and his children, [deli manager] Santo, Mario, Frank, and Sydney Louisa (along with master chef Elias Gomez who has played a major role in Ariemma's success over the past thirty years) maintains a tremendous reputation for itself, serving quality prepared foods and sandwiches[42]. Ariemma's daughter Gabriella, also employed at the deli, greets customers with her infectious personality, and takes care of the clerical work. In 2014, it was featured in the first scene of Christopher Kuban's independent comedy film *Friends and Romans*. Concerning

---

[42] Ariemma Italian Deli's speciality sandwich "Chicken LU-LU" commemorates Ariemma's mother, Ruth Kuczera.

the Ariemma family legacy and business, son Mario concluded, "My family loved being active with the community. One of [my father's] greatest loves was South Beach and being a part of South Beach Robins Baseball & Football... In 1982, when my grandfather passed away, it was a profound loss for our family. He used to come in everyday to work at the deli. I can remember when he pealed the potatoes for the Potato Salad, there wouldn't be a trace of white attached to the pealed skins. He was proud of his service in the Italian Army, his family, and of his heritage!"

{The following captions belong to the following photographs. They are listed in order}

[Mario R. Ariemma at about the age of eighteen in his egg truck "Ary's Fresh Eggs – Grcoceries. M. Ariemma – 14 Vulcan St." Staten Isand. Courtesy – The Ariemma Family]
[Mario R. Ariemma's official "City of New York" peddler's license for the sale of "fruit and vegetables." C. June 1, 1953. Courtesy – The Ariemma Family]
[A Consolidated Edison Co. of New York, Inc. bill for Ariemma's Deli at 1791 Hylan Blvd. C. 1964. Courtesy – The Ariemma Family]

[Mario R. Ariemma works at the newly-established Ariemma's Italian Deli on Hylan Blvd. C. 1956. Courtesy – The Ariemma Family]

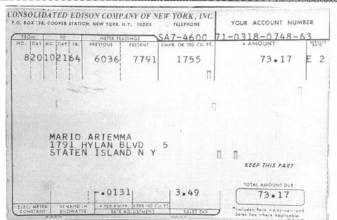

Joseph Vito Lettieri (b. 1921), a longtime Grant City businessman, born to hard-working immigrant parents from the towns of Bitetto (in the metropolitan city of Bari) and Potenza, was the youngest of four children; he was born in "South Brooklyn"—an "obsolete and imprecise" term for the areas of Red Hook, Carroll Gardens, Cobble Hill, etc. Lettieri found a niche in truck-driving early on, as like his father, he began his life's work as a milk man, before delivering groceries and like most Barese, delivering ice in the summer and coal in the winter. After the 9th grade, Lettieri dropped out of Brooklyn Tech H.S. to earn a living. In the spring of 1942, at the age of twenty-one, he enlisted in the U.S. Navy, serving in the American, European (1 star), and Asiatic (3 stars) Theatres. He was an Aviation Machinist Mate 2/c and was stationed on the aircraft carrier, the USS Santee (of which he was a plank owner). For his service, he was awarded the Presidential Unit Citation and the World War II Victory Medal. Following his discharge, Lettieri moved to the small Texas town of Bay City (roughly sixty miles southwest of Central Houston) at the mouth of the Colorado River, and became a shrimper. He operated two bay trawlers for three years. When one of the boats sank in the Colorado River, despite warnings citing "Dangerous Current,"Lettieri nonetheless dove into the water to retrieve his tools and equipment. According to family legend, he is the first known survivor to attempt such a feat. In April 1950, Lettieri returned to New York and despite considerable training as an aviation machinist from the Navy, worked locally as a truck driver, and later became a long-haul driver/owner-operator for Allied Van Lines, driving his truck the Kevinino Puddle Jumper. At this post, he delivered household goods across the country. In 1964, Lettieri started Staten Island Moving & Storage, Agent for Elizabeth, N.J.-based Engel Bros. Van Lines. The company was located alongside Carvel Ice Cream, across from Emily's Keyboard Lounge and Paddy Pasquale's Deli, on Hylan Blvd. between

Greeley Ave. & Lincoln Ave. The company's most sizeable achievement was its dismantling and delivery of the St. George Theatre organ. The iconic instrument—a three-manual, thirty-rank Wurlitzer—valued at its installment in 1929 at $25,000, was to be delivered to Pipe Organ Pizza—a pizzeria in Memorial City, Houston, Texas owned by Constantine Santrizo. *Staten Island Advance* journalist Polly Kummel wrote in Sept., 1973 (the month in which the initial stages of dismantling were commencing), "And so the Lettieris learned that they weren't moving just any organ, but a mammoth pipe organ with literally hundreds, if not thousands, of pieces which were embedded forty-nine years ago in the theater...With a pulley rig over the door, the parts—xylophones, marimbas, drums and cellos sounded by

[Joe Lettieri and his crew from SI Moving & Storage showing Jim Simpson of Victory Van Lines how to move a large safe. Courtesy – Tammy Lettieri]

keys from the console—were brought out slowly and carefully, but surely." Kummel further noted, "In those days, pipe organs provided musical accompaniment for the last of the silent pictures and for sing-alongs, with vaudeville acts in the price of admission." The moving process was supervised by Bud Kurz, an organ expert from San Rafael,

292

Calif. who estimated the organ's weight to be about 15,000 [an estimate provided by Tim Lettieri ranged up to 30,000] pounds. Kurz spent several days in the organ chambers "examining the condition of the equipment, figuring out the sequences for dismantling, and labeling the parts. The organ filled an entire forty-five inch trailer equipped with an air ride suspension system. Lettieri's brother, Kevin assumed the frustrating massive undertaking of itemizing all the parts. The Lettieris moving of the first occupant into the No. 1 World Trade Tower in 1972 marked another milestone in the company's record. Like Lettieri, the first occupant to be moved into the World Trade Tower was a small business owner from Staten Island [43]. Lettieri's most important accomplishment, however, was when he became an Allied Van Lines agent in the early-1970s as this made him the first Allied Van Lines owner-operator to become an Allied Van Lines agent/franchise owner. Humorous stories of Joseph Lettieri are recalled by his daughter Tammy—the author of a children's book series based on her father's adventures. She spoke of her father evading his death after narrowly escaping a bridge which collapsed as he was driving over it in his tractor trailer, the Kevinino Puddle Jumper, in Florida. In the 1950s (a decade before the emergence of monitoring of weather conditions and road closures), J. Lettieri, while crossing the infamous Donner Pass in the Sierra Nevada, saved a truck driver hanging off a cliff who had crashed hauling cattle. "During the Blizzard of 1977", Lettieri recalled, "when my father was fifty-five, my brother was alarmed when my father did not call to ask for assistance backing the trailer into the lot of Dubois Ave. In fact his last call was to say that a major blizzard had shut down most of

---

[43] According to Tim Lettieri, Joseph Lettieri also delivered a lot of carpeting to the World Trade Center. "Two trailer loads of carpeting were delivered to the warehouse on Dubois Ave, and [Lettieri] delivered it to the W.T.C. because he had the extra-long trailers necessary to haul the long rolls of commercial carpeting.

[Joseph Lettieri (right) with Barney Bipp (left) moves office furniture into the World Trade Center wearing his cowboy boots. Courtesy – Tammy Lettieri]

the turnpike and that he was going to try to make it back to Staten Island. Hours passed that Sunday and not a word was heard back from the old Man, as he was affectionately called. So Kevin headed out into the storm...after driving for hours in the general vicinity of [my father's] last known stop, he found the abandoned truck but no sign of my father. Finally about 9pm that evening my father called looking for Kevin. We were dumbfounded. I remember my mother saying, 'He's out looking for you!' to which my father replied that he was home drinking hot chocolate!" In 1973 after being in Grant City in nine years, Staten Island Moving & Storage moved to a warehouse property Lettieri owned on Dubois Ave., off Forest Ave. The tavern around the corner, Lemperle's, was eventually purchased by the former owner of Emily's Keyboard Lounge—the same business located across the street from the original Lettieri site on Hylan Blvd. The old neighborhood had recreated itself.

In an era of hastily vanishing locally-owned businesses, the former- Cangiano's Pork Store at 2271 Hylan Blvd in

Grant City—once a hallmark of excellence in the realm of fine Italian grocery on Staten Island—is merely a discount retail store bearing remnants of the days gone by. Cangiano's derives its namesake from Pasquale Cangiano (b. October 7, 1892), the son of Cosmo Cangiano and Louise Ivarone of Naples. The young Cangiano immigrated to New York City around 1917 at the age of twenty-five, and thereafter, found employment as a butcher at a Carroll Gardens pork store; he later became a partner in the store. In 1932, Cangiano set off to begin his own store, one that specialized in the making of sausage and other pork products (hence, the store's type: *pork store*), at 6508 14th Ave. in Dyker Heights in the building he had purchased in 1930. He resided directly upstairs with his wife and seven children. The initial store was called Jersey Pork Store, and was a "Specialista di Salsiccia" (Specialist in Sausage). Despite the opening of two more locations in Brooklyn, Cangiano himself succumbed to a brain hemorrhage on May 27, 1937. Though the founder had passed, Cangiano's Pork Store at its highest boasted five locations; at one point, Cangiano's claimed to be the largest Italian deli in Brooklyn and Staten Island. Louis Cangiano, —Pasquale's son—along with his wife Saveria, after purchasing the Cangiano's on West 7th St. in Brooklyn, saw the opportunity for a full-grocery store on Staten Island. Cangiano's was opened first as one of many venues in a farmer's market located in Port Richmond in 1960 on Staten Island by Louis and Saveria Cangiano, in partnership with Frank Ritchie; after approximately a dozen years, after locating a different property, Louis opened Cangiano's on Staten Island in 1974 initially as a "gourmet shop for sophisticated Staten Islanders." A May 30, 1977 edition of New York Magazine reads, "Aside from the ferry and python at the zoo, there wasn't ever much that drew us to Staten Island...until the Saturday we happened upon Cangiano's Pork Store, which is not just a pork store. The

Cangianos—brothers, sons, uncles, aunts, nephews, nieces—bake their own Italian cheesecake and bread (Sicilian, brick-oven, and semolina) while you watch, make their own mozzarella (with or without prosciutto) and their own sausages. Delirious customers swoop down on cans of olive oil, pore over a barrel of live snails, shout out their orders for stuffed braciole and marinated roast pork and spiedini[44], wait anxiously in line for 30 cheeses from all over the world." Cangiano's specialized in imported whole Italian tomatoes, Sclafani crushed tomatoes ricotta, Santuzza-blended olive oil, Menucci macaroni, veal cutlets, veal sausage, prosciutto bread, Italian cookies, a full line of

[An advertisement from the Staten Island Advance newspaper advertising the daily savings at Cangiano's Pork Store. C. March 7, 1982. Courtesy – Richard Barbato]

Italian pastries, arancini (Sicilian fried rice balls), mozzarella, cold cuts, and of course bread. The pork store's

---

44 A brief note on translation from Italian: *spiedini* can refer to a small meat roll or skewer, particularly with meat and vegetables. Stuffed *braciole* (pronounced "brahjzool" in Sicilian) refers to fried, rolled thin slices of meat, usually with cheese.

product quality was expressed in their moto: "When you see Cangiano's on the label, you have quality on the table." On Sundays, the store broadcasted Frank Sinatra on the speakers, in addition to other Big Band music (as appropriate for the store's New York-Italian regular clientele). Among favorite Staten Islander memories of Cangiano's are consuming the highly-sought-after bread; often, shoppers who only intended to buy two loaves would have to buy three—one they could eat on the way to the car or while scanning the cold cuts. Conveniently, three loaves of bread were sold together for $1. Other memories include listening to the deli boys who sang behind the cold cuts counter. Former employee for the store Michael Ventrone of Annadale, whose father owned and operated Stapleton Liquor Mart at 100 Canal St. between 1973-1997, remarked, "I began working at Cangiano's when I was only twelve years old! Back in 1972, I was making two bucks an hour, twenty-five bucks a week. My job was to sweep the parking lot, mop the floors, stack milk crates, put away the food...And when I had to make deliveries to homes or businesses one or two miles away, I'd fit whatever I could on the two baskets on my bicycle and ride off. For a kid making twenty-five bucks a week back then, I was rich! I always loved money. I lived across the street from Cangiano's so I saw all my friends' parents coming in and everyone from the neighborhood. The guys working there never called me by my first name—Mike. They'd always say, 'Yo, kid!' I was the only twelve-year old working there; everyone else was pretty much over fifty. They'd say, 'Hey kid! Help that old lady to her car.' And I'd carry out the groceries, and they almost always give me a dollar tip. Everyone working at Cangiano's was so nice to me. I stayed there working until I was sixteen. Those were good days!" Though having earned the respect of a loyal generation of Staten Islanders, Cangiano's ultimately closed on June 13, 2010; the former restaurant beneath the pork store—La Botte—characterized by its "[b]rick arched doorways and mirror-filled windows," became Troy, and is currently Violette's Cellar. Though Cangiano's business ties to Staten Island have officially been severed, the Cangiano-gastronomic legacy lives on in Manhattan. In 2009, Louis and Lauren Cangiano opened Tre Otto[45] trattoria at 1408 Madison Ave. in Carnegie Hill. The restaurant—a fourth generation Cangiano establishment—offers "authentic Italian food prepared from family recipes." Though passer-by may no longer observe the bakers at the old pork store through a glass window from Hylan Blvd., they will forever have a recollection of those people and products at Cangiano's which helped make their gatherings and lives memorable.

~

Among the many Italian newcomers to the Italian South Shore was the Reginella family—natives of Sunset Park, Brooklyn. Celia "Connie" Barone moved with her two children, Gina and Rosemary, to Oakwood in 1977 to a safer, more spacious environment. Though some traditions such as living upstairs from their grandparents were lost in the transition across the Verrazzano-Narrows Bridge, others were preserved, and new ones were adopted. Gina Reginella recalled, "Everything in the front room in my grandmother's house—or as it truly was, the "museum"—was covered entirely in plastic! And you never, ever used the front door! You always needed to come into the house through the side door which led to the basement kitchen...During the summertime, my mother's neighbor on 46th St. would hook up a cap to the fire hydrant, which they called the 'Johnny Pump,' and connect it to the sprinkler system. My sister and I would go into the street with our bathing suits on and enjoy

---

[45] The restaurant's name *Tre Otto* refers to the three eights in Pasquale Cangiano's wife Anna's death date—August 8, 1978.

the water blasting out of the sprinklers on the hot, summer day. The old lady down the block used to get mad at them because her car was getting wet, and she'd call the fire department which would shut the party down! But what I'll always remember most about those days were the stories about 4th of July in Canarsie. Walking through the streets on that night was like going through Vietnam!" ... "We were an Americanized Italian household" Gina explained, "Out of all my mother's siblings, she was the most rebellious in terms of adopting tradition. Her birth name was Consiglia Barone, but her family always called her 'Celia.' In high school, her teacher named her 'Connie' and so she went by that name around friends. Whenever her high school friends would call the house looking for 'Connie,' her mother in her broken English would reply, 'No, there'z a no dog livin' here.'"[46] Upon arriving to Staten Island, Celia worked at Pergament Home Center, and then was employed as a cashier at the Salumeria on Hylan Blvd. in Dongan Hills. Gina continued, "The general rule of thumb was: we'd go out riding down Hylan Blvd. in our convertibles, blaring the radios, or sometimes go down to the roller skating rink where the 'Guidos' hung out, and when we came home, my mom, would immediately go out dancing either to the Brown Derby on 4th Ave. in Brooklyn or to Inn by the Wayside in Dongan Hills! ... I have so many memories of growing up on Staten Island. As we got older, the big thing in the 80s was hanging out in parking lots; sometimes we'd go to Pizza Town in New Dorp or Hylan Plaza." Gina notes how the Staten Island of her generation has undergone some significant amounts of change, particularly within community dynamics. "You don't hear people saying anymore 'Do you know who my uncle is?'" Gina concluded, "It's just not like that." Celia Barone remarked, "I came to

---

[46] The English name "Connie" is homophonic to the Italian word *cane* meaning "dog"

Staten Island to make a better life for my family! I left behind the strict Italian household I grew up in in Sunset Park. I'll remember for the rest of my life: as a young kid at dinner, my father would say, 'If you want to speak English, leave this table! We speak Italian only.' It turns out they weren't even speaking Italian; it was a backward dialect from the town they were from—Torre del Greco, Naples... Before my father passed away in 1962, my mother urged him to become an American citizen;

[A young Johnny Potenza paints a fence in his Midwood home at 1610 Avenue S in Brooklyn. C. 1973. Courtesy – Johnny Potenza]

he was afraid to apply because he had jumped ship twice from Italy. He told me, 'Celia—your mother's going to have me arrested before I die!'... I still try and keep up the Italian customs on Staten Island. Until my kids grew up, we all had dinner every Sunday at two in the afternoon like a true Italian household. I hate to tell you, I make a killer tomato gravy. Everything I put in it is fresh—Italian parsley, crushed tomatoes, garlic, and basinigol. At least that's how they said basil in Torre del Greco!"

Others newcomers to the South Shore of Staten Island include Johnny Potenza—a native of Bensonhurst, raised partly in Midwood, Brooklyn. Potenza, a noted late-night talk show host and musician, Potenza migrated to the neighborhood of Prince's Bay—in his words "Home of the

Italian, Irish, and the Rock n' Roll—in the early-1980s. Of Sicilian and Neopolitan descent, Potenza was raised in a pragmatic household with zero-tolerance for antics. "My father, a plasterer and New York City firefighter, was a 'knock-around kind of a guy. One time, he had this guy who refused to pay him. After trying to negotiate a deal, my father took his sledgehammer to his freshly-plastered walls and shouted, 'There! Now you don't owe me nothing!'" Having

witnessed his first KISS concert at the age of ten at Madison Square Garden, Potenza commenced drum lessons at the age of twelve at local music stores; in 1993 with legendary Jim Chapin—the

[Johnny Potenza (left) interviews television and radio personality, Joe Franklin. C. Aug. 23, 2012. Courtesy – Johnny Potenza]

father of Harry Chapin, the famous folk rock and pop rock musician who rose to prominence in the 1970s. At the age of sixteen, Potenza began entertaining at bars on Staten Island. Though he has been apart of several bands throughout his lengthy musical career, three include The Same (early-1980s), Barrage (1990-1995), and NYB. ("None of Your Business" – 1995-2005). In 1997, Potenza began editing for Public Access Television; his first televised program to edit was "Gangsters of Rock." Since 2008, Potenza has hosted his own late-night talk show, Late Night with Johnny P. For both "Gangsters of Rock" and "Late Night with Johnny P," Potenza has received multiple Nova Awards. Though he has interviewed individuals in the hundreds of quantities, notable interviewees include television and radio personality, Joe Franklin (1926-2015), *The Sopranos* actor Vincent Pastore (portraying Salvatore "Big Pussy" Bonpensiero), reality television personality, Angela "Big Ang" Raiola (1960-2016), and countless celebrities who have starred in *The Sopranos*, *Blue Bloods*, *Goodfellas*, etc. "I can remember – my father would ask me, 'Johnny: what are you going to do with yourself?' I'd say 'I'm going to be a rock star!' And he'd continue to ask me that same question every day. I'd always give the exact same response. Finally one day, I said, 'I want to be a plasterer just like you!' He replied, 'Son – don't be a plasterer! You'll break your ass for the rest of your life.'" Potenza, a talented plasterer, continues his successful lifestyle in the realm of professional entertainment. On July 21, 2018, he received the honorable "Kings of Staten Island" Award at the Richmond County Country Club. As of 2019, Potenza currently is in production for his new entertainment variety show.

Decades before the arrival of those such as Johnny Potenza, Connie Barone and her family, and others from Brooklyn, the South Shore of Staten Island was mostly what natives remember it as: "The Sticks." Among the most nostalgic emblems of the South Shore of Staten Island's past is the famous Al Deppe's restaurant (originally called Al's Place), which stood at the corner of Richmond Rd. & Arthur Kill Rd.—along the former path of N.Y. State Route 440— in Greenridge from 1921 to 1966. Owned by Alfred J. Deppe (b. June 14, 1899), the restaurant, known for its hot dogs (in fact, the diner at this time was only one of three in New York City primarily featuring hot dogs; the others being Feltman's and Nathan's), advertised "famous Home-Made Frankfurters," soft shell crab, a clam bar, wheat cakes, country sausages, homemade ice cream, shore dinners, hamburgers, and French fries. Al Deppe's initiated as a roadside balloon stand, and later evolved through the decades into a full-service restaurant, mini-golf course, small amusement park/indoor arcade, and shooting range. As explained in *Discovering Staten Island: A 350ᵗʰ Anniversary Commemorative History*: "In the 1920s, the business had no running water or electricity, but kerosene, ingenuity, and visits to O'Leary's Ice House kept the food coming and customers happy." Deppe was also renown for his quirky sense-of-humor; on a menu from the late-1950s, it is written: "Tuna Fish Salad, fresh caught tuna. Al throws the cans – Harold catches them" and "Chilled Shrimp Cocktail, of course it's chilled, where do you think we keep them, in the steam table." Asides from being a casual hangout for people throughout the borough, Al Deppe's was among the top destinations for family, Sunday drives, in particular Al Deppe's Playland. Tickets distributed by Elliott Ticket Co. of 409 Lafayette St., Manhattan, which could be saved or redeemed for valuable prizes, guaranteed entry to the indoor arcade where children could play Skee-Ball, ride kiddy-rides, and give a go at the pinball machines. The amusement park further included a German-imported carousel, a machine where one could record their own 45 RPM, vending machines that dispensed photographs of actors and actresses, and a monkey organ-grinder. Perhaps the most memorable of the games was where as many Staten Islanders described it, "you could make Al Deppe's chicken dance for a penny!" In reality, once someone dropped a penny in the machine's slot, a light went on, and the chicken began to move rapidly because shortly after the light's activation, feed would be dropped into the cage. In what was a quite rural area settled initially by Huguenots, Greenridge was made into a popular destination by virtue of Al Deppe's; the triangular corner—known as Deppe's Corner—made up of the tri-intersections of Richmond Ave., Arthur Kill Rd., and Drumgoole Blvd., consisted of a gas station, the Elks Club, a miniature golf course, Al Deppe's, and Fitzgerald's Fairway Club. Ten years after the restaurant's opening in

1931, Al Deppe purchased the mansion at 3250 Richmond Ave. at the corner of Wainwright Ave. The estate was constructed in the 1840s by Obadiah Bowne, and in 1853 was purchased by Edward Banker—a wealthy investor descended from an old New Amsterdam business in the ship chandlery business—who had invested in the Erie Canal, and was a developer of the Staten Island Railroad. After acquiring the property, Deppe constructed a 200-ft. underground tunnel between the restaurant and his home so that he wouldn't have to walk in daylight on the street with his day's receipts. Many believe Deppe to have been paranoid for this reason, and some still speculate money is buried within the tunnel in the present day. In any case, the Elks Lodge took over the site in 1960; the current property is known as "Staten Island Elks Lodge BPO No. 841." In 1965, though Al Deppe's had managed to survive over forty-four years in the same location, it too would be washed away by the malignant tides of Robert Moses. As part of his Richmond Parkway Plan, Moses advised Al Deppe's to sell its property; however, after the restaurant's refusal, Moses went to the courts. Under eminent domain, the City condemned Deppe's property and forcibly removed the restaurant in 1966. *Staten Island Advance* journalist Michael W. Dominowski wrote, "The highway would have cut across the wooded top of Todt Hill and plunged through the Boy Scouts' Pouch Camp and the only glacial lake in New York City. It would have clipped and overshadowed what is now High Rock Park and sundered La Tourette Park, a sylvan place with a rich connection to the American Revolution...[Moses'] road-building troops were hard at work completing the southern end of the Richmond Parkway when New York City mayoral candidate John V. Lindsay, mindful of determined and growing public opposition to the road, suggested Moses realign the unbuilt northern leg to minimize its environmental and social effects." Though Moses' efforts had been halted, Al Deppe's could not be rescued from time. The venerable restaurant, whose gigantic hot dog on the roof was a sweet symbol of children's joyous childhoods, had succumbed to the changing times.

A description of that neighborhood of Arden Heights/Woodrow would be incomplete without the context of quotation remarked by George William Curtis most beloved by Staten Islanders: "God might have made a more beautiful place than Staten Island, but He never did." Curtis—a Republican civil rights advocate and orator from Rhode Island who resided at his home at 234 Bard Ave. constructed in 1853—had substantial reason to make this perhaps almost non-exaggerated statement; many would agree. The homesteads of Woodrow Rd. stretching from Bloomingdale Rd. to Arthur Kill Rd. were such proof. Each property, associated each with an English or German family name from the 1850s, encompassed acres of blossoming pear trees, marshes, and dirt roads. Bob Siclari (b. 1955), a High Mobility Multipurpose Wheeled Vehicle (HMMWV) mechanic at the Tobyhanna Army Depot in Pennsylvania, paints a nostalgic illustration of Staten Island's golden years. Raised until the age of two at 149 Jefferson Ave.[47] in Grant City, Siclari's family had a cultured background. Siclari's parents had a country western band called the "Rhythmn Range Riders." His mother played rhythm guitar, while his father played steel guitar and accordion. His mother and her siblings—the Hoffmann Sisters—performed at various venues on Staten Island, and even recorded with Denver Darling—a New York City radio cowboy noted for his patriotic and American homeland songs. These include "The Devil and Mr. Hitler," "When Mussolini Laid His Pistol Down," and "Cowards over Pearl Harbor"—all released during World War II. The Hoffmann Sisters can be seen

---

[47] At 149 Jefferson Ave. Siclari's older brother, Charlie recalled, "In the early-1930s, my grandfather bought my father a BB gun for a present. My father, only a little kid, shot one of the pigeon's in my grandfather's pigeon coop. My grandfather immediately took the gun and wrapped it tight against a tree!"

[Brothers Charlie "Butch" on his horse, Joker, and Bob on his horse, Flame at the rodeo. C. 1960s. Courtesy – Bob Siclari]

during a recording of Denver Darling's 1942 song: "Shy Anne From Old Cheyenne." Due to their musical backgrounds, Siclari's parents met while performing at WHBI Radio in New Jersey. Siclari's uncle Chris McEwan—a soldier in the 101st Airborne Division—owned and kept a Fairchild PT-19 monoplane with an open cockpit at the Staten Island Airport in New Springville. Siclari's mother, a seamstress who sewed emergency kits into life rafts for the military, helped sew the fabric of the aircraft's wing. An auto enthusiast, Siclari's father purchased an engine—a six-hundred-dollar V-12—which arrived by freight train to Grant City to use in a vehicle. When it was activated in the family backyard, the entire neighborhood was shaken. Siclari's aunts, Rose and Jennie were cooks/waitresses at F.W. Woolworth Co. in Stapleton. During the 1960s, Siclari's uncle Joe, borrowing his brother's auto body grinder, even worked on the Verrazzano-Narrows Bridge. At the age of two, Siclari moved to Arden Heights to 343 Woodrow Rd. The home—construted in originally in 1920 and later moved across the street—sat atop a pig farm, later converted to a horse ranch by Siclari's father, Charlie (1920-1965). Siclari recalled scavenging for toys in the foundation of the original site of the home, left uncovered for decades for people to abandon their household garbage. Charlie Siclari, an equestrian enthusiast who raced horses against freight trains and was a member of the Sheriff's Mounted Posse[48], famously was featured in a *Staten Island Advance* article for the scaled Western town he constructed on his property. The town included a Montanti General Store (named for L. Montanti & Sons Leathercraft Supplies Inc. on Richmond Terrace) in a transformed Weissglass Milk truck, a Wells Fargo Bank, and a lifesize bar complete with all accessories inside. Siclari stated, "My dad built the scaled town just for us so we could play. But by the time we were young teenagers, we were playing more World War II-type games, as opposed to Western ones. The worst was getting hit with a hand grenade, which was essentially a big hunk of dirt!" Another incident, as described by Charlie Siclari, involved a runaway calf from the Siclari property. "I noticed this calf my father had picked up had run

[The Siclari family poses in front of the "Golden Horseshoe Saloon" – one of many buildings in their scaled Western town. C. 1962. Courtesy – Bob Siclari]

---

[48] The Sheriff's Mounted Posse in Sept. 1962 possessed twenty-five active members, of whom Charlie Siclari was the leader. A highlight of the group's "colorful history" was an appearance at the 1939 New York World's Fair. The group also accompanied Gov. Nelson Rockefeller into the annual Republican picnic, held in Pleasant Plains in 1962.

away when I was bringing out some seed to feed it! It roamed the entire South Shore for six-eight weeks. Eventually, we found it at the home an old woman on Arthur Kill Rd. The woman was mostly blind and thought she had been feeding a 'large dog' every evening! ... And that wasn't the only time one of our animals went missing! Sometime, in the 1960s, I woke up to find two of horses had vanished. The first order of business was to immediately tell Mom I couldn't go to school, and the second – to call friends who lived down the street. They saddled their horses and met me at my house where I had saddled my horse. I tracked them through the woods from Annadale almost to Great Kills where we lassoed them and brought them home!"" Following his lively youth, Bob Siclari went on to become an auto mechanic at the Annadale Service Station on Amboy Rd. & Annadale Rd. for thirty years. After growing tired of servicing automobiles, and having his former house developed into a uniform collection of dwellings, Siclari left this time to the greener pastures of Pennsylvania.

At the age of eleven, Siclari and his brother had worked at Mount Loretto driving the tractors. Paid in hay, Siclari stored his earnings in his family's backyard barn. The fifteen tons of hay he amassed, which stacked to the height of the barn's roof, eventually went into flames during a blaze on the property. Mount Loretto was founded by Father John Christopher Drumgoole (1816-1888). Originally from the town of Granard, County Longford, Ireland, Drumgoole arrived in New York City in 1824. His mother, widowed at an early age, met him at the Quarantine Station off Staten Island, and from there brought him to St. Patrick's Church. First appointed sexton at St. Mary's Church, he would go on to graduate from the Seminary of Our Lady of Angels near Niagara Falls in 1865, be ordained a priest four years later, found Mission of the Immaculate Virgin in 1870 on Great Jones St. & Lafayette Pl., and later be named chaplain of St. Vincent's Home for Homeless Newsboys on Warren Street in Newspaper/Park Row in 1871. Located at 53 Warren Street, St. Vincent's provided shelter for impoverished newsboys and bootblacks at a price of 5¢; Drumgoole offered courses in woodworking, shoemaking, and baking. His time working with the newsboys was commended by the naming of "Drumgoole Plaza" in 2003 on Frankfort Street, beneath the Brooklyn Bridge. On November 22, 1883, Drumgoole opened the Mount Loretto Orphanage (whose namesake derived from the Sisters of Loretto) after having purchased a 253-acre parcel of land from the Bennett Farm at a price of $40,000; by a few months into operation, the grounds would span a total of 600 acres, encompassing the former farms of Seguine, Jessup, Vail, and Nance. Mount Loretto would continue its expansion until its final purchase of six acres of land which included the historic Prince's Bay Lighthouse erected in 1828, from the U.S. Department of Commerce in 1926. The grounds, compromised of a total of forty-seven buildings, would reach their maximum size at 700 acres in 1947. The construction of the entirety of the facilities would cost more than $1 million; regardless of the hefty price, Father Drumgoole left the orphans without any debt. The orphanage was divided into four distinct sections: St. Elizabeth's Home for Girls, St. Joseph's Asylum for Blind Girls, the Duval Cottage for orphaned baby girls, and St. Joseph's Home for Boys. Other divisions include the reading hall, billiard room, and Trades' School which offered classes in shoemaking, butchering, sawing, moulding, knitting, upholstering, printing, stenography, typewriting. The cows which grazed on the campus' voluminous pastures were a frequent sight viewed by Staten Islanders who embarked on Sunday drives down Hylan Blvd. to Tottenville; until 1967, the cows were used to provide milk for the orphans. At its peak, Mount Loretto housed roughly 2,000 destitute children who as television and radio news broadcaster Frank Cipolla described in his book *It Shocked Even Us!* were, "wayward kids from some of the toughest, grimiest neighborhoods in the city. These were not the cute 'Bowery Boys' kind of mischievous kids we used to watch on Sunday morning TV. These were 'Don't Screw with Me or Else I'll Slit Your Throat' kind of kids." Nevertheless, Fr. Drumgoole remarked 118 years before, in 1893, "The child who was absolutely destitute, applying for admission, must never be refused; the child who, though not destitute, was in a position where his faith was endangered, must not be refused." Refugees included those from the 1960-1962 Operation Peter Pan—a mission established by the Catholic Welfare Bureau to rescue over 14,000 children fleeing from Castro's forming communist dictatorship in Cuba. Others included many starving, Irish orphans from the streets of Manhattan; "the general environment of the City at the time" Drumgoole felt, "was a great threat to younger children." The farm on Staten Island was a pleasant reminder of both Fr. Drumgoole and Irish children's upbringing in the old country; the orphanage did much for Irish orphans who would normally be sent west to other distant facilities. The Irish culture, formerly present at Mount Loretto, in the present day is celebrated at the "Staten Ireland Irish Fair." The fair is hosted by the Saint Columcille Irish Culture Center and Catholic Charities, and celebrates over a century of Staten Island-Irish history in the form of the playing of traditional Irish music (by the Richmond County Pipes & Drums Inc., Celtic Cross Pipes & Drums, etc.), cooking of Irish-American cuisine (e.g. Fish & Chips, Corned Beef Sandwiches, and sausages), and distribution of awards to extraordinary individuals of Irish descent. Catholic Charities of New York—the current operator of the former Mount Loretto—in 1986 also developed "Project Irish Outreach." The project assists Irish immigrants with naturalization, employment, and legal representation.

Among the many Irish and Scandinavians who inhabited the isolated neighborhood of Tottenville (just southwest of Mount Loretto) in early-mid-20th century Staten Island,

several Italians also managed t
themselves. Frank Barsalona (b. 1?
of Sciacca, Sicily in 1899 to Little .
he would meet his future wife, J
immigrated in about 1904). Presen
included longtime Italian, Rosebank
Montalbano—the owner of Montalb,
St. Upon his move to Tottenville b
began F. Barsalona Seafood at 43 Be
constructed in 1917 by Barsalona, as   ..., Dimino,
Marinello (mostly from Brooklyn and Queens), and
Montalbano families. Barsalona had sought a less-crowded
residence than his current one in Little Italy, and desired "to
be in the country surrounded by water." Three times a week,
the newly-arrived immigrant made the trek to the Fulton Fish
Market in the early morning hours to prepare for deliveries
along his route. Due to the large presence of Norwegians and
Swedes in Tottenville, Barsalona was able to sell a wide
variety of seafood: flounder, fluke, tuna, clams, mussels,
squid, octopus, and lobsters. In the time before refrigeration,
Barsalona relied on local ice man, Vito Scarangello to supply
cooling for the seafood. Barsalona's grandson Jim, owner of
Team New Jersey Softball, who grew up at 124 Nashville St.
(constructed by his parents in 1955) reminisced, "I can
remember my grandpa sitting on the porch smoking his cigar
on Sundays. He never went to church! " "Whenever my
grandparents would get into arguments in Italian, and my
grandma accused Frank of always 'just want[ing] to eat,' my
grandpa would quit and go sit on the porch for hours. Then
my grandma would wink at me and whisper 'He's mad!'"
Barsalona recalled seeing his grandfather constantly with a
soda bottle in hand; little did he know, the can was filled with
homemade wine. "I remember watching them make the wine.
Making the wine, and the large Italian feast that would be
included, truly I will assume the same as they did in the
village in Italy. Many if not all traditions never changed for

immigrant families that came over from Italy." ...ona's son, Gus went on to found G. & S. Paint Store(s) 1951 in Tottenville; the store later expanded to 164 New Dorp Lane, Eltingville, Port Richmond, and Great Kills. "My father was a character by all means" Barsalona elaborated, "he actually served on the USS Alabama during World War II, and played on the Pacific Fleet Baseball Team with Major League Baseball pitcher for the Cleveland Indians, Bob Feller!" As Staten Island began to see rapid change and industrialization in the 1950s, the neighborhood in which as Jim Barsalona described it, "some people never even left," changed—in this case, for the worst. Deemed a health hazard, Frank Barsalona's horses were forced out of operation on public streets. Determined to continue his business, nevertheless, Barsalona learned to drive, although "not very well." In the current day, the property no longer stands. Jim Barsalona concluded, "I went back to Staten

[Frank Barsalona his delivery vehicle at 43 Bedell Ave. in semi-rural Tottenville. C. 1947. Courtesy – Carol Gorshoff Barsalona]

Island one day and found the property completely different. My house was gone. I felt violated."

FINAL REFLECTION

Italians were known throughout the Island for their willingness to negotiate, their specialized skills, and their sociability. Among notable Italians possessing such traits was Carmine Rizzo—an immigrant from the small town of Sacco, Salerno who became famous for his one-word, accented request, "Shin-ee?" Carmine Rizzo had moved to America to Astoria, Queens around 1970 to be with his brother who had immigrated in 1955. Since October of 1972 (until 2005), Rizzo, along with his sidekick Angelo Passero, wandered the Staten Island Ferry offering to shine shoes for a measly rate of $2.50 per shine. In the later years of their shining, between 6am and 12 noon, they were fortunate enough to barely earn $20. The elusive pair could be seen daily with their shoe shine kit—a "reasoning artifact for ferry riders...[which] held the brushes, cloth, and black, brown, oxblood, and neutral shine that helped many commuters win the job, date, or respect they desired." Dan Barry wrote in his article *About New York; All Feet on Deck, Forlorn* (2004), "Once summoned, [Carmine] would place a small pillow on the ground and kneel before the patron, as in supplication. From this vantage point he could not see the glint of morning sunlight off Lady Liberty's torch, or gaze into the fog that seems to set the Verrazzano-Narrows Bridge in the backdrop of a dream. There on his knees, all he saw were the words "Life Preservers" stenciled beneath the scarred, dark-wooden benches; trouser legs; and other people's shoes." Rizzo's employment was in reality a generational one; each set of soon-to-retire shiners would pass their equipment and position to the next one. Rizzo's assumption of this trade was actually entirely impromptu. When a close friend of Rizzo's from the old country—

Francesco DiCicca—died due to drowning, DiCicca's son took over the position for a short duration of time before moving back to Italy and becoming a farmer. DiCicca's grandchildren notified Rizzo of the potential job, and Rizzo gladly accepted. Rizzo would shine shoes until 2000, where

[A typical day shining shoes for the diligent Mr. Carmine Rizzo. C. early-2000s. Courtesy – Angelo Rizzo]

he would then eventually come out of retirement and continue until 2005; for several months, he drove his wife crazy, contemplating whether to go back to work or not. Rizzo's son Angelo, who joined his father on the immigration voyage to the United States, exclaimed, "My dad never liked having a boss! He was an independent spirit. When my father first came to New York, he was a construction worker. He absolutely hated having someone telling him what to do! (Of course, he could only do certain things. He had broken his back in 1967 when he fell from an olive tree, harvesting olives in Italy). And when his brother tried to convince him to get a job at a factory, my dad was adamant in his denial! Even back when my father used to go from farm to farm plowing the land with his oxen, he didn't have a boss...But people liked my father because he was an honest guy. And a gentleman too; he'd take the ladies' boots off first, then shine them. It was

314

funny...On Columbus Day, my father used to wear 'Kiss Me, I'm Italian' pins, and on St. Patrick's Day, he'd dress up in green and wear 'Kiss Me, I'm Irish' pins. Some of the other shoe shiners used to like to sneak peeks up the ladies' dresses, but my father never did. And then they'd ask my father, 'Why does everyone get their shoes shined by you, and not by me?' My dad would just tell them, 'I don't know, you should ask them.' My father, who paid for my brother and I to go to college, and believed in respecting people and being honest, always told me, 'You can go and clean bathrooms, as long as it's honest work. Back in Sacco, there were so many *camorristas* (members of the Italian criminal, Mafia-type organization *Camorra*). They'd go around as tax collectors demanding the property tax each year. Let's say the people owed three-hundred lire, and said they would pay the rest at the end of the year. The camorrista would go down to Salerno and report the people had only paid one-hundred lire, and he would pocket the rest! Then, come end of the year, he would make the people pay money they didn't even owe. But *my father*...No! They never fooled him. He made sure they accurately wrote what he had paid in their book...My father for these reasons believed in having a tight-knit family and being able to outsmart evildoers... I'll never forget...He'd cautiously say, "*Buoi e femmine del paese tuo*—oxen and women from your town."

EPILOGUE

Whether for better or worse, though by many opinions expressed in this work of literature a specific choice is clear, Staten Island continues to change at an unprecedented pace. As demographics shift, native Islanders are pushed toward the boundaries of New Jersey and Pennsylvania, and development rages on in a bountiful real estate market, Staten Island faces serious prospects of urbanization. The Verrazzano-Narrows Bridge, though still a factor in population increase, becomes less of a symbol of "unhinged development" in the twenty-first century. Though the gravel roads of Mid-Island and farms of the South Shore have absorbed into time's daunting continuum, they shall live eternally within the confines of this work. Though certain fears about development are indeed justified on several rational bases, "Creative Patriot" painter Scott LoBaido originally of Dongan Hills pointed out in a telephone interview: "Who knows what will really happen – we all thought it was the end of the world when the A&W went into business on Hylan Blvd.!" Politically-speaking, Staten Island is yet another fascinating case study. Founder of 123 Publish Incorporated and descendant of Mario Esposito— former vice president of the Stapleton-based Canal and Cardinal Lumber Co.'s, Joseph Pidoriano, a political organizer for the Island's Republican Party, remarked, " "Staten Island's modern politics is ever changing. As the younger population gets older and more politically diverse, it is imperative my political party (The Republican Party) become more acquiescent and use a combination of informative/persuasive communication to those groups of voters. Many younger people are leaving Staten Island, and one of the biggest messages that Republicans must focus on would be improving the infrastructure in a differentiated way that the Democrats would claim to fix infrastructure, reduce taxes so they can keep more of what they bring home, and reform student loans without raising taxes on the middle class. Staten Island should be a model for the rest of the nation in the ever-evolving political arena". As for the Democratic Party on Staten Island, a recent political victory was scored during the 2018 U.S. House of Representative midterms by Max Rose. Though politics, development, and the future of the Island will continue to remain somewhat unpredictable going forward, one thing is clear—in the words of John Franzreb III: "Staten Island has been found."

Source Notes

(Listed in Order Used)

1. *"...conservative bastion in a liberal city."* Adopted from Kramer, Daniel C., et. Flanagan, Richard M. "Staten Island: Conservative Bastion in a Liberal City." Lanham: University Press of America, 2012. Print.

2. *"[f'in] Guinea Gangplank"* The term "Guinea Gangplank" originated sometime in the mid-1960s. It derives from "the stereotype that Italians, escaping from Brooklyn, use this bridge to get to the one neighborhood they can escape to" (Urban Dictionary, 2005). The vulgarity in brackets was adopted from W. Roccaro, personal communication, May 21, 2018.

3. *"...laborers to work when they have made them angry"* ibid.

4. *"outdated bus routes."* Furfaro, Danielle. "Fuming residents say Staten Island bus route revamp is a disaster." New York Post. Sept. 26, 2018.

5. *"gavones."* Gavone (singular) derives from the Italian word *cafone*, meaning a laborer or peasant. In Italian-American slang, it has come to be associated with one who "is overly aggressive and hungry, particularly of a man of Southern Italian descent." Adopted from A. Supino, personal communication, Jan. 5, 2018.

6. *"four regional dialects."* The American-English language consists of four basic accents (with slightly varied lexicon): California/Pacific West, Deep South, Midwest, and Northeast (e.g. New York, Bostonian, New Jersey). The Staten Island speech/form of speaking is distinctive in style. All characteristics of the accent i.e. inflection of vowels, utilizing spontaneity, etc. are adopted from M. Ragucci, personal communication, Dec. 9, 2017.

7. *"Staten Italy."* This title of the "forgotten borough" pays homage to Basille, Sal et. Garcia, Francis. "Staten Italy: Nothin' but the Best Italian-American Classics, from Our Block to Yours." Grand Central Life & Style. March 31, 2015.

8. *"...1950s and 60s were Jewish"* M. Ragucci, personal communication, Dec. 9, 2017.

9. *"...would honor one another's parking space."* Though this fact seems to be a changing factor in the entirety of American society, it is particularly of interest in Staten Island's South Shore. Adopted from V. Popolano, personal communication, Jul. 10, 2018.

10. *"matchbox cities."* Adopted from "...to some quirks of fate that spared Annadale-Huguenot the matchbox-house development of neighboring

318

towns." Sterne, Michael. "The New York times guide to where to live in and around New York." Times Books. Nov. 1, 1985.

11. *"Annadale-Huguenot" and relevant historical information.* Adopted from "Interview with Borough President Robert T. Connor, Staten Island: The Forgotten Borough." New York Illustrated. Late-1960s.

12. *"...studies of this painfully accurate description of Staten Island."* This testimony of education on modern Staten Island is adopted from C.B. Reiss, personal communication, Dec. 6, 2018.

13. *"[exclusion] from the Five-Borough Ferry Plan."* Based on F. Morano, personal communication, May 7, 2018...and..."Staten Island NYC Is Excluded in Five Borough Ferrt Plan, BP Oddo Seeks Correction." Staten Island NYC Living. Jan. 9, 2017.

14. *"at 450 acres owned by Staten Island Marine Development."* Satow, Julie. "Staten Island Property Puts a NASCAR Failure Behind It." The New York Times. Oct. 29, 2013.

15. *"...what my mother would call a schnapps idea."* Feuer, Alan. "Plan for NASCAR Speedway Is Scrapped on Staten Island." The New York Times. Dec. 5, 2006.

16. *"S. Robert Molinari" and relevant biographical information.* Adopted from "Molinari is Dead; Ex-Legislator, 59; Staten Island Realty Broker Served in State Assembly, '43-'44, and in City Bureau." The New York Times. June 2, 1957.

17. *"Independent Subway System."* Adopted from "The New York Red Book." New York: William Press, 1944.

18. *"South Shore Sales & Rentals – Homes Built."* Text extracted from a photograph taken by N.Y.C. Department of Records & Information Services between 1939-1941. 153 New Dorp Lane.

19. *"...frying pan before you got home."* Adopted from M. Gallucci, personal communication, May 24, 2018.

20. *"...known for his courtroom theatrics."* From Kilgannon, Corey. "Character Study – Stylish, Tenacious Defender." The New York Times. Dec. 24, 2015.

21. *"...to thousands of people struggling with addiction."* Carl's Recovery Center – Carl V. Bini Memorial Fund. Web. May, 2018.

22. *"Peter Cundari" and relevant biographical information and anecdotes.* Adopted from P. Cundari, personal communication, May 28, 2018.

23. *"Enza Giordano Mammi" and relevant descriptions and stories.* Taken from E.G. Mammi, personal communication, Dec. 22, 2018.

24. *"Community Service Award in 2013."* Taken from "About Joseph – Licensed Associate Real Estate Broker." Compass.com. Web.

25. *"flood-build-repeat cycle."* Fox Beach 165 – Oakwood Beach Buyout.

26. *...[m]y tenants were hysterical, crying..."* Craig, Caroline. "This NYC's Realtor's Most Memorable Deal? Selling His Flood-Ravaged Neighborhood to the Government." Natural Resource Defense Council., Inc. (NRDC). Feb. 22, 2018.

319

27. *"...began Original Shoe Repair."* "Tirone – Carmelo Tirone Way (Staten Island). NYC Streets. LL: 2006/13"

28. *" later moved to 164 Port Richmond Ave in 1975."* Rich, Kiawana. "Port Richmond icon Tirone's Family Shoe Store closing after 60 years in business." Staten Island Advance. 2011.

29. *"...flipped us the bird."* J. Tirone, personal communication, May 19, 2018.

29. *"Staaten Eylandt"* History, Story, Legend of the Old King's Highway: Now the Richmond Road ..." pg.1, Staten Island Antiquarian Society, 1916.

30. *"Sri Lankans."* Staten Island in 2019 houses the largest Sri Lankan concentration in the United States. "Little Sri Lanka" exists in the St. George and Tompkinsville areas, and is not clearly defined. Adopted from Khona, Rachel. "On Staten Island, Savoring Flavors of Sri Lanka." The New York Times. Jul. 15, 2015.

31. *"triggered a two-fold population increase."* U.S. Decennial Census. 1900-1990.

32. *" a total of 11,724 acres."* From Eisenstadt, Peter R. "The Enyclopedia of New York State." pg. 1457. Syracuse University Press, 2005.

33. *"I've been told that Italian women..."* Harting, Emilie. "The Meyer Farms of New Springville, Staten Island, New York: 1903-late 1950s."

34. *"at the Criaris Farm at 2289 Richmond Ave."* Wilson, Andrew. "Port Richmond Branch Library, The First 50 Years: 1905-1955." New York Public Library. Mar. 26, 2009.

35. *"spreading manure, picking weeds,..."* Hughes, Langston. "The Big Sea: An Autobiography." Re-published Farrar, Straus, and Giroux. Mar. 2, 2015. Web.

36. *"Pizzagaina."* The baking of this traditional dish is recognized by thousands of Staten Island families. This particular information is adopted from M. Ragucci, personal communication, Dec. 26, 2017.

37. *"Novelli's Pork Store."* Silvestri, Pamela. "Eastern grain pie. Novelli's keeps an Italian tradition alive on Staten Island." Staten Island Advance. April, 2018.

38. *"seven hundred stores on Staten Island, Brooklyn..."* Scutts, Joanna. "The Extra Woman: How Marjorie Hills Lead a Generation of Women to Live Alone ..." pg. Liveright Publishing, Nov. 14, 2017.

39. *"All of the stores out of the confines..."* Husson, Joseph. "Semi-trailers Get Grocer New Trade in Bigger Territory." The Commercial Vehicle, Inc. Dec. 1, 1915.

40. *"...your nickel is as good as your dollar."* "Brooklyn's Greatest Cash Grocer – Thos. Roulston." Staten Island Advance, Nov. 3, 1921, pg. 10

41. *"herd of cows in Mahway, N.J."* Schuyler, Philip. "The Hundred Year Book: Being the Story of the Members of the Hundred Year Association of New York, A.S. Barnes, 1942.

42. *"Swill Milk Scandal in New York."* "Sheffield Farms, The Milk Industry, and the Public Good." Manhattanville: A New York Nexus. Columbia University, In the City of New York.

43. *"May 22, 1923."* "Dairy Produce, the Dairy and Poultry Magazine." Vol. 40, pg. 28. 1933.

44. *"Emilio Grasso"* Sublett, John L. "Staten Island: A Walk Down Memory Lane." pg. 107. CreateSpace Indepdent Publishing Platform. Jan. 28, 2009.

45. *"Antonio Pillitteri...Austin Ave. in South Beach."* Year: *1940*; Census Place: *New York, Richmond, New York*; Roll: *m-t0627-02763*; Page: *6B*; Enumeration District: *43-171*.

46. *"essentiality for public welfare."* From Coal Age Magazine. "Anthracite Operators' Advertising Campaign to Show That Producers' Profits Are Modest." Vol. 20, pg. 509. McGraw-Hill, Sept. 29, 1921.

47. *"sixteen percent of the nation's energy consumption."* Dublin, Thomas et. Licht, Walter. "The Face of Decline: The Pennsylvania Anthracite Region in the Twenteith Century." Pg. 1. Cornell University Press, Oct. 3, 2016.

48. *"Lehigh & Wilkes-Barre written on the side..."* Discenza, Frank. "New Dorp Coal, The Lumber Yard was right there also, I don't know if many people knew about it." Shared to the F.B. Group: New Dorp Beach. Feb. 17, 2014.

49. *"...transported to a silo."* Pitanza, Marc. "Staten Island Rapid Transit." Pg. 96. Arcadia Publishing, Jun. 22, 2015.

50. *"at 451 St. Marks Pl."* "451 St. Marks Pl. B-6, L-9" 1939-1941. DOF: Staten Island 1940s Tax Photos. NYC Department of Records & Information Services.

51. *"Eagle Confectionery Store at 239 Sand Lane."* "239 Sand Lane. B – 3110, L – 32" 1939-1941. DOF: Staten Island 1940s Tax Photos. NYC Department of Records & Information Services.

52. *"Pitarresi, an immigrant from Palermo."* J. Pitarresi, personal communication, Aug. 17, 2018.

53. *"collective grocer organizations such as 'United Service Grocers.'"* "423 [sic] Olympia Blvd., B-3253, L- 31" Address incorrectly marked in accompaniment with original photograph. Correct address appears to be "211 Olympia Blvd., B-?, L-?" DOF: Staten Island 1940s Tax Photos. NYC Department of Records & Information Services.

54. *"The Great American Tea Co."* Hammond, Richard. "Smart Retail: Practical Winning Ideas and Strategied from the Most Successful Retailers in the World." Pearson, U.K., Sept. 26, 2012.

55. *"The evidence before Walter Lindsey's..."* Levinson, Marc. "The Great A&P and the Struggle for Small Business in America." Pg. 4. Farrar, Straus, and Giroux, Aug. 30, 2011.

56. *"in 2005 by the Federal Trade Commission."* "FTC Challenges A&Ps Proposed Acquisiton of Pathmark Supermarkets." Federal Trade Commission – Press Releases. Nov. 27, 2007.

57. *"owned by brothers Dave and Bob..."* Wilson, Ron. "Dugan's Bakery (Queens) and the End." Newark Memories – Old Newark.

58. *"...Gertenschlagger..."* Roman, Harry T. "Dugan's Bakery." Old Newark Memories.

59. *"...on the day of President Kennedy's assassination."* DiMaio, Shane. "Historic Jack's Grinding truck for sale on Craigslist." Staten Island Advance, 2016.

60. *"Amboy Road in 1924."* Sperr, P.L. "Amboy Road (left), east from about Barclay to about Arden Ave." Spring, 1924. Irma and Paul Milstein Division of United States History, Local History and Geneaology. New York Public Library – Digital Collections.

61. *"...more officers than The Bronx."* Barron, Seth. "New York's Red Borough." City Journal, Winter, 2018.

62. *"favoring the placement of more jails in individual boroughs."* "Smaller, Safer, Fairer: A Roadmap to Closing Riker's Island." NYC Mayor's Office of Criminal Justice.

63. *"...National Prohibition Park in 1888."* Haller, Vera. "Westerleigh, STATEN ISLAND, Built on Temperance." The New York Times. Apr. 8, 2014.

64. *"...What the Brooklyn Bridge has done for Brooklyn."* Adapted from text located within Sperr, P.L. "Forest Avenue (formerly Washington Avenue), west from about Elizabeth Grove Road." Mar. 3, 1927. Irma and Paul Milstein Division of United States History, Local History and Geneaology. New York Public Library – Digital Collections.

65. *"...similar to the one in Laurelton, Queens."* "Giffords Gardens Villas (1928-29) – 163 Jumel St. – Great Kills, Staten Island." Flickr, May 29, 2015. Used with permission of Matthew X. Kiernan

66. *"health alternative[s] to modern medicine."* Nicholas Georgianis. "Uncategorized - Spanish Camp 2016, Staten Island NY." Feb. 7, 2016.

67. *"...autobiographical book published in 1924."* Bowers, Paul. "An Introduction to *The Eleventh Virgin*." The Catholic Worker Movement.

68. *"[those of] Beverly Hills or Saddle River."* Engels, Mary. "Bungalow Site Sold, Residents Get Boot." Special to the New York Daily News. Jul. 28, 1997.

69. *"[DiScala] had already been sanctioned..."* Barrett, Wayne. "The Story of the Demolition of Spanish Camp and the Dorothy Day Cottage." The Village Voice, republished on PBase. Web. May 2-8, 2001.

70. *"Founded as the first retreat center..."* Sherry, Virginia N. "It's Mount Manresa's Centennial Year." Staten Island Advance, 2011.

71. *"...considered an ecological gem."* Manson, Jamie. "Paradise lost: Jesuits sell oldest house, pristine forest to developers." National Catholic Reporter, Oct. 23, 2013.

72. *"Rev. Vincent Cooke stated..."* Foderaro, Lisa W. "Trying to Save a Quiet Place on Staten Island." The New York Times, Apr. 26, 2014.

73. *"Next, as possessing the powers of borough president..."* Rizzi, Nicholas. "Oddo spells Revenge by Picking Mt. Manresa Street Names Inspired by 'Greed.' DNA Info. Web. Dec. 16, 2015.

74. *"...shows 'Father Knickerbocker'."* Sachs, Charles L. "Made on Staten Island: Agriculture, Industry, and Suburban Living in the City." Pg. 113. University Publishing Association; Library Ed edition, Oct. 1, 1988.

75. *"from S.P.E. Realty Associates..."* Adapted from text featured in Sperr, P.L. "Amboy Road, at the N.E. Corner of Arden Ave." May 4, 1926. NYPL catalog ID (B-number): b19806373

75. *"Bungalows, in fact...13 Weed Ave."* M. Savitsky, personal communication, Jan. 28, 2019.

76. *"such as Annadale Beach in 1925."* Adapted from text located within Sperr, P.L. "Amboy Road, east from about Philip Avenue." May 4, 1926. New York Public Library – Digital Collections.

77. *"acres from James W. Hughes."* Secret Staten Island, F.B. Group. "Update on the 'Paterno's Case.'" Apr. 20, 2011.

78. *"lured by prospective benefits..."* R. Nazzaro-Paterno, personal communication, Dec. 30, 2018.

79. *"Minogue & Minogue."* Adaped from text located within Sperr, P.L. "Willowbrook Road, north from near Watchogue Road." May 13, 1926. New York Public Library – Digital Collections.

80. *"In 1971, for instance, Republican State Senator John Marchi..."* Kroessler, Jeffrey A. "The Limits of Liberal Planning: the Lindsay's Administration's Failed Plan to Control Development on Staten Island." Pg. 4. CUNY John Jay College – Publications and Research.

81. *"Paul Margarella...Stephen Margarella" and relevant biographical, historical information and dates* adopted from S. Margarella, personal communication, Jun. 7, 2018.

82. *"sell periodically for $6-8 a pelt..."* M. Notarfrancesco, personal communication, May 13, 2018.

83. *"Voorlezer's House in South-Central Staten Island."* Greenwood, Richard. "National Register of Historic Places Inventory – Nomination Form." National Park Service, Jul. 17, 1975.

84. *"A son, John Van Pelt, Jr."* "John Van Pelt, Jr." Penn Yan & How It Got That Way." Penn Yan History.

85. *"...boat waving the ' flag of truce.'"* Whitehead, William A. "Contributions to the Early History of Perth Amboy and Adjoining Country: With Sketches of Men and Events in New Jersey during the Provincial Era." Pg. 335. D. Appleton, 1856.

86. *"[Lord Howe] entered into a discourse of considerable length..."* Franklin, Benjamin et. Franklin, William. "Memoirs of the Life and Writings of Benjamin Franklin." Pg. 302. H. Colburn, 1818.

87. *"independence was now an unchangeable fact..."* Fleming, Thomas. "Ben Franklin: Inventing America." Pg. 158. Voyageur Press, Sept. 15, 2016.

88. *"to over one-thousand, six hundred acres of land."* Seaberg, Maureen et. Anarumo, Theresa. "Hidden History of Staten Island." Arcading Publishing, Dec. 11, 2017.

89. *"Christopher Billopp would become a representative..."* Sabine, Lorenzo. "Biographical Sketches of Loyalists of the American Revolution...Vol. I" Little Brown, 1864.

90. *"...confined in the jail at Burlington."* Billopp, Charles F. "A history of Thomas and Anne Billopp Farmar, and some of their descendants in America" pg. 57-58. Grafton Press, 1908.

91. *"numerous gatherings with General Wilhelm Von Knyphausen."* Hicks, George W. "Revolutionary War Amid Southern Chaos." PublishAmerica, Aug. 8, 2008.

92. *"A poem from 'Evacuation Day.'"* Riker, James. *"Evacuation Day, 1783: Its Many Stirring Events: with Recollections of Capt. John Van Arsdale."* 1883.

93. *"St. Andrew's was founded by..."* The Church of Saint Andrew – Staten Island. Web.

94. *"The Moravians argued that the Anglican Church..."* Papas, Phillip. "That Ever Loyal Island: Staten Island and the American Revolution." Pg. 25. NYU Press, 2009.

95. *"Staten Island's days of being shrouded and saved by its isolation..."* Dominowski, Michael W. "2010 Census: How NYC 'master builder' Robert Moses made Staten Island what it is today." Staten Island Advance, 2011.

96. *"I can remember my bed rumbling the day..."* M. Lombardi, personal communication, Jul. 24, 2018.

97. *"which would model Boston, Massachusetts' Commonwealth Avenue..."* Kroessler, Jeffrey A. "Beyond the Bridge: The Unfinished Staten Island Parkways of Robert Moses and the Preservation of the Greenbelt." Vol. 94, No. 1-2 (Winter/Spring 2013), pp. 111-129. Fenimore Art Museum.

98. *"angered over the rejection of his proposal..."* "Radical Infrastructure Schemes: The Brooklyn-Battery Bridge." The Weekly Nabe. Web. Jul. 3, 2013.

99. *"...advanced his urbanizing tyrannical agenda."* Kensinger, Nathan. "New Dorp Bungalows." Nathan Kensinger Photography: The Abandoned & Industrial Edges of New York City, Feb. 28, 2011.

100. *"...persuaded by Borough President Anthony Maniscalco."* Curtis High School, Alumni News. "50ᵗʰ Anniversary of Verrazzano-Narrows Span." 1994.

101. *"...cites New Brighton as one of the first potential 'suburbs.'"* Jackson, Kenneth T. "Crabgrass Frontier: The Suburbanization of the United States." Oxford University Press, USA, Apr. 16, 1987.

102. *"Staten Island is fortunte in its terrain..."* Barron, Ann Marie. "Robert Moses: Master planner saw Verrazzano-Narrows Bridge as crucial link for commerce." Staten Island Advance, 2015.

103. *"enough concrete in in its anchorages..."* Friedrich, Augustine J. "Sons of Martha: Civil Engineering Readings in Modern Literature." American Society of Civil Engineers, 1989.

104. *"to begin a combination freight and passenger tunnel."* The Commercial and Financial Chronicle, Vol. 110, Issue I. National News Service, 1920.

105. *"In all, 467 acres of marsh..."* Steinberg, Ted. "Gotham Unbound: The Ecological History of Greater New York." Simon and Shuster, Jul. 21, 2015.

106. *"In a report written by... atomic bombs."* P. DeRienzo, personal communication, Jun. 11-12, 2018.

107. *"a violation of the Clean Air Act of 1963."* "The Fresh Kills Story: From World's Largest Garbage Dump to a World-Class Park." Published electronically, Sept. 20, 2012.

108. *"whose captain would reside at a farmstead."* Adapted from information added by the Staten Island Museum Collection to Sperr, P.L. "Westcott Blvd. at Kemball Ave." 1905. New York Public Library.

109. *"chemist and mining geologist..."* Buck, C. Elton. "Report... Upon the Mines of Staten Island of the Richmond Iron Mining Co." Root, Anthony, and Company, 1868.

110. *"additional mines were discovered in Todt Hill..."* Real Estate SINY – "About Todt Hill, Staten Island."

111. *"...called Moses' Mountain."* Wollney, Clay. "Staten Island nature: What is Moses Mountain?" Staten Island Advance, 2018.

112. *"New York's worst neighborhood name..."* Ephemeral New York – Chronciling an ever-changing city through faded and forgotten artifacts. "New York's Worst Neighborhood Name Ever." Jan. 28, 2010

113. *"unusual, wear-resistant, elastic..."* Hornbostel, Carol. "Construction Materials: Types, Uses and Applications." John Wiley & Sons, Jan. 16, 1991.

114. *"Battleship Linoleum."* Simpson, Pamela H. "Cheap, Quick, and Easy: Imitative Architectural Materials, 1870-1930." Univ. of Tennessee Press, 1999.

115. *"manufactured by Hayes-Diefenderfer..."* Hill, A.A. et. Richardson, M.T. "Automobile Dealer and Repairer: A Practical Journal Exclusively for These Interests." Vol. 23-24; pg. 65. Motor Vehicle Publishing Co., 1917.

116. *"The first-celebrating pastor, Rev."* "The Catholic Church in the United States of America: Undertaken to Celebrate the Golden Jubilee of His Holiness, Pope Pius X." Pg. 394. Catholic Editing Co., 1914.

117. *"He would go on to serve at Our Lady of Peace..."* Troeger, Virginia B. McEwan, Robert J. "Woodbridge: New Jersey's Oldest Township." Arcadia Publishing, 2002.

118. *"some Sunday mornings all I want to be is..."* P.F. Battaglia, personal communication, May 16, 2018.

119. *"boasting over 1,400 workers."* "Soap, Cosmetics, Chemical Specialities." Vol. 33, pg. 44. PTN, 1957.

120. *"...P&G had distributed $12,000,000 in cash."* "Michigan Purchasing Management." Pg. 1943. Oakland Publishing, 1937.

121. *"99 44/100%"* Bernays, Edward L. "Biography of an Idea: The Founding Principles of Public Relations." Chpt. 26. Open Road Media, Apr. 7, 2015.

122. *"one could also mix ivory soap with ammonia..."* Procter & Gamble Company. "Unusual Uses of Ivory Soap (Classic Reprint)." Fb&c Limited, Nov. 21, 2017.

123. *"...$128,549,649"* "The Magazine of Wall Street." Volume XXI, pg. 969. Ticker Publishing Co., Late-1910s.

124. *"[adding] soap powder to its mix in 1912..."* Wallace, Mike. "Gotham: A History of New York City from 1898 to 1919." Pg. 308. Oxford University Press, Sept. 4, 2017.

125. *"provided with freight interchanges by..."* "Industrial, Offline Terminal Railroads & Rail Marine Operations of Brooklyn, Queens, Staten Island, Bronx, and Manhattan." TrainWeb. Used with permission of Phillip M. Goldstein.

126. *"...alongside the S.S. Ross at Pier 6."* American Maritime Cases, Volume II; pg. 1481

127. *"...derived from 1,117 captured whales."* Time Magazine; 28 May 1934 edition.

128. *"For many Staten Islanders, working at Procter & Gamble was a family affair."* Lundrigan, Margaret et. Navarra, Tova. "Staten Island." Pg. 93. Arcadia Publishing, 2006.

129. *"The plant unfortunately shut down on..."* Regan, Claire M. "P&G plant is long closed, but retirees share a bond that lasts forever." Staten Island Advance, 2018.

130. *"The Russians who were big wartime customers..."* Coquillette, Robert M.T. "A Family Saga: A Record of One Man's Experiences in the 20th Century." iUniverse, 2009.

131. *"...built daytime radio for the networks..."* Allen, Robert C. "To Be Continued... Soap Operas Around The World." Routledge, Jan. 4, 2002.

132. *"Samuel Stockton White, D.D.S."* Judd, Homer et. Spalding, Christopher W. et. Chase, Henry S. "The Missouri Dental Journal." Vol. 12, pg. 87. Levison & Blythe, 1880.

133. *"...and Henry D. Justi."* Edmonson, James M. "American Surgical Instruments: The History of Their Manufacture and a Directory of Instrument Makers to 1900." Norman Publishing, 1997.

134. *"...porcelain teeth made with feldspar."* Holloway, Laura C. "Famous American Fortunes and the Men who Have Made Them: A Series of Sketches of Many of the Notable Merchants, Manufacturers, Capitalists, Railraod Presidents, Bonanzo and Cattle Kings of the Country." Pg. 694. Bradley & Co., 1884.

135. *"...in London in 1851."* Lemelson Center for the Study of Innovation and Invention. Web.

136. *"...paid-in capital of one-million dollars."* White, Samuel S. "Samuel S. White Catalogue of Dental Instruments and Equipment." Pg. 23. Norman Publishing, 1995.

137. *"...and later, candle-making."* Morris, Ira K. "Morris's Memorial History of Staten Island, New York, Vol. 2." Pg. 472. Memorial Publishing Co., 1900.

138. "...and members of the Board of Directors." The Dental cosmos; a monthly record of dental science. [Vol. 62] Pg. 420. Philadelphia: S. S. White Dental Manufacturing Co., 1920

139. "...by a water-proof coating as set forth." "Annual Report of the Commissioner of Patents." Pg. 517. U.S. Government Printing Office, 1863.

140. "the Machine-cut Engine Bur..." "Seventy-Five Years of Service, 1844-1919, a history of the House of White." Pg. 43. Philasdelphia: S.S. Dental Manufacturing Co., 1920

141. "...Motor Car Co. trucks."Artman, James. "The Commercial Car Journal." Vol. 18, pg. 90. Chilton Company, 1919.

142. "...workmanship and elegance in finish." "Transactions", Vols. 1-12. California Dental Association, 1873.

143. "...plans for condominium development were made by" Cullen, Terence. "Muss Absolved, Yet Again, of Wrongdoing in $38M Staten Island Development Sale." Commercial Observer, Feb. 9, 2016.

144. "...wings spread sits at her feet." "Pleasant Plains Plaza, Amboy Rd., Bloomingdale Rd., Staten Island" Official Website of the New York City Department of Parks & Recreation.

145. "...then at the Dubois Mansion in West New Brighton." Matteo, Thomas. "The World Leaders Who Walked Among Us." Staten Island Advance, Sept. 18, 2011.

146. "...rubber-like material to no avail." Redclift, Michael. "Chewing Gum: The Fortunes of Taste." Pg. 25. Routledge, May 27, 2004.

147. "...and peanuts in glass jars." Smith, Andrew F. "Fast Food and Junk Food: An Encylopedia of What We Love to Eat." Vol. 1, pg. 731. ABC-CLIO, 2012.

148. "...of the Roman-Catholic Mass in Aprl of 1839." Lundrigan, Margaret. "Staten Island: Isle of the Bay." Arcadia Publishing, 2004.

149. "The company's guns would be reviewed..." Newton, John. "Report upon the Results of Firing to determine the Pressure of the Blast from 15-inch smooth bore guns made at Staten Island, New York in 1872 and 1873." U.S. Government Printing Office, 1874.

150. "Buy Today You Pay More Tomorrow." Adapted from text located within Sperr, P.L. "Willowbrook Road, south side, about 200 feet west of Sunset Avenue (formerly Gun Factory Road), showing the remains of an old stone-and-wood dwelling." NYPL Digital Collection

151. "damasks, feathers, etc." Dickens, Miller. "Household Words" Vol. 3. Bradbury & Evans, 1851.

152. "[i]n the [receiving] department about..." Clute, J.J. "Annals of Staten Island, from its Discovery to the Present Time, Vol. 2." Pg. 322. Press of C. Vogt., 1877.

153. "A bronze statue of him was erected..." "Barrett Triangle – Clarence T. Barrett Memorial." Official Website of the New York City Department of Parks & Recreation.

154. *"...in the Vietnam War in 1967."* Dalton, Kristin F. "Plaque unveiled to honor Cpl. Lawrence Thompson, first African-American Islander killed in Vietnam." Staten Island Advance, 2016.

155. *"...American Institute of Mining Engineers."* "Cassier's Magazine, Vol. 8." Pg. 362. L. Cassier Company, Limited, 1865.

156. *"Describing the enormous Staten Island factory."* Arnold, Harold L. "The factory manager and accountant: some examples of the latest American factory practice." Engineering Magazine, 1903.

157. *"wheelbarrows, and steam shovels."* American Industrial Mining Co. "C.W. Hunt Locomotives and Insutrial Railways, Staten Island, N.Y." Web.

158. *"Hunt once wrote in a speech he delivered as..."* "Transactions of the American Society of Mechanical Engineers." Vol. 20, pg. 28. The Society, 1899.

159. *"...and Building Material Exchange."* The National Cyclopaedia of American biography:..." Pg. 156, J.T. White Company, 1910.

160. *"...at a rate of nine knots per hour..."* The Nautical Gazette, Vol. 84." Pg. 4. The Gazette, 1913.

161. *"...and perfect wall material."* "The Northern American Review, Vol. 156, No. 434, Jan., 1893." Published electronically by University of Northern Iowa.

162. *"...in Austin between 1882 and 1888."* Cox, Mike. "Legends and Lore of the Texas Capitol." Pg.148. Arcadia Publishing, Jun. 26, 2017.

163. *"two-hundred million board feet."* "U.S. Gypsum in New Brighton produced America's Sheetrock." Staten Island Advance, 2019.

164. *"...New Jersey, and Connecticut."* "Staten Island: Old U.S. Gypsum Plant to Host LUMEN Festival." Editorial Staff at The New York History Blog. May 31, 2010.

165. *"...brought his scrap metal business from Manhattan to Tottenville."* "Hardware: A Review of the American Hardware Market" Vol. 17. 1898.

166. *"...was once the largest freight customer on..."* Pitanza, Marc. "Staten Island Rapid Transit." Pg. 112. Arcadia Publishing, Jun. 22, 2015.

167. *"...of the modern linotype machine."* "New York City Signs – 14th to 42nd Streets." Web. Used with permission of Walter Grutchfield.

168. *"...supplied to Western Electric Co."* "Popular Mechanics." Vol. 77, pg. 192. Heart Magazines, Jan., 1942.

169. *"...team uniforms and equipment."* "Tottenville." Pg. 23. Arcadia Publishing, 2011.

170. *"...as well as layers of clean soil."* Porpora, Tracey. "Old Nassau Smelting site bought for $30M; to be mixed-use development." Staten Island Advance, Mar. 10, 2016.

171. *"John Francesco's scrap yard...which is currently under development."* M. Notrarfrancesco, Jr., personal communication, May 13-20, 2018.

172. *"Just nearby the scrap yard...in his pajamas."* A. Supino, personal communication, Jan. 5, 2018.

172. *"Lester Kehoe Machinery Inc...television shootings."* E. Drury, personal communication, Jun. 22, 2018.

173. *"...corbelled brick ornament."* Landmarks Preservation Commission October 30, 2007, Designation List 397 LP- 2250, pg. 1

174. *"...manufactured by the Standard Varnish Works."* "Bowery Boys History. "Staten Island Has Many Charms Worthy of Consideration: Ten Ways to sell a borough (and a proposed subway) in 1912.""

175. *"5,000 tons to 75,000 tons."* "New International Yearbook: A Compendium of the World's Progress." Pg. 413. 1922.

176. *"223 feet across Richmond Terrace."* "The Tammany Times, Vols. 22-23." Tammany Publishing Co., 1903.

177. *"The works have a capacity for producing."* Bayles, Richard M. "History of Richmond County (Staten Island), New York: From Its Discovery to the Present Time, Part 1." Pg. 736. L.E. Preston, 1887.

178. *"...of soil to ensure public safety."* EPA Seeks Public Input on Cleanup Options for Lead-Contaminated Site in Staten Island, N.Y. Mar. 8, 2011.

179. *"...and Shark River oysters."* New Jersey Board of Health 1908: 266-67.

180. *"Investigation by Great Britain's..."* "Annual Report of the State Board of Health of New York." Pg. 319. The Board, 1896.

181. *"[w]hile oysters are being..."* Shrady, George F. et. Stedman, Thomas L. "Medical Record." Vol. 65, pg. 888. W. Wood., 1904.

182. *"fine private field with..."* "Aeronautics." Vols. 13-14. Pg. 113. Published 1913.

183. *"organizer of the first Junior..."* Manhanti, Subodh. "Kalpana Chawla." Publications Division Ministry of Information & Broadcasting, Aug. 22, 2017.

184. *"...first air mail postal service."* Aviation Hall of Fame & Museum of New Jersey. Web.

185. *"Quite an assortment of individuals."* LaGuardia, Fiorello H. "American in the Making." Jun., 1948. Web. The Atlantic.

186. *"Bellanca then gained a significant amount..."* Longden, Tom. "Clarence Chamberlin – Aviaition Pioneer." Des Moines Register. Web

187. *"...Galati, Romania..."* Cooper, Ralph. "George Gh. Fernic: 1900-1930." Early Aviators, Web.

188. *"Professor Alexander Klemin."* "Flying Magazine." Feb., 1930.

189. *"Rock Island Railroad Co."* The Tammany Times, Volumes 22-23; pg. 19.

190. *"...were built at Bethlehem's Staten Island Yard."* Information courtesy of the Tin Can Sailors

191. *"...more passengers than the average ferry."* "Ships and the Sea." Vol. 3, pg. 42. Published 1953.

192. "Schutzen Corps..." . Lundrigan, Margaret. Navarra, Tova. "Staten Island: Volume II; A Closer Look." pg. 35. Arcadia Publishing, 1999.

193. *"...Sisters of St. Francis."* "Magazine of Western History." Vol. 14, pg. 328. Publisher not identified, 1891.

194. *"Grandpa Moses."* Lundrigan, Magaret. "Irish Staten Island." Pg. 35. Arcadia Publishing, 2009.

195. *"judges, lawyers, and even celebrities..."* Adapted from a caption beneath Jack Demyan (1923-99), "Jazz Players." From the Noble Maritime Collection. Web.

196. *"...Francis Ford Coppola's highly-popular..."* Benanti, Carol A. "Everything old is Nu again at Hofbrau redux." Staten Island Advance, Mar. 5, 2010.

197. *"...rented for $75 per day..."* Porpora, Tracey. "Secrets behind the Godfather movie revealed." Staten Island Advance, 2018.

198. *"...Flick Room became a..."* Adapted from text from a digitized advertisement for Demyan's Hofbrau from Silvestri, Pamela. "20 restaurants we miss on Staten Island." Staten Island Advance, 2017.

199. *"...dined at the hofbrau."* "Federal Supplement." Vol. 542, pg. 1389. Published in 1982.

200. *"Bechtel's Brewery contained..."* Hall, Henry. "America's Successful Men of Affairs: The city of New York." Pgs. 68-70. New York Tribune, 1895.

201. *"The Beer King...plan for the future."* W. Roccaro, personal communication, May 21, 2018.

202. *"...Heil's Parks in Fort Wadsworth."* Goyens, Tom. "Beer and Revolution: The German Anarchist Movement in New York City, 1880-1914." Pg. 30. Univ. of Illinois Press, Nov. 12, 2007.

203. *"...deposits beneath the bedrock."* Rosenberg, Stephanie. "Hydrogeology of Staten Island, New York – Stony Brook Univ., Dept. of Geosciences." 2013.

204. *"can still be discovered in the present day..."* Bindley, Katherine. "The Secret Spring of Clove Lakes Park." The New York Times, Oct. 10, 2008.

205. *"The four companies operated a total of..."* Annual Report of the State Water Supply Commission of New York, 1906.

206. *"commemorating the freedom of the masonry practice..."* "The Jubilee: Celebratiion in the Lodges Under the Jurisidiction..." Pg. 164. Freemasons, Grand Lodge of the State of New York. De Leeuw & Oppenheimer, 1890.

207. *"The Club Rooms hosted a variety..."* Proceedings, pg. 50, Staten Island Institute of Arts and Sciences., 1948.

208. *"The company...in 1835.."* "The National Magazine: A Monthly Journal of American History." Vol. 13, pg. 651. Magazine of Western Publishing Co., 1891.

209. *"...having a flat undersurface."* Blatchford, Samuel. "Reports of Cases Argued and Determined in the Circuit Court of the United States for the Second Circuit," Vol. 22, pg. 268. Derby and Miller, 1885.

210. "...or ornamental pressed brick." King, Moses. "King's Handbook of New York City: An Outline History and Description of the American Metropolis." Pg. 880. Moses King, 1892.

211. "...Robert Young, in 2005." Rashbaum, William K. "Grisly Mob Killing at STATEN ISLAND Mansion Is Detailed." The New York Times, May 12, 2006.

212. "fireplaces...in every stucco." Sietsema, Robert. "Killmeyer's and the Kreischer Mansion: Meat and Murder in Staten Island." The Village Voice, Dec. 3, 2010.

213. ".New York in 1898." Marine Progress, Vol. 4.

214. "...Methodist Chapel at Kreischerville." Neighborhood Preservation Center, Kreischerville; 1994.

215. "...during the Great War." Tottenville Historical Society

216. "Born on January 31, 1845...1878." Elbe-Weser Triangle, Germany, Lutheran Baptisms, Marriages, and Burials, 1574-1945 [database on-line]. Provo, UT, USA: Ancestry.com Operations, Inc., 2016. Original data: Mikrofilm Sammlung. Familysearch.org ONiedersächsisches Landesarchiv, Standort Stade, Deutschland.

217. "...and a portable cake oven." "The Northwestern Miller." Vol. 110, pg. 544. Miller Publishing Co., 1917.

218. "Known as a kind man..." Ferrer, Margaret L. "Richmond Town and Lighthouse Hill." Pg. 29. Arcadia Publishing, Jun. 1, 1996.

219. "...throughout the metropolitan region." Sachs, 1988.

220. "The invention consisted of a perforated..." Knorpp, P. et. Mayer, G.A. (Jul. 30, 1889) U.S. 407935A.

221. "...with a porch on three sides." Diamondstein-Speilvogel, Barbaralee "The Landmarks of New York, Fifth Edition: An Illustrated Record of the City's Historic Buildings." Pg. 178. SUNY Press, Sept. 1, 2011.

222. "...reflecting light against their jewels." Zinn Brilliant, History. Web,

223. "...originally from New Jersey...Staten Island business." W. Buda, personal communication, Jan. 10-May 20, 2018.

224. "The business...grasslands." Somma-Hammel, Jan. "The Weissglass family: Titans of Staten Island." Staten Island Advance, 2017.

225. "There is a hugde demand nationwide..." Porpora, Tracey. "2 businessmen bring the 'milkman' back to Staten Island." Staten Island Advance, 2018.

226. "Though the Weissglass name...Sterner &." G. LeBlanc, personal communication, Feb. 18, 2018.

227. "...and Bruno Sammartino." Matteo, Thomas W. et. Lundrigan, Margaret. "Legendary Locals of Staten Island." Pg. 55. Arcadia Publsihing, 2017.

228. "[Eugene] Ferkauf could undercut..." Lichtenstein, Nelson. "The Retail Revolution: How Wal-Mart Created a Brave New World of Business." Pg. 36. Henry Holt & Co., Jul. 21, 2009.

229. *"...former grounds of a chicken farm."* Benanti, Carol A. "A look back: Check out vintage photos of New Springville." Staten Island Advance, 2018.

230. *"...barricade of seventeen ship piers."* Hulbert, Murray. "Letters to the Editor." The New York Times, Dec. 31, 1944.

231. *"...and tropical plants."* Martin, Julia. "Artists Invade Enclave of Staten Island Shops." The New York Times, May 27, 1973.

232. *"Columbia Meat Market...ice were stored."* Sherry, Virginia N. "Local butcher shop turns 90." Staten Island Advance, 2010.

233. *"Among those who have...understood that one bit."* P. Passarella (D. Garcenot), personal communication, Sept. 21, 2018.

234. *"The practice of performing...John Denver."* A. Granito-Bergstromc, personal communication, Sept. 22, 2018.

235. *"Similar Italian, Staten Island...whatever he had."* M. Bonamo, personal communication, Jun. 26, 2018.

236. *"Maria Bonamo's cousin...evil spirits."* J. Gatti, personal communication, Jan. 28, 2018.

237. *"Joanne Bennetti...hell of a person."* J. Bennetti, personal communication, Oct. 10, 2018.

238. *"Benntti's classmate...Church of the Assumption."* J. Darrigo, personal communication, Oct. 14, 2018.

239. *"In the age when...would prove otherwise."* A. Navarino, personal communication, Oct. 15, 2018.

240. *"They ddnt need Willowbrook...and have a family."* G. Ricciardi, personal communication, Oct. 28, 2018.

241. *"Scarano's Market...they were."* D.S. Amaturo, personal communication, Sept. 30, 2018.

242. *"Amaturo's childhood friend...Getta outta here."* T. Iommi, personal communication, Jan. 6, 2019.

243. *"Iommi's former neighbor...shortly afterward."* J. DeVito, personal communication, Jun. 12, 2018.

244. *"Mike Pistilli...dating their sisters."* M. Pistilli, personal communication, Aug. 31, 2018.

245. *"Continuing in the Italian vein...he was my everything."* J.F. Brogna, personal communication, Sept. 29, 2018.

246. *"Gloria Santo...at the end of Walker St."* G. Santo, personal communication, Nov. 17, 2018.

247. *"What hits you first..."* Yalof, Ina. "Food and the City: Professional Chefs, Restauranteurs,..." Penguin, May 31, 2016.

248. *"The establishment began...in June of 2003."* P. Denino, personal communication, Aug. 19, 2018.

249. *"Zinicola's Bakery...at PS21."* B. Zinicola, personal communication, Aug. 4, 2018.

250. *"As a small kid...with the water."* S. Lombardi, personal communication, Jul. 29, 2018.

251. *"Located formerly...and I'll never forget it."* D. Musto and M. Musto (special thanks to F.A. Capitini for making arrangements), personal communication, Sept. 10, 2018.

252. *"John Hershkowitz...Joe Montanti."* J. Herskowitz, personal communication, Jan. 28, 2019.

253. *"Staten Island used to be...so many memories were made."* J. Montanti, personal communication, Sept. 24, 2018.

254. *"The story of Sedutto's...just one more time."* J. Sedutto, personal communication, Jul. 31, 2018.

255. *"Of Staten Island's...pleasing people."* A. Lambert, personal communication, Mar. 9, 2018.

256. *"The Mariners Harbor...St. George Theater."* V. Medugno, personal communication, Jun. 4, 2018.

257. *"Staten Island is only...Sara Lee."* E. Casazza, personal communication, Aug. 6, 2018.

258. *"A staple of Mariners Harbor...remember about Staten Island."* L. Sander, personal communication, Jan. 12-15.

259. *"The famed pizzeria...'He already did.'"* A.A. Morton, personal communication, Aug. 15, 2018.

260. *"Forest Ave...tomato sauce will be compared."* L.L. Stanzione, personal communication, Aug. 13, 2018.

261. *"LiGreci's Staaten...to work that money off."* K. LiGreci, personal communication, Aug. 25, 2018.

262. *"Born in 1924...and I never will."* V. D'Antuono and L. D'Antuono, personal communication, Aug. 9, 2018.

263. *"The Franzreb Stables...relatively untouched."* J. Franzreb, personal communication, Feb. 12, 2018.

264. *"...both the English and Western styles."* "New York Magazine." Vol. 17, No. 41, pg. 60. New York Media, L.L.C., Oct. 15, 1984.

265. *"...shut down in June of 1994."* D'Anna, Eddie. "The memory of Staten Island stables lies in the shadow of business." Staten Island Advance, 2009.

266. *"...which aims to preserve the 415-acre..."* "Mall-city median partnership and a model for other commercial areas (editorial)." Staten Island Advance, 2016.

267. *"As in other areas...making the American Dream come true."* Msgr. F. Berardi, personal communication, Nov. 18, 2018.

268. *"Born in September...of candy anyway."* R. Pucillo, personal communication, Dec. 1-4, 2018.

369. *"Natives of Edwain Markham Gardens..."* Year: *1940*; Census Place: *New York, Richmond, New York*; Roll: *m-t0627-02761*; Page: *5B*; Enumeration District: *43-73*

370. *"Michele Gambetta...Howard Ct."* M.B. Gambetta, personal communication, Jan. 5, 2019.

371. *"Adjourning Davis Ct...tight family structure."* K. Prestia, personal communication, Jan. 21, 2019.

372. *"Of course...different times."* K. Mittenhuber, personal communication, Jan. 23, 2019.

373. *"Perhaps one of the...businesses in the community."* P. Scamardella, personal communication, Dec. 11, 2018.

374. *"Tony Del Bove...one-hundred-two"* J. Ogden, personal communication, Jan. 13, 2019.

375. *"Fellow neighborhood...miss that smell."* M. Cucuzza-Ciaburri, personal communication, Feb. 1, 2019.

376. *"Just around the corner...fail to benefit from them..."* S. Pillarella, persona communication, Jan. 1, 2019.

377. *"The Pillarella family...who love the Lord."* B. Pietracatella, personal communication, Jan. 3, 2019.

378. *"Johnny Latanzio...helped build America."* M.P. Ventrudo, personal communication, Sept. 5, 2018.

379. *"In part, the conception...was half-obliterated."* P.B. Foggin, personal communication, Dec. 14, 2018.

380. *"Similar to Chicken Delight's...coming years."* W. Roccaro, personal communication, May 21, 2018.

381. *"One establishment on Jewett...Island households."* J. Carrozza, personal communication, Jun. 21, 2018.

382. *"Meiers Corners...Business Improvement District (BID)."* A. Campitiello, personal communication, Jun. 1, 2018.

383. *"Alfono's is only one...into the heart of suburbia."* V. Zummo, personal communication, Jun. 4, 2018.

384. *"When they weren't playing pinochle..."* Zummo, Sandra. "The house on Nanny Goat Hill." Staten Island Advance, Jul. 17, 2010.

385. *"Another testimony...an accordion in my hand."* D. Comis=, personal communication, Oct. 4, 2018.

286. *"in reams of 480 sheets."* "Annual Report of the Public Printer for the fiscal year ended June 30, 1910." Pg. 243.

287. *"...not to be exceeded in quality."* "United States Investor." Vol. 30, pg. 677. F.B. Bennett, 1919.

288. *"The area surrounding the site..."* R. Simpson, personal communication, Jan., 2018.

289. *"...August 7th and 17th."* Sciorra, Joseph. "Bult with Faith: Italian American Imagination and Catholic Material Culture in New York City." Pg. 130. Univ. Tennessee Press; 1st edition, Feb. 27, 2015.

290. *"...to Rosebank in 1895."* Zeitlin, Steven J. et. Reaven Marci. " Hidden New York: A Guide to Places That Matter." Pg. 330. Ribergate Books, Oct. 5, 2006.

291. *"...many topped by crosses."* Del Giudice, Luise. "Sabato Rodia's Towers in Watts: Art, Migrations, Development (Critical Studies in Italian America). – 1st Edition." Pg. 192. Fordham Univ. Press, Jun. 15, 2014.

292. *"The reverend...was born in Armento..."* Mele, Andrew P. "Italian Staten Island." Pg. 81. Arcadia Publishing, 2010.

293. "...his homebound parishioners." Holy Rosary Church, Parish History. Web.

294. "...old country customs and religion." Gavan, Peggy. "1900: The Goats That Goaded the Fox Hill Golfers on Staten Island." Adapted from The Hatching Cat in Animal Tales, Goats of New York. Apr. 8, 2015.

295. "...instruction of the Ordnance Department." Conti, Flavio G. et. Perry, Alan R. " Italian Prisoners of War in Pennsylvania: Allies on the Home Front, 1944-45." Pg. 138. Fairleigh Dickinson Univ. Press, Oct. 19, 2016.

296. "Twenty-five Italian officers..." Moreo, Dominic W. "Riot at Fort Lawton, 1944." Pg. 99. iUniverse, 2004.

297. "Paul Mattiola...192 Garfield Ave." P. Mattiola, personal communication, Dec. 1, 2018.

298. "Cozy neighborhood pharmacy..." O'Shea, Karen. "Cozy neighborhood pharmacy on Staten Island faces, 'Goliath,'" Staten Island Advance, 2010.

299. "Fraternal organizations...1912." Fioravanate, Janice. "If You're Thinking of Living In/ Rosebank; Clinging to Tradition on Staten Island." The New York Times. Sept. 18, 1994.

300. "Those included the DeRosa's... & Engine 152." G. DeRosa, personal communication, Dec. 28, 2018.

301. "Lorraine Guerrera...life of the party." L.G. Maciejowski, personal communication, Jan. 19, 2019.

302. "Just approximately...lost my mother." A. Simon, personal communication, Jan. 24, 2019.

303. "...of several hundred feet." De Biasi, Agostino. "Il Carroccio." Vol. 4, pg. 262. Published digitally – Fb&c Limited, Nov. 16, 2016. Article translated manually from Italian to English.

304. "...such a home on just such a site." Adapted from a caption beneath "Villa Tocci, Staten Island – New York." Original Photographs. Iber Libro.

305. "...intending to construct residential housing." Lore, Diane C. "Archdiocese selling 90-year old Staten Island church." Staten Island Advance, 2018.

306. "Making All Things New." Lore, Diane C. "10 once-thriving Catholic churches, schools, now closed or merged." Staten Island Advance, 2018.

307. "New York Paraffin Candle Co." "Italy Italy." Vol. 9, Issue 2, Pg. 53. Italy-Italy Corp., 1991.

308. "My invention consists in the method..." Meucci, Anthony. Jan. 25, 1859. US22739A

309. "...and foremost Italian in New York." Sacramento Daily Union, Volume 91.12, 1896; Fonderia USA.

310. "...costing only half the price." Judd, Orange. "American Agriculturalist." Vol. 23. Published electronically by Fb&c Limited, Jan. 30, 2018.

311. "...he would sit in a corner of a room." Hibbert, Christopher et. King, Ross. "Garibaldi: Hero of Unification." Pg. 121. Macmillan, Jul. 22, 2018.

312. *"...was officially recognized as the inventor of the telephone."* U.S. House of Representatives Resolution 269 – 107th Congress (2001-2002).
313. *"On July 30, 1871..."* Yates, Maura. "Annivesary of "The Vessel of Death."" Staten Island Advance, 2009.
314. *"His home of nearly forty years...'Industrial Workers of the World' members."* M. Marchiano, personal communication, May 28, 2018.
315. *"Paul Caglianone..."* Siuzdak, Colleen. "Developing pride in the Italian-American woman." Staten Island Advance, 2018.
316. *"The club was formed in 1950...school-age children."* Information courtest of the Italian Club of Staten Island Foundation, Inc. (special thanks to A. Maniscalco, V. Popolano, and R. Macri), personal communication, Feb. 27, 2018.
317. *"The earliest Italian-culture promoting...Rosebank Youth & Parents."* H. Murphy, personal communication, Dec. 4, 2018.
318. *"Among the strict, disciplined...You don't have that anymore."* V. Tucciarone, T. Csorba, and A. Csorba, personal communication, Aug. 7, 2018.
319. *"Similar to the riuals...either fish or crabs..."* R. Nazzaro-Paterno, personal communication, Dec.30, 2018.
320. *"The day they changed the zoning laws...wonderful upbringings I had."* P. Gati, personal communication, Aug. 31, 2018.
321. *"There's really something special...to all the women in Rosebank."* J. Burns, personal communication, Sept. 13, Oct. 10, 2018.
322. *"The first of the Scaramuzzo's...he was a father to me, in Rosebank."* S. La Scalla, personal communication, Sept. 6, 2018. And M. Scaramuzzo, personal communication, Sept. 8, 2018.
323. *"Carlo Sorrentino...in which my grandparents lived."* C. Sorrentino-Higgins, personal communication, Oct. 13-14. 2018.
324. *"That world...toward Hylan Blvd."* F. Martucci, personal communication, Jan. 23, 2019.
325. *"The original Montalbano's...Tomahawks in one day."* C. Parrelli, personal communication, Aug. 17, 2018.
326. *"De Luca's General Store."* Rosenblum, Constance. "More New York Stories: The Best of the City Section of The New York Times." Pgs. 82-83. NYU Press, Nov. 24, 2010.
327. *"On a recent visit to the store..."* Lyons, Bill. "Unconventional creativity at De Luca General Store, a humble Rosebank institution." Staten Island Advance, 2015.
328. *"The quintessential manifestation...in its golden years."* V. Moschella, personal communication, Aug. 9, 2018.
329. *"Years ago, all you need was some..."* Monahan, Matthew. "A life spent watching – and caring." Staten Island Advance, May 16, 1982.
330. *"The era of simple...until 1971."* C. Perrino, personal communication, Jan. 9-10, 2018.
331. *"A bakery just north...Navarino family."* A. Baglio, personal communication, Nov. 5, 2018.

332. *"...'Clifton Berley' may call itself 'New York.'"* "Country Life in America." Vol. 5, pg. 484. Doubleday, Page & Co., 1904.

333. *"Although a certain segment..."* "Domestic Engineering." Vol. 69, pg. 116. Domestic Engineering Co., 1914.

334. *"Nearly fifty years later."* "Ernest Flagg Estate, Todt Hill." Forgotten NY. Mar. 4, 2018. Web.

335. *"A native of the forgotten borough...walking on sunshine."* R. Barbato, personal communication, Jul. 25, 2018.

336. *"Joseph Primiano...done you a favor."* M.F. Iammatteo and M. Iammatteo, personal communication, Sept. 26, 2018.

347. *"Integrated into all...stronger than ever."* G. DiLeo, personal communication, Sept. 8, 2018.

348. *"buckboards and the like..."* "The Staten Island Historian." Vols. 1-10. Pg. 41. Staten Island Historical Society.

349. *"depicting the persecution of Jews..."* Hamm, Michael F. "Kiev: A Portrait, 1800-1917." Pg. 151. Princeton Univ. Press, 1995.

350. *"Many film stars of the..."* Helmreich, William B. "The New York Nobody Knows: Walking 6,000 Miles in the City." Pg. 163. Princeton Univ. Press, Oct. 20, 2013.

351. *"...leadership of Irish, Father Kearney."* Moses, Paul. "An Unlikely Union: The Love-Hate Story of New York's Irish and Italians." Pg. 49. NYU Press, Jul. 3, 2015.

352. *"Prior to the rectory's...surrounding homes."* L. Winkler, personal communication, Jan. 28, 2018.

353. *"From the Italian community of South Beach... a thousand watermelons."* V. Picone, personal communication, Jun. 18, 2018.

354. *"The old Italian South Beach...behind the building."* S. Marino, personal communication, May 28, 2018.

355. *"Many local businesses...the last Christmas he would ever live."* A. LaRosa, personal communication, Jun. 20, 2018.

356. *"What Castellano liked best...ending disputes."* Sifakis, Carl. "The Mafia Encylopedia." Pg. 39. Infobase Publishing, 2006.

357. *"The exotic delicasies...steeple and baptismal hall."* R. Crocitto, personal communication, Jul. 14, 2018.

358. *"which meant 'take it away.'"* Perito, Nick. "I Just Happened to Be There: Making Music With The Stars." Pg. 68. Xlibris Corp., Sept. 29, 2004.

359. *"...and then to Cape Coral, Florida."* "Singer Johnny Maestro Loses Cancer Battle." Associated Press, Mar. 25, 2010.

360. *"The Staten Island bungalow...childhood."* Evanier, David. "Roman Candle: The Lify of Bobby Darin." Pgs. 3, 17. Excelsior Editions, Aug. 1, 2010.

361. *"..., and Dement's."* Bailey, Rob. "28 musicians you didn't know lived on Staten Island." Staten Island Advance, 2017.

362. *"[t]he banquet was held on Staten Island."* "Rivista della massoneria Italiana liberta, uguaglianza, fratellancza." Pg. 190. Ti. Letterania, 1902. Translated manually from Italian to English.

363. *"...and dancing into the night."* "The Clothier and Furnisher." Vol. 87, pg. 75. Published, 1915.

364. *"with a mansard roof and 'widow's walk."'* Fioravante, Janice. "If You're Thinking of Living In/Arrochar; A 'Brigdadoon' at the Verrazzano Bridge." The New York Times, May 7, 1995.

365. *"On his first day, a snowstorm..."* Benanti, Carol A. "Dr. Francis J. Romano, revered family physician, dies at 94." Staten Island Advance, 2016.

366. *"Debated to be the oldest...took control of operations."* Certain details throughout this article are extracted from Staten Island Advance Entertainment Desk. "Basilio Inn: What Makes It Staten Island's Oldest Restaurant." Staten Island Advance, 2018.

367. *"A recognizable face...Staten Island back then."* M. Burns, personal communication, May 29, 2018.

368. *"Licastri's Bakery...son-of-a-bitch!"* S. Licastri and C. Licastri, personal communication, Aug. 15, 2018.

369. *"The southern end...today in South Beach."* G. Anastasio, personal communication. Nov. 24, 2018.

370. *"Among those children...of his heritage."* M.A. Ariemma, personal communication, Jan. 25, 2019.

371. *"Joseph Vito Lettieri...recreated itself."* T. Lettieri, personal communication, Oct. 1-3, 2018.

372. *"In an era of hastily vanishing...lives memorable."* P. Cangiano, Aug. 11, 2018.

373. *"I began working at Cangiano's..."* M. Ventrone, personal communication, May 13, 2018.

374. *"Among the many Italian...Torre Del Greco."* C.C.R. Barone and G.R. Kokolis, personal communication, Jul. 23, 2018.

375. *"Other newcomers...entertainment variety show.."* J. Potenza, personal communication, Jan. 29, 2019.

376. *"In the 1920s, the business had..."* Staten Island 350th Anniversary Committee. "Discovering Staten Island: A 350th Anniversary Commemorative History." Arcadia Publishing, Feb. 18, 2011.

377. *"The estate was constructed in the 1940s by..."* Lee, Jamie. "Signs of tunnels still exist in Staten Island's Elks Lodge." Staten Island Advance, 2010.

378. *"In any case, the Elks Lodge..."* "Local Lodges Online – Staten Island, NY 841." Elks USA. Web.

379. *"The highway would have cut across..."* Dominowski. Michael W. "Unused Staten Island overpasses being dismantled, and so is an era." Staten Island Advance, 2017.

380. *"Curtis—a Republican civil rights advocate.."* Somma-Hammel, Jan. "Cool Spaces: George William Curtis House is a landmark in Livingston." Staten Island Advance, Aug., 2018.

381. *"Bob Siclari...blaze on the property."* B. Siclari, personal communication, Dec. 23, 2018.

382. *"...Newspaper/Park Row in 1871."* McNamara, Patrick. "New York Catholics: Faith, Attitude, and the Works." Section 15, Pg. 2. Orbis Books, 2014.

383. *"shoemaking, and baking."* Burgan, Michael. "The American Newsboy." Pg. 24. Capstone, 2007.

384. *"stenography, and typewriting."* Fathers, Paulist. "The Catholic World, Vol. 58: A Monthly Magazine of Genera Literature and Science; Oct. 1893, to March, 1894 (Classic Reprint)." Pgs. 29-30. Fb&c Limited, Jan. 18, 2017.

385. *"wayward kids from some..."* Cipolla, Frank. "It Shocked Even Us!" Pg. 223. Lulu.com, Jun. 1, 2011.

386. *"...west to other distant facilities."* Lundrigan, Margaret. "Irish Staten Island." pg. 50. Arcadia Publishing, 2009.

387. *"Among the many Irish...felt violated."* J. Barsalona, personal communication, Nov. 24, 2018.

388. *"Italians were known throughout...from your town."* A. Rizzo, personal communication, Aug. 11, 2018.

389. *"Founder of 123...political arena."* J. Pidoriano, personal communication, Jan. 27, 2019.

Index

341

343

WRITTEN AND RESEARCHED BY

Lorenzo Lucchesi (b. 2001) is the author of three books, *American Advent, Diarrhea of a Black Man,* and *Staten Island: Like It or Not!,* as well as a novella *The Battle for North Beach.* His literature genres of specialization include biographical, political-fiction, and history. A second-generation San Franciscan and native of the Excelsior District, Lucchesi is also a musician, polyglot, political-enthusiast, and scholar of Italian-American history. Since November of 2017, he has meticulously chronicled the history of Staten Island, New York dating back to the commencement of the nineteenth century, through referencing thousands of archives and conducting a series of several hundred interviews. Lucchesi's hobbies include foreign language-learning, studying geography, and cooking European cuisine.

Cover Design by Andre Hunt © 2019

Made in the USA
Columbia, SC
24 May 2020